The
Vegetarian
Cookbook

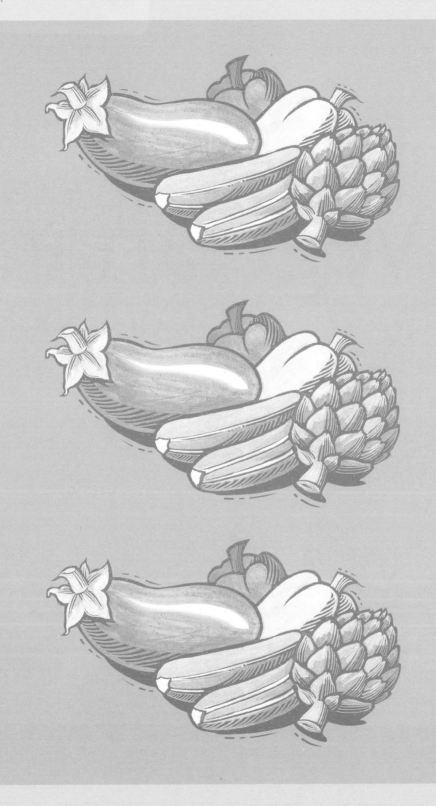

The
Vegetarian
Cookbook

Nicola Graimes

HERMES
HOUSE

This edition is published by Hermes House

Hermes House is an imprint of Anness Publishing Ltd
Hermes House, 88–89 Blackfriars Road, London SE1 8HA
tel. 020 7401 2077; fax 020 7633 9499; info@anness.com

© Anness Publishing Ltd 2003

Publisher : Joanna Lorenz
Managing Editor : Helen Sudell
Editor: Valerie Ferguson
Jacket and Text Design: Chloe Steers
Tyesetting :Diane Pullen
Illustrations:Angela Wood
Production Controller : Joanna King
Recipes : Catherine Atkinson, Alex Barker,Michelle Berriedale-Johnson,
Angela Boggiano, Kathy Brown,Carla Capalbo, Kit Chan, Jacqueline Clarke,
Carole Clements, Trish Davies, Roz Denny, Patrizia Diemling, Matthew Drennan,
Sarah Edmonds, Rafi Fernandez,Christine France, Silvano Franco, Shirley Gill, Nicola Graimes,
Rosamund Grant,Carole Handslip,
Deh-Ta Hsiung, Patricia Lousada, Lesley Mackley, Sue Maggs,
Kathy Man,Sally Mansfield, Norma Miller, Sallie Morris, Annie Nichols,Maggie Pannell,
Katherine Richmond, Jennie Shapter,Anne Sheasby,Liz Trigg,Hilaire Walden,Laura Washburn,
Steven Wheeler, Elizabeth Wolf-Cohen, Jeni Wright

1 3 5 7 9 10 8 6 4 2

Previously published as part of a larger compendium, Vegetarian

Note
Bracketed terms are intended for American readers

For all recipes, quantities are given in both metric and imperial measures and where appropriate,
measures are also given in standard cups and spoons.
Follow one set, but not a mixture, because they are not interchangeable.

Standard spoon and cup measures are level
1tsp=5ml, 1tbsp=15ml,1 cup=250ml/8fl oz

Australian standard tablespoon are 20ml. Australian readers should use 3tsp in place of 1 tbsp for
measuring small quantities of flour, salt, etc

Medium(US large) eggs are used unless otherwise stated

CONTENTS

INTRODUCTION

There is a common myth that a vegetarian diet that avoids all meat, poultry and fish, and their derivatives and products, is lacking in certain nutrients. However, research into the effects of food on health has proved that vegetarians who follow a diet that is rich in fruit and vegetables, wholegrains, nuts, seeds and beans with a moderate quantity of eggs and dairy products are less likely to suffer from many of the diseases that plague modern Western and industrialized cultures. These include obesity, cancer, heart disease, gallstones, diabetes, constipation and diverticular disease.

Yet, vegetarianism is not purely about achieving and maintaining good health. A meat-free diet is enjoyable, delicious and varied. The choice of fresh vegetables, fruit, herbs, noodles, pasta, grains and cheeses is now more extensive than ever before, enabling cooks to experiment with different flavours, textures and colours, and vegetarian food has become a popular cuisine in its own right.

The first section of this book provides an extensive guide to vegetarian ingredients, from vegetables and fruit to herbs and spices and store-cupboard (pantry) essentials. This comprehensive reference guide highlights the range of ingredients available and gives information on buying and storing them.

The recipes have an international feel, taking their inspiration from many of the culinary traditions of the world. You will find dishes influenced by Indian, Chinese, Thai, Italian, South American and North African styles of cooking. The recipes celebrate the diversity of vegetarian food. While some are based on traditional, classic dishes, others take components from various cuisines around the globe to create a contemporary fusion of flavours and culinary styles. There are ideas to cater for all eating occasions, from quick, nutritious light meals to flavourful main dishes and sophisticated creations for entertaining, but the emphasis is always on high-quality raw ingredients.

Today, much of our food is processed and bears little resemblance to the original ingredients, so the recipes in this book specify fresh, unrefined foods whenever possible. These whole foods retain all their natural goodness and are not processed, over-refined, subjected to chemicals during production or loaded with harmful additives, colourings or flavourings.

In the recipes, organic free-range (farm-fresh) eggs are recommended. Sometimes white flour is used in combination with wholemeal (whole-wheat) flour to give a lighter end result even though it is less nutritious. You should use organic unbleached white flour for these recipes because it is untreated with chemicals. Unsalted (sweet) butter is used rather than margarine. It is high in fat but, if eaten in moderate amounts, it is hugely preferable in taste. Margarine is also subject to intense processing and the addition of emulsifiers, colourings, flavourings and stabilizers. High-fat Parmesan is used in preference to low-fat alternatives for the simple and basic reason of taste – a little goes a long way. Unrefined pure honey and other natural sweeteners replace refined sugar where possible and much is made of the delicious monounsaturated fat, olive oil, which is at the heart of the healthy Mediterranean diet.

Each recipe is easy to follow with numbered step-by-step instructions, and is often accompanied by suggestions for alternative ingredients and advice on selecting or preparing key ingredients.

Whether you want to embark on a healthier lifestyle or simply expand on your repertoire of vegetarian recipes, this book is mouthwatering proof that vegetarian cooking is not only healthy and nutritious, but also exciting and delicious.

NICOLA GRAIMES

A Balanced Diet

To maintain optimum health, it is essential to eat a balanced diet. For a vegetarian this means eating a wide variety of foods that provide the right proportions of nutrients and water. A balanced diet should always include enough calories to provide the body with vital energy, but not an excess, which leads to weight gain and health problems.

When choosing a vegetarian diet, do not simply swap meat and fish for cheese and eggs. Vegetarians should aim to eat a wide variety of nutrient-rich foods. The following guide will help you plan a balanced, healthy and varied diet.

Whole Grains and Potatoes

This group should form the main part of the diet. It includes cereals such as oats and wheat, and foods made from them such as bread and pasta, grains such as rice, and starchy vegetables such as potatoes. Wholemeal (whole-wheat) foods such as pasta and bread, brown rice and unpeeled potatoes are the most nutritious.

Recommended daily intake: Aim for 6–11 servings a day. (A serving is equivalent to 1 slice of bread, ½ cup of cooked cereal, rice or pasta or 1 potato.)

Fruit and Vegetables

These foods provide significant amounts of vitamins, minerals and fibre and are low in fat and calories. Cruciferous vegetables, such as broccoli and cabbage, provide antioxidants, which may protect against certain cancers. Bright orange, yellow and red fruit and vegetables are rich in beta carotene and vitamin C.

Recommended daily intake: Aim for at least 5 servings a day. (A serving is equivalent to 1 piece of fruit, 2 tablespoons of vegetables, a glass of juice, or a bowl of salad.)

Legumes, Nuts and Seeds

Beans, peas and lentils, tofu, tempeh and other legumes, nuts and seeds provide protein, fibre, iron, calcium, zinc and B vitamins and vitamin E. Legumes are low in fat and provide plenty of fibre. Nuts and seeds are nutritious but they are high in fat so should be eaten in moderation.

Recommended daily intake: 2–3 servings a day. (A serving is equivalent to a small handful of nuts and seeds, ½ cup cooked beans or 115g/4oz tofu or tempeh.)

Dairy Foods and Non-dairy Alternatives

This group includes milk, cheese, yogurt and soya milk and provides protein, calcium, vitamins B_{12}, A and D, but can be high in fat. Eggs are also included.

Recommended daily intake: 2–3 servings a day. (A serving is equivalent to 1 egg, a slice of cheese, or a small pot of yogurt.)

Fatty and Sugary Foods

Chocolate, crisps (US potato chips), cakes, biscuits (cookies), and fats provide few nutrients. Eat sparingly.

Maintaining Good Health

There are six essential nutrients needed for good health – carbohydrates, fibre, protein, fats, vitamins and minerals. If these are consumed in the correct proportions, they will provide the body with both sustained energy and the nutritional requirements for continued good health and metabolic function. It is also vital to drink sufficient water for optimum health.

CARBOHYDRATES

At one time carbohydrates, which are made up of starches and sugars, were considered to be fattening and less valuable than protein-rich foods. However, they are now recognized as the body's major source of energy and many carbohydrate-rich foods supply a substantial amount of protein, vitamins, minerals and fibre, with very little fat. About half the food we eat should be made up of unrefined complex carbo-hydrates, such as wholegrain cereals, wholemeal (whole-wheat) bread and pasta, and brown rice. These high-fibre foods are broken down slowly by the body and provide a steady supply of energy, whereas simple carbohydrates or sugars are quickly absorbed into the bloodstream and give only a short-term energy boost. Always try to choose unrefined carbohydrates, as the refined versions, such as white flour, rice and sugar, are stripped of many of their nutrients, including essential vitamins, minerals and fibre.

FIBRE

Fruits, vegetables, grains, legumes, nuts and seeds are our main sources of fibre, of which there are two types: insoluble and soluble. Insoluble fibre, which is found in whole wheat, brown rice, bran and nuts, provides bulk to the diet and helps to combat constipation. Soluble fibre, which is found in legumes, vegetables and oats, binds with toxins in the gut and promotes their excretion, and also helps to reduce blood cholesterol. Both types of fibre reduce the risk of bowel disorders, including diverticulitis, colon and rectal cancer and irritable bowel syndrome, although adding bran to meals is not advised.

Few people eat enough fibre. We should consume about 18 grams of fibre a day, but on average most people only eat about 12 grams. People who wish to lose weight will find that a high-fibre diet is beneficial as it provides bulk and naturally limits the amount of food eaten as there is a greater feeling of fullness after a meal that lasts for a longer period of time.

HOW TO INCREASE YOUR FIBRE INTAKE

• *Base your diet on wholemeal (whole-wheat) bread and pasta, brown rice and fresh fruit and vegetables. Heavily refined and processed foods contain less fibre and fewer nutrients.*

• *Start the day with a wholegrain cereal, such as porridge (oatmeal) or bran flakes.*

• *Eat plenty of dried fruit – add it to cereals or yogurt, or use to make a compote.*

• *Add beans and lentils to salads and soups to boost their fibre content.*

• *Wherever possible, avoid peeling fruits and vegetables, as the skins contain valuable fibre.*

PROTEIN

This is essential for the maintenance and repair of every cell in the body, and also ensures that enzymes, hormones and antibodies function properly. Protein is made up of amino acids of which there are 20, and eight of these need to be supplied by diet. A food containing all eight of these amino acids is known as a complete or high-quality protein. For vegetarians, these complete proteins include eggs, dairy products and soya beans. Protein from plant sources, such as nuts and legumes, do not usually contain all eight amino acids and need to be eaten with cereals, such as bread, rice or pasta, to make them into complete proteins. We should aim to get 10–15 per cent of our calories from protein.

Vegetarians are often concerned that their diet may lack protein when they cut out meat and fish from their diet. Yet in reality, most people in the industrialized world eat too much protein, and deficiency is virtually unheard of. High-protein foods, such as dairy products and nuts, are a source of fat, and have been found to leach calcium from the body, which then increases the risk of developing osteoporosis.

It is a common misconception that vegetarians have meticulously to combine protein foods in every meal to achieve the correct balance of all eight amino acids. Nutritionists now believe that provided a balanced and varied diet of grains, legumes, dairy produce, eggs and vegetables is eaten on a daily basis, intentionally combining protein foods is unnecessary.

FATS

A small amount of fat in the diet is essential for good health. Fat provides vitamins A, D and E and essential fatty acids and contributes greatly to the taste, texture and palatability of food. It contains a large number of calories, and should make up no more than 30 per cent of your diet. The type of fat is as crucial as the quantity.

Saturated fat (found mainly in dairy products in the vegetarian diet) has been associated with an increased risk of cancer and coronary heart disease. Eating too much saturated fat can increase excess body weight and raise blood cholesterol levels leading to narrowed arteries, more so than eating foods such as eggs and cheese that are high in cholesterol.

HOW TO REDUCE DIETARY FAT

While a vegetarian diet can be lower in fat than one based on meat, it is easy to eat too many dairy products, oil-laden salad dressings and sauces and high-fat ready-meals. There are many simple ways to reduce fat in your diet.

- *Use strong, mature (sharp) cheese such as Parmesan because only a small amount is needed to add flavour to a dish.*
- *Make low-fat salad dressings using miso, orange juice, yogurt, herbs, spices or tomato juice in place of oils.*
- *Stir-fry foods using only a little oil. For best results make sure the wok or frying pan is very hot before adding the oil.*
- *Avoid blended oils because they may contain coconut or palm oil, which are saturated fats.*
- *Opt for low-fat cheeses such as cottage, curd (farmer's) or ricotta instead of high-fat cheeses such as Cheddar.*
- *Use low-fat yogurt instead of cream in cooked recipes. Stir in a spoonful of cornflour (cornstarch), mixed to a paste with a little water, to prevent the yogurt from curdling when heated.*
- *Choose filling complex carbohydrates in preference to high-fat protein foods.*

Unsaturated fats, both polyunsaturated and monounsaturated, can help to reduce harmful LDL cholesterol (the type that furs up arteries) and, importantly, increase the beneficial HDL cholesterol, which is thought to reduce cholesterol levels in the body. Monounsaturated fats, such as olive oil, sesame oil and rapeseed (canola) oil, are less vulnerable to oxidation, which is harmful to health, than polyunsaturated fats. Polyunsaturated fats provide essential fatty acids, omega-3 and omega-6. Omega-3 (linolenic acid), which is found in walnuts, soya beans, wheatgerm and rapeseed oil, has been found to reduce the risk of heart disease, while omega-6 (linoleic acid), which is found in nuts, seeds and oils, is thought to reduce blood cholesterol.

WATER
Although it is possible to survive for weeks without food, we can live for only a few days without water. It plays a vital role in the body: it transports nutrients, regulates temperature, transports waste via the kidneys, and acts as a lubricating fluid. Most people do not drink enough water. It is thought that an adult requires around 2.5 litres/4¼ pints per day. A shortage of water can provoke headaches and loss of concentration. Fizzy drinks, tea and coffee all act as diuretics, speeding up water loss, which causes dehydration.

VITAMINS AND MINERALS
These are vital for good health and the functioning of our bodies, and, with a few exceptions, must be supplied by diet. The levels our bodies require vary depending on health, lifestyle and age. Contrary to popular belief vitamins and minerals do not provide energy in themselves but assist in the release of energy provided by carbohydrates, fats and proteins.

Vitamins are either water-soluble or fat-soluble. Water-soluble vitamins – the B vitamins and vitamin C – cannot be stored and must be replaced on a daily basis. If you drink alcohol or smoke, increase your intake of foods rich in B vitamins and vitamin C. Vegetarians should make sure they have enough vitamin B_{12}, mostly found in animal sources, although this should not be difficult as it is required only in tiny amounts. It is found in dairy products, fortified breakfast cereals, yeast extract, miso and eggs. Fat-soluble vitamins A, D, E and K are stored in the liver for some time.

There are 16 essential minerals; some, like calcium, are required in relatively large amounts, while trace elements such as selenium and magnesium, are needed in tiny quantities but are nevertheless vital to the healthy functioning of the body. Minerals have a variety of roles but primarily regulate and balance the body and maintain a healthy immune system. A deficiency of iron affects one-fifth of the world's population, and vegetarians especially need to make a point of eating iron-rich foods.

Essential Vitamins & Minerals

A balanced intake of these vital nutrients is crucial for good health and maintaining every function of the body. As they are readily available in a wide range of vegetarian foods there is little need to be concerned about deficiencies if a varied diet is eaten. The chart below explains where they can be found and their benefits.

VITAMIN/ MINERAL	BEST VEGETARIAN SOURCES	ROLE IN HEALTH	SYMPTOMS OF DEFICIENCY
A (retinol in animal foods, beta carotene in plant foods)	Milk, butter, cheese, egg yolks and some margarine, carrots, apricots, squash, red (bell) peppers, broccoli, green leafy vegetables, mango and sweet potatoes.	Essential for vision, bone growth, and skin and tissue repair. Beta carotene acts as an antioxidant and protects the immune system.	Deficiency is characterized by poor night vision, dry skin and lower resistance to infection, especially respiratory disorders.
B_1 (thiamin)	Wholegrain cereals, brewer's yeast, potatoes, nuts, pulses and milk.	Essential for energy production, the nervous system, muscles and heart. Promotes growth.	Deficiency is characterized by depression, irritability, nervous disorders, loss of memory. Common among alcoholics.
B_2 (riboflavin)	Cheese, eggs, milk, yogurt, fortified breakfast cereals, yeast extract, almonds and pumpkin seeds.	Essential for energy production and for the functioning of vitamin B_6 and niacin as well as tissue repair.	Deficiency is characterized by lack of energy, dry cracked lips, numbness and itchy eyes.
Niacin (part of B complex)	Pulses, potatoes, fortified breakfast cereals, milk, cheese, eggs, peas, mushrooms, green leafy vegetables, prunes.	Essential for healthy digestive system, skin and circulation. It is also needed for the release of energy.	Deficiency is unusual but characterized by lack of energy, depression and scaly skin.
B_6 (piridoxine)	Eggs, wholemeal (whole-wheat) bread, breakfast cereals, nuts, bananas, broccoli and cabbage.	Essential for assimilating protein and fat, to make red blood cells and a healthy immune system.	Deficiency is characterized by anaemia, dermatitis and depression.
B_{12} (cyanocobal-amin)	Milk, eggs, fortified breakfast cereals, cheese and yeast extract.	Essential for formation of red blood cells and maintaining a healthy nervous system.	Deficiency is characterized by fatigue, increase risk of infection, anaemia.
Folate (folic acid)	Green leafy vegetables, fortified breakfast cereals, bread, nuts, pulses, bananas and yeast extract.	Essential for cell division; makes genetic material. Extra is needed pre-conception and during a pregnancy.	Deficiency characterized by anaemia and appetite loss. Linked with neural defects in babies.
C (ascorbic acid)	Citrus fruit, melons, strawberries, tomatoes, broccoli, potatoes, (bell) peppers and green vegetables.	Essential for the absorption of iron, healthy skin, teeth and bones. An antioxidant that strengthens the immune system and fights infection.	Deficiency characterized by increased susceptibility to infection, fatigue, poor sleep and depression.
D (calciferol)	Sunlight, margarine, vegetable oils, eggs, cereals and butter.	Essential for bone and teeth formation, helps the body to absorb both calcium and phosphorus.	Deficiency characterized by softening of the bones, muscle weakness and anaemia.

VITAMIN/ MINERAL	BEST VEGETARIAN SOURCES	ROLE IN HEALTH	SYMPTOMS OF DEFICIENCY
E (tocopherol)	Seeds, nuts, vegetable oils, eggs, wholemeal (whole-wheat) bread, green leafy vegetables, oats and cereals.	Essential for healthy skin, circulation and maintaining cells – an antioxidant.	Deficiency characterized by increased risk of heart attack, strokes and certain cancers.
Calcium	Milk, cheese, yogurt, green leafy vegetables, sesame seeds, broccoli, dried figs, pulses, almonds, spinach and watercress.	Essential for building and maintaining bones and teeth, muscle function and the nervous system.	Deficiency characterized by soft and brittle bones, osteoporosis, fractures and muscle weakness.
Iron	Egg yolks, fortified breakfast cereals, green leafy vegetables, dried apricots, prunes, pulses, wholegrains and tofu.	Essential for healthy blood and muscles.	Deficiency characterized by anaemia, fatigue and low resistance to infection.
Zinc	Peanuts, cheese, whole grains, sunflower and pumpkin seeds, pulses, milk, hard cheese and yogurt.	Essential for a healthy immune system, tissue formation, normal growth, wound healing and reproduction.	Deficiency is characterized by impaired growth and development, slow wound healing and loss of taste and smell.
Sodium	Most salt we eat comes from processed foods, – crisps (US potato chips), cheese and canned foods. It is also found naturally in most foods.	Essential for nerve and muscle function and the regulation of body fluid.	Deficiency is unlikely but can lead to dehydration, cramps and muscle weakness.
Potassium	Bananas, milk, pulses, nuts, seeds, whole grains, potatoes, fruits and vegetables.	Essential for water balance, normal blood pressure and nerve transmission.	Deficiency is characterized by weakness, thirst, fatigue, mental confusion and raised blood pressure.
Magnesium	Nuts, seeds, whole grains, pulses, tofu, dried figs and apricots and green vegetables.	Essential for healthy muscles, bones and teeth, normal growth and nerves.	Deficiency is characterized by lethargy, weak bones and muscles, irritability and depression.
Phosphorus	Milk, cheese, yogurt, eggs, nuts, seeds, pulses and all whole grains.	Essential for healthy bones and teeth, energy production and the assimilation of nutrients, particularly calcium.	Deficiency is rare.
Selenium	Avocados, lentils, milk, cheese, butter, brazil nuts and seaweed.	Essential for protecting against free radical damage and may protect against cancer – an antioxidant.	Deficiency is characterized by reduced antioxidant protection.
Iodine	Seaweed and iodized salt.	Aids the production of hormones released by the thyroid gland.	Deficiency can lead to the formation of a goitre and a sluggish metabolism and apathy as well as dry skin and hair.
Chloride	Table salt and foods that contain salt.	Regulates and maintains the balance of fluids in the body.	Deficiency is rare.
Manganese	Nuts, whole grains, pulses, tofu and tea.	Essential component of various enzymes that are involved in energy production.	Deficiency is not characterized by any specific symptoms.

VEGETABLES

Using vegetables offers the cook an infinite number of culinary possibilities. The choice is immense and the growing demand for organic produce has meant that pesticide-free vegetables are now increasingly available. Vegetables are an essential component of a healthy diet and have countless nutritional benefits. They are at their most nutritious when freshly picked.

ROOTS AND TUBERS

Vegetables such as carrots, parsnips, swedes (rutabaga) and potatoes, are comforting and nourishing, and it is not surprising that they should be popular in the winter. They are extremely versatile as they can be used in soups, salads, stir-fries, casseroles and even desserts. Their sweet, dense flesh provides sustained energy, valuable fibre, vitamins and minerals.

CARROTS

The best carrots are not restricted to the cold winter months. Summer welcomes the slender sweet new crop, often sold with their green, feathery tops. (These are best removed after buying as they rob the root of moisture and nutrients.) Buy organic carrots if you can because high pesticide residues have been found in non-organic ones. As an added bonus, organic carrots do not need peeling.

Look for firm, smooth carrots – the smaller they are, the sweeter they are. Carrots should be prepared just before use to preserve their valuable nutrients. They are delicious raw, and can be steamed, stir-fried, roasted or puréed.

BEETROOT

Deep, ruby-red in colour, beetroot (beet) adds a vibrant hue and flavour to all sorts of dishes. It is often pickled in vinegar, but is much better roasted, as this emphasizes its sweet earthy flavour. Raw beetroot can be grated into salads or used to make relishes. It can also be added to risottos or made into delicious soups. If cooking beetroot whole, wash carefully, taking care not to damage the skin or the nutrients and colour will leach out. Trim the stalks to about 2.5cm/ 1in above the root. Small beetroots are sweeter and more tender than larger ones.

CELERIAC

This knobbly root is closely related to celery, which explains its flavour – a cross between aniseed, celery and parsley. Similar in size to a small swede, it has ivory flesh and is one of the few root vegetables that must be peeled before use. When grated and eaten raw in salads, celeriac has a crunchy texture. It can also be steamed, served with a white sauce, baked in gratins or combined with potatoes and mashed with butter or margarine and grainy mustard. Celeriac can also be used in soups and broths.

SWEDE

The globe-shaped swede has pale orange-coloured flesh with a delicate sweet flavour. Trim off the thick peel, then treat in the same way as other root vegetables: grate raw into salads; dice and cook in casseroles and soups; quarter, par-boil and roast or steam, then mash with a little olive oil and serve as an accompaniment to a wide variety of dishes.

Parsnip

This vegetable has a sweet, creamy flavour and is delicious roasted, puréed or steamed. Parsnips are best purchased after the first frost of the year as the cold converts their starches into sugar, enhancing their sweetness. Scrub well before use and peel only if the skin is tough. Avoid large roots, which can be woody.

Turnips

This humble root vegetable has many health-giving qualities, and small turnips with their green tops intact are especially nutritious. Their crisp, ivory flesh, which is enclosed in white, green and pink-tinged skin, has a pleasant, slightly peppery flavour, the intensity of which depends on their size and the time of harvesting. Small turnips can be eaten raw and are tasty grated in salads. Alternatively, steam, bake or use in casseroles and soups.

Potatoes

There are thousands of potato varieties, and many lend themselves to particular cooking methods. Small potatoes, such as Pink Fir Apple and Charlotte, and new potatoes, such as Jersey Royals, are best steamed. They have a waxy texture, which retains its shape after cooking, making them ideal for salads. Main crop potatoes, such as Estima and Maris Piper, and sweet potatoes (preferably the orange-fleshed variety which have a better flavour than the cream-fleshed type), are more suited to roasting, baking or mashing, and can be used to make chips (French fries). Discard any potatoes with green patches as these indicate the presence of toxic alkaloids.

Vitamins and minerals are stored in, or just beneath the skin, so it is best to use potatoes unpeeled. New potatoes and salad potatoes need only be scrubbed.

Potatoes are not fattening – it is the cooking method that bumps up the calories. Steam and bake instead of frying to retain nutrients and to keep fat levels low.

Jerusalem Artichokes

This small knobbly tuber has a sweet, nutty flavour. Peeling can be awkward, although scrubbing and trimming is usually sufficient. Store in the refrigerator for up to one week. Use them in the same way as potatoes – they make good creamy soups.

Radishes

There are several types of this peppery-flavoured vegetable. The round ruby-red variety is most familiar; the longer, white-tipped type has a milder taste. Mooli or daikon radishes are white and very long; they can weigh up to several kilos or pounds. Radishes can be used to add flavour and texture to salads and stir-fries.

Horseradish

This pungent root is never eaten as a vegetable. It is usually grated and mixed with cream or oil and vinegar, and served as a culinary accompaniment.

Buying and Storing Root Vegetables

Seek out bright, firm, unwrinkled root vegetables and tubers, which do not have soft patches. When possible, choose organically grown produce. Store root vegetables in a cool, dark place.

BRASSICAS

This large group of vegetables boasts an extraordinary number of health-giving properties. Brassicas range from the dark, crinkly-leafed Savoy cabbage to the small, walnut-size Brussels sprout.

BROCCOLI

This nutritious vegetable should be a regular part of everyone's diet. Two types are commonly available: purple-sprouting, which has fine, leafy stems and a delicate head, and calabrese, the more substantial variety with a tightly budded top and thick stalk. Choose broccoli that has bright, compact florets. Yellowing florets, a limp woody stalk and a pungent smell are an indication of overmaturity. Trim stalks before cooking, although young stems can be eaten, too. Serve raw in salads or with a dip. Steamed purple sprouting broccoli can be dressed in vinaigrette. If you cook broccoli, briefly steam or stir-fry it to preserve the nutrients and keep the cooking time brief to retain the vivid green colour and crisp texture.

PREPARING BROCCOLI
Trim the stalks from broccoli and divide it into florets. The tender stems of young broccoli can be thinly sliced and eaten, too but not mature ones.

CAULIFLOWER

The cream-coloured compact florets, or curds, should be encased in large, bright green leaves. There are also varieties with green or purple florets.

To get the most nutrients from a cauliflower, eat it raw, or bake or steam lightly. Raw or cooked cauliflower has a mild flavour and is delicious tossed in a vinaigrette dressing or combined with tomatoes and spices.

CABBAGE

Frequently overcooked, cabbage is best eaten raw, or cooked until only just tender. Stir-frying or braising are preferable to boiling. There are several varieties: Savoy cabbage has substantial, crinkly leaves with a strong flavour and is perfect for stuffing; firm white and red cabbages can be shredded and used raw in salads, as can Chinese leaves (Chinese cabbage); pak choi (bok choy) is best cooked in stir-fries.

BRUSSELS SPROUTS

These miniature cabbages grow on a long tough stalk. They have a strong nutty flavour. Brussels sprouts are sweeter when they have been picked after the first frost and are best cooked lightly. Steam or stir-fry to keep their colour and crisp texture.

Buying and Storing Brassicas

Seek out brightly coloured, firm brassicas with no signs of discoloration, wilting or slime. Avoid cauliflowers that have black spots or yellowing leaves. Make sure that cabbages have a heavy heart. Chinese leaves should be compact and heavy for their size. Choose small Brussels sprouts with tightly packed leaves. Store cabbages and Brussels sprouts in a cool, dark place for up to a week. Broccoli and cauliflower should be stored in the refrigerator for only 2–3 days. Use Chinese greens on the day of purchase.

PREPARING BRUSSELS SPROUTS
These should be prepared just before cooking using a small, sharp knife.

1 Peel off any outer damaged leaves from the Brussels sprouts.

2 Before cooking, cut a cross in the base of each sprout, so that they cook quickly.

Green Leafy Vegetables

For years we have been told to eat up our greens and now we are beginning to learn why. Research into their health benefits has indicated that eating dark green leafy vegetables, such as spinach, spring greens (collards), Swiss chard and kale, on a regular basis may protect against certain forms of cancer as they are rich in many essential nutrients.

Spinach

This dark, green leaf is a superb source of cancer-fighting antioxidants. It contains about four times more beta carotene than broccoli. It is also rich in fibre, which can help to lower harmful levels of LDL cholesterol in the body, reducing the risk of heart disease and stroke. Spinach does contain iron but not in such a rich supply as was once thought. It also contains oxalic acid, which inhibits the absorption of iron and calcium in the body. However, eating spinach with a vitamin C-rich food will increase absorption. You could also cook the spinach with a bunch of sweet Cicily, an easy-to-grow herb that absorbs oxalic acid. Spinach also contains vitamins C and B_6, calcium, potassium, folate, thiamine and zinc. Nutritionally, it is most beneficial when young leaves are eaten raw in a salad, but it is also good lightly steamed, then chopped and added to omelettes or mixed with curd cheese and nutmeg and used as a delicious stuffing for pancakes.

Swiss Chard

A member of the beet family, Swiss chard has large, dark leaves and thick, white, orange or red edible ribs. It can be used in the same way as spinach, or the stems may be cooked on their own. Swiss chard is rich in vitamins and minerals, although, like spinach, it contains oxalic acid.

Spinach Beet

Similar to Swiss chard, this form of the beetroot (beet) plant is grown only for its leaves and has a sweet, mild flavour. Hardier than tender spinach, it is an ideal vegetable for the winter months. Use in the same way as spinach.

Spring Greens

These leafy, dark green, non-hearting, young cabbages are full of flavour but are only available for a relatively short period. Rich in vitamin C and beta carotene, spring greens contain indoles, one of the phytochemicals that are thought to protect the body against breast and ovarian cancer.

Buying and Storing Green Leafy Vegetables

These do not keep well – up to 2–3 days at most, as they quickly wilt and lose their nutritional benefits. Eat soon after purchase to enjoy them at their best. Look for brightly coloured, undamaged leaves that are not showing any signs of yellowing or wilting. Wash the leaves thoroughly in cold water before use and eat them raw, or cook lightly, either by steaming or stir-frying to preserve their valuable nutrients.

SQUASHES

Popular in the USA, Africa, Australia and the Caribbean, squashes come in a vast range of shapes, colours, sizes and flavours. They are broadly divided into winter and summer types.

WINTER SQUASHES

These have tough inedible skins, dense, fibrous flesh and large seeds. Most can be used in both sweet and savoury dishes.

Acorn Squash This small to medium-size squash has an attractive, fluted shape and looks rather like a large acorn. The orange flesh is sweet with a slightly dry texture, and the skin colour ranges from golden to dark green. Its large seed cavity makes this squash perfect for stuffing.

Butternut Squash A large, pear-shaped squash with a golden-brown skin and vibrant orange flesh. The skin is inedible and should be removed along with the seeds. Roast, bake, mash or use in soups or casseroles. The flesh has a rich, sweet, creamy flavour when cooked and makes a good substitute for pumpkin.

Pumpkins These are native to America, where they are traditionally enjoyed at Thanksgiving. Small pumpkins have sweeter, less fibrous flesh than the larger ones. Deep orange in colour, pumpkin can be used in both sweet and savoury dishes, such as pies, soups, casseroles, soufflés and even ice cream. Avoid boiling pumpkin as it can become waterlogged and soggy. The seeds are edible and highly nutritious.

SUMMER SQUASHES

Picked when still young, summer squashes have thin, edible skins and tender, edible seeds. Their delicate flesh cooks quickly.

Patty Pan Squash These pretty, baby squash are similar in taste to a courgette and are best steamed or roasted. They may be yellow or bright green, and although they can be expensive to buy, there is no waste.

Courgettes The most widely available summer squash, courgettes have most flavour when they are small and young. Young courgettes have glossy, bright green or yellow skin and creamy coloured flesh. Extremely versatile, they can be steamed, grated raw into salads, stir-fried, griddled, puréed or used in soups and casseroles. Their deep yellow flowers are a delicacy and are perfect for stuffing.

Marrows The grown-up equivalent of courgettes, marrows have a mild flavour and are best baked either plain or with a stuffing. Spices and tomatoes are good flavourings.

Cucumbers The long, thin, smooth-skinned variety is the most familiar. Their refreshing, mild flavour makes cucumbers perfect to use raw in salads or thinly sliced as a sandwich filling. They can also be pickled and steamed, baked or stir-fried.

Buying and Storing Squashes

Look for squashes that are firm, bright and unblemished and that are heavy for their size. Whole winter squash can be kept for several weeks in a cool, dry place. Once cut, they should be kept in the refrigerator and eaten as soon as possible. Summer squash should be stored in the refrigerator for only a few days.

Pods & Seeds

While most of these vegetables are delicious eaten fresh, many of them – peas, corn and broad (fava) and fresh beans, for example – can also be bought frozen. High in nutritional value, these popular vegetables can be enjoyed all year. Other types of pea include mangetouts (snow peas) and sugar snap peas, which can be eaten whole.

Peas

These are one of the few vegetables that taste just as good when frozen. Because freezing takes place soon after picking, frozen peas often have a higher nutritional value than fresh. Another advantage is that frozen peas are readily available all year round. Peas in the pod have a restricted availability and their taste diminishes if not absolutely fresh, because their sugars rapidly turn to starch. However, when they are at the peak of freshness, peas are delicious and have a delicate, sweet flavour. Pop them from the pod and serve raw in salads or steam lightly. Delicious cooked with fresh mint, peas also make satisfying purées and soups, and can be added to risottos and other rice dishes. Mangetouts and sugar snaps can be served steamed as an accompanying vegetable, raw in salads or added to stir-fries

Broad Beans

When young and fresh these tasty beans are a delight to eat. Tiny pods can be eaten whole; simply trim, and then slice. Usually, however, you will need to shell the beans as their skins can become tough. Older beans are often better skinned after they are lightly cooked as this improves their flavour.

Green Beans

All varieties of green beans are eaten pod and all. They should be bright green and crisp-textured. Simply trim and lightly cook or they can be stir-fried or steamed. Serve green beans hot, or leave to cool slightly and serve as a warm salad with a squeeze of fresh lemon juice or a vinaigrette dressing. Young, crisp beans can also be served raw as crudité with a dip or pâté. Simply string, top and tail them before use.

Peas and beans are a good source of protein and fibre and are rich in vitamin C, iron, thiamine, folate, phosphorous and potassium.

Buying and Storing Pods and Beans

Look for bright green, smooth, plump pods and keep in the refrigerator for no more than a day or two.

Corn

The cobs are best eaten soon after picking, before their natural sugars start to convert into starch when the flavour fades and the kernels toughen. However, as with peas, frozen corn is nutritious as it is frozen soon after picking retaining its vitamins. Remove the green outer leaves and the silks and cook whole or slice off the kernels with a sharp knife. Cook for only 4–5 minutes so that they retain their texture. Baby corn cobs can be eaten raw in salads, and are also good in stir-fries, stews and casseroles. **Buying and Storing:** look for very fresh, plump kernels that show no signs of discoloration, wrinkling or drying and eat as soon after purchase as possible. If you do not intend to eat them immediately, store them in the coolest part of the refrigerator.

Vegetable Fruits

Through cultivation and use, tomatoes, aubergines (eggplant) and (bell) peppers are all vegetables, but are botanically classified as fruit. Part of the nightshade family, they have only recently become appreciated for their health-giving qualities.

Tomatoes

There are dozens of varieties to choose from, which vary in colour, shape and size. The egg-shaped plum tomato is perfect for cooking, as it has a rich flavour and a high proportion of flesh to seeds – but it must be used when fully ripe. Too often, store-bought tomatoes are bland and tasteless because they have been picked too young. Vine-ripened and cherry tomatoes are sweet and juicy and are tasty in salads or uncooked sauces. Large beefsteak tomatoes have a good flavour and are also excellent for salads. Sun-dried tomatoes add a rich intensity to sauces, soups and stews. Genetically engineered tomatoes are now sold in some countries, but at present they are sold only canned as a concentrated purée (paste). Check the label.

Buying and Storing: look for deep-red fruit with a firm, yielding flesh. Tomatoes that are grown and sold locally will have the best flavour. To improve the flavour of a slightly hard tomato, leave it to ripen fully at room temperature. It is best to avoid refrigeration because this stops the ripening process and adversely affects the taste and texture of the tomato.

Peeling and Seeding Tomatoes

Tomato seeds can give sauces a bitter flavour. Removing them and the tomato skins will also give a smoother result.

1 Immerse the tomatoes in boiling water and leave for about 30 seconds – the base of each tomato can be slashed to make peeling easier.

2 Lift out the tomatoes with a slotted spoon, rinse in cold water to cool slightly, and peel off the skin.

3 Cut the tomatoes in half, then scoop out the seeds with a teaspoon and remove the hard core. Dice or coarsely chop the flesh according to the recipe.

Aubergines

The dark-purple, glossy-skinned aubergine is the most familiar variety, although it is the small, ivory-white egg-shaped variety that has inspired the name "eggplant" in the USA. There is also the bright green pea aubergine that is used in Asian cooking, and a pale-purple Chinese aubergine. Known in the Middle East as "poor man's caviar", aubergines give substance and flavour to spicy casseroles and tomato-based dishes, and are delicious roasted, griddled and puréed into garlic-laden dips. It is no longer essential to salt sliced or chopped aubergines to remove any bitterness, as this has been selectively bred out of most modern varieties. However, this method, known as degorging, prevents the absorption of excessive amounts of oil if you are frying aubergines.

Buying and Storing: when buying, look for small to medium-size aubergines with bright, shiny skins. Those with shrivelled skin are overmature and are likely to be bitter and tough. Store in the refrigerator for up to two weeks.

CHILLIES

Native to America, this member of the capsicum family now forms an important part of many cuisines, including Indian, Thai, Mexican, South American and African. There are more than 200 different types of chilli. Red chillies are not necessarily hotter than green ones – but they will probably have ripened for longer in the sun. The heat in chillies comes from capsaicin, a compound found in the white membranes, the seeds and, to a lesser extent, in the flesh. Chillies range in potency from the mild and flavourful to the blisteringly hot. Dried chillies tend to be hotter than fresh. Smaller chillies, such as bird's eye chillies, contain proportionately more seeds and membrane, which makes them more potent than larger ones. It is very important to wash your hands with warm soapy water after preparing chillies as they can badly irritate the skin and eyes. Immediately splash affected areas with copious amounts of cold water.

Buying and Storing Choose unwrinkled bright, firm chillies and store in the refrigerator for up to one week. They can also be frozen and there is no need to thaw them before using.

PREPARING CHILLIES

Chillies add a distinct flavour, but remove the seeds as they are fiery hot.

1 Chillies can irritate the skin; always wear rubber gloves and never rub your eyes after handling chillies. Halve the chilli lengthways and remove and discard the seeds.

2 Slice or finely chop and use as required. Wash the knife and board thoroughly in hot, soapy water. Always wash your hands thoroughly after preparing chillies.

PEPPERS

Like chillies, sweet (bell) peppers are also members of the capsicum family. They range in colour from green through to orange, yellow, red and even purple. Green peppers are fully developed but not completely ripe, which can make them difficult to digest. They have refreshing, juicy flesh with a crisp texture. Other colours of peppers have sweeter flesh, and are more digestible than green peppers. Roasting or chargrilling peppers will enhance their sweetness. They can also be stuffed, sliced into salads or steamed. They contain significant amounts of vitamin C, as well as beta carotene, some B complex vitamins, calcium, phosphorus and iron.

Buying and Storing Choose firm and glossy peppers with an unblemished skin and store whole in the refrigerator for up to a week.

AVOCADOS

Although avocados have a high fat content, the fat is monounsaturated, and is thought to lower blood cholesterol levels in the body. Avocados also contain valuable amounts of vitamins C and E, and iron, potassium and manganese. They are said to improve the condition of the skin and hair.

Once cut, avocados should be brushed with lemon or lime juice to prevent the flesh from turning brown. They are usually eaten raw. Avocado halves can be dressed with a vinaigrette, or filled with sour cream, hummus or mayonnaise. Slices or chunks of avocado are delicious in salads. They can be made into the Mexican dip Guacamole and used in soups and stews, when they are added towards the end of cooking.

Buying and Storing Choose avocadoes that "give" slightly when gently pressed. Store at room temperature or in the refrigerator for two to three days.

SHOOT VEGETABLES

This highly-prized collection of vegetables ranges from the aristocratic asparagus to the flowerbud-like globe artichoke.

FENNEL

Florence fennel is closely related to the herb and spice of the same name. The short, fat bulbs have a similar texture to celery and are topped with edible feathery fronds. Fennel has a mild aniseed flavour, which is most potent when eaten raw. Cooking tempers the flavour, giving it a delicious sweetness. When using fennel raw, slice it thinly or chop coarsely and add to salads. Alternatively, slice or cut into wedges and steam, or brush with olive oil and roast or cook on a griddle.

ASPARAGUS

There are two main types: white asparagus is picked just before it sprouts above the surface of the soil; while green-tipped asparagus is cut above the ground and develops its colour when it comes into contact with sunlight. Before use, scrape the lower half of the stalk with a vegetable peeler, then trim off the woody end. Briefly poach whole spears in a frying pan containing a little boiling salted water, or tie the spears in a bundle and boil upright in an asparagus boiler or tall pan. Asparagus is delicious served with melted butter, or dipped into mayonnaise or vinaigrette. It can also be roasted in a little olive oil.

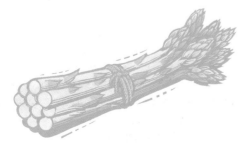

CHICORY

This shoot has long, tightly packed leaves. Red chicory (Belgian endive) has a more pronounced flavour, while the white variety has crisper leaves. The crisp texture and slightly bitter flavour means that chicory is particularly good in salads. It can also be steamed or braised, although the red-leafed variety will fade to brown. Before use, remove the outer leaves and wash thoroughly, then trim the base.

CELERY

This was once grown primarily for medicinal reasons. Serve raw, steamed or braised. Celery leaves have a tangy taste and are also useful for adding flavour to stocks. Celery is rich in vitamin C and potassium.

GLOBE ARTICHOKES

Once cooked, the purple-tinged leaves of globe artichokes have an exquisite flavour. Each leaf should be dipped into garlic butter or vinaigrette dressing, then drawn through the teeth to remove the fleshy part. The heart is then dipped in the butter or dressing.

Buying and Storing Shoot Vegetables

When buying, always choose the freshest-looking specimens. Asparagus spears should have firm stalks. Chicory should be neither withered nor brown at the edges – the best white chicory is sold wrapped in blue paper to keep out the sunlight and to stop it turning green and bitter. Fennel bulbs should be crisp and white and have plenty of fresh fronds. Globe artichokes should have tightly closed, stiff leaves and still have the stalk attached.

Store shoot vegetables unwrapped in the salad drawer of the refrigerator. Asparagus, chicory and fennel will keep for 2–3 days, globe artichokes for up to a week, and celery for about 2 weeks.

THE ONION FAMILY

Onions and garlic are highly prized as both vegetables contain allicin, which has been found to stimulate the body's antioxidant mechanisms, raising levels of beneficial HDL cholesterol and combating the formation of clogged arteries. Additionally, these vegetables are indispensable in cooking. The wide variety of onions, available throughout the year, can be enjoyed raw or cooked and, with garlic, add flavour to a huge range of savoury dishes.

ONIONS

Every cuisine in the world includes onions in one form or another. They are an essential flavouring, offering a range of taste sensations, from the sweet and juicy red onion and powerfully pungent white onion to the light and fresh spring onion (scallion). Pearl onions and shallots are the babies of the family. Tiny pearl onions are generally pickled, while shallots are good roasted with their skins on, when they develop a caramel sweetness, or sautéed and then marinated in a strong vinaigrette dressing.

Buying and Storing: when buying, choose onions that have dry, papery skins and are heavy for their size. They will keep for 1–2 months in a cool, dark place.

GARLIC

For centuries, this wonder food has been the focus of much attention, and is praised for its medicinal powers, which range from curing toothache and preventing cancer to warding off evil demons. It is known to have antiviral, antibacterial and antifungal properties when eaten raw. The flavour of garlic is milder when whole or sliced; crushing or chopping releases the oils making the flavour stronger. Slow-cooking also tames the pungency of garlic, although it still affects the breath.

Buying and Storing: most garlic is semi-dried to prolong its shelf life, yet the cloves should still be moist and juicy. Young garlic, which is available in early summer, has a long green stem and soft white bulb, with a white, pink-tinged or purple-tinged skin. It has a fresher flavour than semi-dried garlic, but can be used in the same ways. Pungency varies, but the general rule when buying garlic is: the smaller the bulb, the more potent the flavour. If stored in a cool, dry place, but not in the refrigerator, garlic will keep for up to about eight weeks. If the air is damp, garlic will sprout and if it is allowed to get too warm, the cloves will eventually turn to grey mildewed powder.

LEEKS

Like onions and garlic, leeks have a long history and are very versatile, having their own distinct, subtle flavour. They are less pungent than onions, but are still therapeutically beneficial. Excellent in soups and casseroles, leeks can also be used as a pie filling or in flans, layered in a terrine or simply steamed and served hot with a light, creamy sauce, ideally with a hint of lemon, or cooled slightly and dressed with a vinaigrette. They have a particular affinity with eggs and so go well in omelettes and quiches. They are also delicious sliced or shredded and then stir-fried with a little garlic and ginger.

Commercially grown leeks are usually about 25cm/10in long, but you may occasionally see baby leeks, which are very mild and tender and are best lightly steamed or roasted with a little olive oil.

Buying and Storing: choose firm leeks with bright green leaves which should also be used. Avoid those without their roots as they will deteriorate more quickly. Leeks will keep well for up to a week in the salad drawer of the refrigerator.

MUSHROOMS

Thanks to their rich earthiness, mushrooms add substance and flavour to all sorts of dishes. There are more than 2,000 edible varieties, but only a tiny proportion are readily available. These fall into three camps: common cultivated mushrooms, such as the button (white); wild varieties that are now cultivated, such as the shiitake; and the truly wild types that have escaped cultivation, such as the morel.

BUTTON, CAP AND FLAT MUSHROOMS
The most common cultivated variety of mushrooms, these are actually one type in various stages of maturity. The button mushroom is the youngest and has, as its name suggests, a tight, white, button-like cap. It has a mild flavour and can be eaten raw in salads. Cap mushrooms are slightly more mature and larger in size, while the flat mushroom is the largest and has dark, open gills. Flat mushrooms have the most prominent flavour and are good grilled (broiled) or baked on their own, or stuffed.

CHESTNUT MUSHROOMS
The brown-capped chestnut mushroom looks similar to the cultivated button but has a more assertive, nutty flavour. They are ideal for antipasto, serving in a cream sauce or in mushrooms à la grecque.

PORTABELLO MUSHROOMS
Similar in appearance to the cultivated flat mushroom, the portabello is simply a large chestnut mushroom. It has a rich flavour and a firm, meaty texture and is good grilled or sautéed.

FIELD MUSHROOMS
This wild mushroom has an intense, rich flavour. It is ideal for grilling and stuffing and makes excellent soup.

CHANTERELLES
This egg-yolk-coloured mushroom has a pretty, funnel shape, and a fragrant but delicate flavour. Also known as the girolle, it is sold fresh in season and dried all year round. If buying fresh, eat as soon as possible and wipe rather than wash as the skin is porous. Sauté, bake or add to sauces.

CEPS
This wild mushroom, which is also known by its Italian name, porcini, has a tender, meaty texture and woody flavour. Dried ceps are used for their rich taste.

MORELS
Slightly sweet-flavoured mushrooms with a distinctive, pointed, honeycomb cap and a hollow stalk. They can be awkward to clean. Morels are costly to buy fresh because they have a short season, but they can be bought dried in small packets.

OYSTER MUSHROOMS
Now cultivated and widely available, oyster mushrooms have an attractive shell-shaped cap and thick stalk. They are usually pale, grey-brown, although yellow and pink varieties are also available.

SHIITAKE MUSHROOMS
These are available fresh or dried and are popular in Asian cooking. They are thought to boost the immune system. When using dried shiitake remove and discard the stems before adding to a dish.

Buying and Storing Mushrooms
Buy mushrooms that smell and look fresh. Avoid ones with damp, slimy patches and any that are discoloured. Store in a paper bag in the refrigerator for up to 4 days. Wipe mushrooms with damp kitchen paper before use but never wash or soak them.

Salad Leaves

Today, salad leaves come in a huge variety of shapes, sizes, colours and flavours.

Round Lettuce

The soft-leaf round (butterhead) lettuce has a mild flavour and is a good sandwich filler.

Cos Lettuce

Known since Roman times, the cos or romaine lettuce has long, sturdy leaves and a strong flavour. Little Gem (Bibb) is a baby variety with firm, densely packed leaves.

Iceberg Lettuce

This round, firm, pale green lettuce has a crisp texture. It has a mild, slightly bitter flavour and is best used as a garnish.

Oak Leaf

This attractive lettuce has red-tinged, soft-textured leaves with a slightly bitter flavour. In salads, combine with green lettuces for a contrast of tastes and textures.

Lollo Rosso

The pretty, frilly leaves of lollo rosso are green at the base and a deep, crimson red around the edge. Its imposing shape means it is best mixed with other leaves if used in a salad. Lollo biondo is a pale green version.

Frisée Lettuce

Also known as curly endive, frisée has spiky, ragged leaves that are dark green on the outside and fade to an attractive pale yellow-green towards its centre. It has a distinctive bitter flavour.

Lamb's Lettuce

Also known as mâche and corn salad, this tiny plant has a cluster of rounded, velvety leaves with a delicate flavour. Serve on its own or mix with other leaves.

Radicchio

A member of the chicory family, radicchio has deep red, tightly packed leaves that have a bitter peppery flavour. It is good in salads and can be sautéed or roasted.

Rocket

Classified as a herb, rocket (arugula) is a popular addition to salads, or it can be served as an appetizer with thin shavings of Parmesan cheese. It has a strong, peppery flavour, which is more robust in wild leaves than in cultivated ones. Lightly steamed rocket has a milder flavour than the raw leaves, but it is equally delicious.

Sorrel

The long pointed leaves of sorrel have a refreshing, sharp flavour that is best when mixed with milder tasting leaves.

Watercress

The hot, peppery flavour of watercress complements milder tasting leaves and is classically combined with fresh orange. It does not keep well and is best used within two days of purchase.

Buying and Storing Salad Leaves

Salad leaves do not keep well and are best when they are very fresh. Avoid leaves that are wilted, discoloured or shrivelled. Store in the refrigerator, unwashed, for between 2 days and 1 week, depending on the variety. As salad leaves are routinely sprayed with pesticides, they should be washed thoroughly, but gently, in cold water and then dried in a dishtowel. Better still, choose organically grown produce.

HERBS

Herbs have been highly prized by natural practitioners for centuries because, in spite of their low nutritional value, they possess many reputed healing qualities. In cooking, herbs can make a significant difference to the flavour and aroma of a dish and they have the ability to enliven the simplest of meals. Fresh herbs can easily be grown at home in the garden or in a pot.

BASIL

This delicate aromatic herb is widely used in Italian and Thai cooking. The leaves bruise easily, so are best used whole or torn, rather than cut with a knife.

BAY

These dark-green, glossy leaves are best left to dry for a few days before use. They have a robust, spicy flavour and are an essential ingredient in bouquet garni.

CHIVES

A member of the onion family, chives have a milder flavour and are best used as a garnish, chopped and sprinkled over egg or potato dishes, or added to salads or flans.

CORIANDER

Warm and spicy, coriander (cilantro) is popular in Indian and Thai curries, stir-fries and salads. It looks similar to flat leaf parsley but its taste is completely different. It is often sold with its root intact. The root has a more intense flavour than the leaves and can be used in curry pastes. It is especially popular in Thai cooking.

DILL

The mild, yet distinctive, aniseed flavour of dill goes well with potatoes, courgettes (zucchini) and cucumber. It makes a good addition to creamy sauces and can be added to a wide variety of egg dishes. It can also be used as a flavouring for dressings and marinades and is a good partner for mustard. An attractive herb with delicate, wispy leaves, add dill to dishes just before serving. It is also useful as a garnish to the finished dish.

MARJORAM

Closely related to oregano, marjoram has a slightly sweeter flavour. It goes well in Mediterranean-style vegetable dishes, such as ratatouille, or in casseroles and tomato sauces, but should be added at the last minute as its flavour diminishes when heated. It can also be added to a marinade.

MINT

The most familiar types are spearmint and peppermint, but there are other distinctly flavoured varieties, such as apple, lemon, Moroccan and pineapple mint. It is used as a flavouring in many cuisines and a wide variety of dishes, from stuffings to fruit salads. Mint is an essential ingredient in the Middle Eastern bulgur wheat salad, tabbouleh, and is also used with natural (plain) yogurt to make raita, a cooling accompaniment to hot curries.

OREGANO

This is a wild variety of marjoram, but it has a more robust flavour that goes well with tomato-based dishes.

PARSLEY

There are two types of parsley: flat leaf and curly. Both taste relatively similar, but the flat leaf variety is preferable in cooked dishes. Parsley is an excellent source of vitamin C, iron and calcium. Chewing parsley after eating garlic or onions can neutralize the smell and freshen breath.

ROSEMARY

The leaves of wonderfully aromatic rosemary are traditionally used in meat dishes, but can also add a smoky flavour to hearty bean and vegetable dishes.

SAGE

The leaves of this herb, which may be silver-grey or purple, have a potent aroma and only a small amount is needed. Sage is commonly added to meat dishes but, if used discreetly, it is delicious with beans, cheese, lentils and in stuffings.

TARRAGON

A popular herb in French cooking, tarragon has an affinity with all egg- and cheese-based dishes. The short, slender-leafed French variety has a warm, aniseed flavour and is considered to be superior to and more palatable than the more invasive Russian tarragon.

THYME

This robustly flavoured aromatic herb is good in tomato-based recipes, and with roasted vegetables, lentils and beans. It is also an essential ingredient in a classic bouquet garni.

Buying and Storing Herbs

Fresh herbs are widely available, sold loose, in packets or growing in pots. The packets do not keep for as long and should be stored in the refrigerator. Place stems of fresh herbs in a jar half-filled with water and cover with a plastic bag. Sealed with an elastic band, the herbs should keep in the refrigerator for a week. Alternatively, wrap in a damp dishtowel and store in the vegetable drawer of the refrigerator. Growing herbs should be kept on a sunny windowsill. If watered regularly, and not cut too often, they will keep for months. Pinch out flowers to maintain leaf growth.

CHOPPING HERBS

Herbs should be prepared just before use to retain colour, texture and flavour.

1 Remove the leaves and place on a clean, dry chopping board. Use a large, sharp cook's knife (a blunt knife will bruise, not chop, the herbs).

2 Chop the herbs, as finely or as coarsely as required, by holding just the tip of the blade on the board and firmly rocking the handle up and down.

3 Alternatively use a mezzaluna which is a half-moon-shaped utensil with a curved blade and handles at either end. It should be moved with a seesaw motion.

4 Chives and dill can be snipped directly into a dish, using sharp kitchen scissors. This is quicker, easier and gives more even results than chopping them.

Sprouted Seeds, Pulses and Grains

Sprouts are quite remarkable in terms of nutritional content. Once the seed (or pulse or grain) has germinated, the nutritional value rises dramatically. There are almost 30 per cent more B vitamins and 60 per cent more vitamin C in the sprout than in the original seed, pulse or grain. Supermarkets and health-food stores sell a variety of sprouts, but it is easy to grow them at home – all you need is a jar, some muslin and an elastic band.

Mung Beansprouts

The most commonly available beansprouts, these are popular in Chinese and Asian cooking, where they are used in soups, salads and stir-fries. They are large, with a crunchy texture and a delicate flavour.

Alfalfa Sprouts

These tiny, wispy white sprouts have a mild, nutty flavour. They are best when eaten raw in salads or sandwiches to retain their crunchy texture.

Wheat Berry Sprouts

Sprouts grown from wheat berries have a crunchy texture and sweet flavour and are excellent in breads. If they are left to grow, the sprouts will become wheatgrass, a powerful detoxifier that is is usually made into a juice.

Chickpea Sprouts

Sprouts grown from chickpeas have a nutty flavour and add substance to dishes. They can be used in salads, casseroles or stir-fries.

Lentil Sprouts

These sprouts have a slightly spicy, peppery flavour and thin, white shoots. Use only whole lentils: split ones will not sprout.

Aduki Beansprouts

These fine wispy sprouts have a sweet nutty taste. Use in salads and stir-fries. They can take a little longer than lentils to sprout.

Buying and Storing Sprouted Seeds, Pulses and Grains

Choose fresh, crisp sprouts with the seed or bean still attached. Avoid any that are slimy. Sprouts are best eaten on the day they are bought but, if fresh, they will keep, wrapped in a plastic bag, in the refrigerator for 2–3 days. Rinse and pat dry before use.

How to Use Beansprouts

Sprouted pulses and beans have a denser more fibrous texture, while sprouts grown from seeds are lighter. Use a mixture of the three for a variety of tastes and textures. They are at their most nutritious when only 5mm/¼in long.

Mung beansprouts These are often used in Asian food, particularly stir-fries, and require little cooking.

Alfalfa sprouts These are good as part of a sandwich filling as well as in salads. They are not suited to cooking.

Sprouted grains These are good in breads, adding a pleasant crunchy texture. Knead them in after the first rising, before shaping the loaf.

Use chickpea and lentil sprouts in casseroles and bakes.

Sea Vegetables

Highly nutritious sea vegetables are highly versatile and can be used as the main component of a dish, to add texture and substance, or as a seasoning. Some sea vegetables, such as wakame, hijiki and kombu (or kelp) can be used in soups, stews and stir-fries, while others, such as agar-agar, are used as a setting agent in jellies, mousses and cheesecakes.

Nori
This useful sea vegetable has a delicate texture and mild flavour. It is sold in thin purple-black sheets, which turn a pretty, translucent green when toasted or cooked. It is one of the few sea vegetables that does not require soaking. In Japanese cooking, the sheets are used to wrap delicate, small parcels of vinegared rice and vegetables that are eaten as sushi. Once toasted and crisp, nori is crumbled and used as a garnish.

Arame
Sold in delicate, black strips, arame has a mild, slightly sweet flavour. If you have not tried sea vegetables before, it is a good start. Arame needs to be soaked before using in stir-fries or salads, but for moist or slow-cooked dishes, such as noodles and soups, it can be added straight from the packet.

Wakame
This sea vegetable is often confused with its relative, kombu, because it looks very similar until it is soaked, when it changes colour from brown to a delicate green.

Wakame has a mild flavour and is one of the most versatile sea vegetables. Soak briefly and use in salads and soups or toast, crumble and use as a condiment.

Kombu
Also known as kelp in the West, kombu is a brown sea vegetable and is usually sold dried in strips, but may be pickled. It has a very strong flavour and is used in slowly cooked dishes, soups and stocks – it is an essential ingredient in the Japanese stock, dashi. A small strip of kombu added to beans while they are cooking will soften them and increase their digestibility.

Hijiki
This sea vegetable looks similar to arame, but is thicker and has a slightly stronger flavour. Once soaked, hijiki can be sautéed or added to soups and salads, but it does require longer cooking than most sea vegetables. It expands considerably during soaking, so only a small amount is needed.

Agar-agar
The vegetarian equivalent to the animal-derived gelatine, agar-agar can be used as a setting agent in both sweet and savoury dishes. It can be bought as flakes or strands, both of which need to be dissolved in water before use. Agar-agar has a neutral taste and its gelling abilities vary according to the other ingredients in a dish, so you may need to experiment, if substituting it for gelatine in a recipe.

Buying and Storing Sea Vegetables
Sea vegetables are usually sold dried and will keep for months. Once the packet is opened, transfer the sea vegetables to an airtight jar. Fresh sea vegetables may be stored in the refrigerator, but will only remain fresh for 1–2 days. Rinse well before use.

FRUIT

Perhaps the ultimate convenience food, most fruits can be simply washed and eaten and, because the nutrients are concentrated just below the skin, it is best to avoid peeling. Cooking fruit reduces valuable vitamins and minerals, so, if you can, eat it raw. Fruit is a source of energy and provides valuable fibre and antioxidants, which are said to reduce the risk of heart disease and cancers.

ORCHARD FRUITS

These fruits have a long history, spanning thousands of years and offer an incredible range of colours and flavours. This group includes many favourites, from crisp, juicy apples, which are available all year round, to luscious, fragrant peaches – a popular summer fruit.

APPLES

There are thousands of varieties of apple, although the choice in stores is often restricted to a mere few. Some of the best-liked eating varieties are Cox's Orange Pippin, Granny Smith, Gala, Braeburn, Golden and Red Delicious and McIntosh. The Bramley Seedling, with its thick, shiny, green skin and tart flesh, is the most familiar cooking apple and is perfect for baking or as the basis of apple sauce. Some lesser-known varieties, many of which have a short season, are often available from farm stores. Apples are delicious when they are eaten raw with their skin on. This versatile fruit is often used in breakfast dishes, main meals, salads, desserts, pies and even soups. Large cooking apples are ideal puréed, stewed and baked, but their tartness means that sugar has to be added. Some varieties of eating apple are just as good cooked and do not need any sugar.

To preserve the maximum amount of vitamins and minerals, cook apples over a low heat with little or no water.

Buying and Storing: when buying apples, choose bright, firm fruits without any bruises or signs of insect damage. Organic apples are more prone to blemishes than non-organic ones, and the fruits can look a little unappealing, but the taste will often be superior. Smaller apples tend to have a better flavour and texture. Store at room temperature or in the refrigerator if you prefer cold apples.

APRICOTS

The best apricots are sunshine gold in colour and full of juice. They are delicious baked or used raw in salads.
Buying and Storing: an apricot is at its best when truly ripe. Immature fruits are hard and tasteless and rarely attain perfect sweetness. Store apricots in the refrigerator, but bring back to room temperature before eating for the best flavour.

CHERRIES

There are two types: sweet and sour. Some are best eaten raw, like Bing, while others, such as Morello, are best cooked.
Buying and Storing: choose firm, bright, glossy fruits that have fresh, green stems. Discard any that are soft, or have split or damaged skin. Store in the refrigerator.

NECTARINES AND PEACHES

These summer fruits are prized for their perfume and luscious juiciness. Peaches range in colour from gold to deep red when perfectly ripe, and the flesh can be orange or creamy white.

Like a peach without the fuzzy skin, nectarines are named after the drink of the gods – nectar – and are delicious baked or used raw in salads or pavlovas. **Buying and Storing:** avoid fruit that is overly soft. Peaches and nectarines are extremely fragile and bruise easily, so buy when slightly under-ripe. To ripen them quickly, place in a brown paper bag with an already ripened fruit. Store ripe nectarines and peaches in the refrigerator, but bring back to room temperature before eating.

PEARS

These have been popular for thousands of years and were extensively cultivated by both the Greeks and the Romans. Pears come into their own in the late summer and autumn (fall) with the arrival of the new season's crops. Particular favourites are green and brown-skinned Conference; Williams, with its thin, yellow skin and sweet, soft flesh; plump Comice, which has a pale yellow skin with a green tinge; and Packham, an excellent cooking pear.

Like certain apples, some pears are good for cooking, others are best eaten raw, and a few varieties fit happily into both camps.

Pears can be used in both sweet and savoury dishes including salads, and can be baked, poached and used in pies and tarts. Once cut, brush the flesh with lemon juice to prevent discoloration. **Buying and Storing:** choose firm, plump fruit that are just slightly under-ripe. Pears can ripen in a day or so and then they pass their peak very quickly and become woolly or squashy. To tell if a pear is ripe, feel around the base of the stalk, where it should give slightly when gently pressed, but the pear itself should be firm.

PLUMS

Ranging in colour from pale yellow to dark, rich purple, plums come in many different varieties, although only a few are available in stores. They can be sweet and juicy or slightly tart; the latter are best cooked in pies and cakes, or made into a delicious jam. Sweet plums can be eaten as they are, and are good in fruit salads, or they can be puréed and combined with custard or yogurt to make a fruit fool. **Buying and Storing:** plums should be just firm, and not too soft, with shiny, smooth skin that has a slight "bloom". Store ripe plums in the refrigerator. Unripe fruits can be kept at room temperature for a few days to ripen.

DRIED FRUIT

A useful source of energy, dried fruit is higher in calories than fresh fruit, and packed with vitamins and minerals. Apricots and prunes are the most popular types, but dried apple rings, cherries and peaches are also available. Look for unsulphured fruit as this has a better colour and flavour.

Buying and Storing Dried Fruit

Look for plump fruit that does not look too shrivelled and buy in small quantities from a source with a quick turnover. Store in an airtight container in a cool cupboard.

Citrus Fruits

Juicy and brightly coloured, citrus fruits, such as oranges, grapefruit, lemons and limes, are best known for their sweet, slightly sour juice, which is very rich in vitamin C. They add an aromatic acidity to many dishes, from soups, salads and sauces to desserts and pies.

Oranges

Best eaten as soon as they are peeled, oranges start to lose vitamin C from the moment they are cut. Thin-skinned oranges tend to be the juiciest.

Popular varieties include the Navel which contains no pips and so is good for slicing; sweet, juicy Jaffa and Valencia; and Seville (Temple), a bitter orange used to make marmalade.

The outermost layer of the orange rind can be removed using a vegetable peeler or paring knife. This thin rind contains aromatic oils, which give a delightful flavour to both savoury and sweet dishes.

Grapefruit

The flesh of the grapefruit ranges in colour from vivid pink and ruby red to white; the pink and red varieties are sweeter. Heavier fruits are likely to be juicier. Served juiced, halved or cut into slices, grapefruit can provide a refreshing start to the day. The fruit also adds a refreshing tang to salads or a contrast to rich foods. Grilling (broiling) mellows the tartness, but keep cooking times brief to preserve the nutrients.

Lemons

Both the juice and rind of this essential cooking ingredient can be used to enliven salad dressings, vegetables, marinades, sauces and biscuits (cookies). Lemon juice can also be used to prevent some fruits and vegetables from discolouring when cut.

Lemons should be deep yellow in colour, firm and heavy, with no hint of green in the skin as this is a sign of immaturity, while a thin, smooth skin is a sign of juicy flesh.

Limes

Once considered to be rather exotic, limes are now widely available. Avoid fruits with a yellowing skin as this is a sign of deterioration. The juice has a sharper flavour than that of lemons and if you substitute limes for lemons in a recipe, you will need to use less juice. Limes are used in Asian cooking and the rind can be used to flavour curries, marinades and dips.

Buying and Storing Citrus Fruits

Look for plump, firm citrus fruit that feels heavy for its size, and has a smooth thin skin; this indicates that the flesh is juicy. Fruits with bruises, brown spots, green patches (or yellow patches on limes) and soft, squashy skin should be avoided, as should dry, wrinkled specimens. Citrus fruits can be kept at room temperature for a few days, but if you want to keep them longer, they are best stored in the refrigerator and eaten within two weeks. Most citrus fruits are waxed or sprayed with fungicides, so scrub them thoroughly to remove any residues. If you can, buy organic or unwaxed fruit.

BERRIES AND CURRANTS

These baubles of vivid red, purple and black are the epitome of summer and autumn (fall), although they are now often found all year round. Despite their distinctive appearance and flavour, berries and currants are interchangeable in their uses in jams, jellies, pies and tarts. Raspberries, blueberries, blackberries and currants all freeze well.

STRAWBERRIES

These are the favourite summer fruits and do not need any embellishment. Serve ripe (avoid those with white or green tips) and raw, on their own, or with a little cream or some natural (plain) yogurt. Wash only if absolutely necessary and just before serving.

RASPBERRIES

Soft and fragrant, raspberries are best served simply and unadulterated – maybe with a spoonful of natural yogurt. Those grown in Scotland are regarded as the best in the world. Raspberries are very fragile and require the minimum of handling, so wash only if really necessary. They are best eaten raw as cooking spoils their flavour and vitamin C content.

BLUEBERRIES

Dark purple in colour, blueberries are very popular in the USA. When ripe, the berries are plump and slightly firm, with a natural "bloom". Avoid any that are soft and dull-skinned, and wash and dry carefully to avoid bruising. Cultivated blueberries are larger than the wild variety. Both types are sweet enough to be eaten raw, but are also good cooked in pies and muffins, used for jellies and jams or made into a sauce to serve with nut or vegetable roasts. Unwashed blueberries will keep for up to a week in the bottom of the refrigerator.

BLACKBERRIES

These are a familiar sight in early autumn, growing wild in hedgerows. Cultivated blackberries have a slightly longer season. Juicy and plump, blackberries can vary in sweetness, which is why they are so often cooked. Wash them carefully to prevent bruising the fruits, then pat dry with kitchen paper. Use in pies and tarts, or make into jams and jellies. The berries can also be lightly cooked, then puréed and sieved to make a sauce to serve with other fruits.

GOOSEBERRIES

These range from the hard and sour green type to the sweeter, softer purple variety. Slightly unripe gooseberries make wonderful pies, crumbles (crisps), jams and jellies. Ripe, softer fruits can be puréed and mixed with cream, yogurt or custard, to make a delicious fruit fool.

BLACKCURRANTS, REDCURRANTS AND WHITECURRANTS

These pretty, delicate fruits are usually sold in bunches on the stem. To remove the currants from the stalk, run the prongs of a fork down through the clusters, taking care not to damage the fruit. Wash the fruits carefully, then pat dry. Raw blackcurrants are quite tart, but this makes them ideal for cooking in sweet pies. They make delicious jams and jellies, and are especially good in summer pudding when they are partnered by other berries. Sweeter whitecurrants make a delightful addition to fruit salads.

Buying and Storing Berries and Currants

Look for firm, glossy berries and currants. Make sure that they are not squashed or mouldy. Ripe fruits do not keep well and are best eaten on the day of purchase – store in the refrigerator. Unripe fruits can be kept for longer.

GRAPES, MELONS, FIGS AND DATES

These fruits were some of the first ever to be cultivated. They are available in a vast variety of shapes, colours and sizes, and with the exception of melons, they can also be bought dried. As well as being a good source of nutrients, these fruits are high in soluble fibre.

GRAPES & DRIED VINE FRUITS

There are many varieties of grape, each with its own particular flavour and character. Most are grown for wine production. Grapes for eating are less acidic and have a thinner skin than those used for wine-making. Seedless grapes are easier to eat and contain less tannin than the seeded fruit. Grapes range in colour from deep purple to pale red, and from bright green to almost white. The finest eating grapes are Muscat grapes, which have a wonderful, perfumed flavour. They may be pale green or golden, or black or red. Italia grapes, another popular eating variety, have a luscious musky flavour.

Serve grapes with cheese, in salads or as a topping for a tart. Before cooking them, remove the skin by blanching the grapes in boiling water for a few seconds, then peel with a small knife.

Raisins, sultanas (golden raisins) and currants are the most popular dried fruits. Traditionally, they are used for fruit cakes and breads, but they are also good in desserts and savoury dishes. In Indian and north African cookery they are often used for their sweetness.

Buying and Storing: choose grapes that are plump and firm with no sign of blemish. They should be evenly coloured and firmly attached to the stalk. Unwashed fruit may be stored in the refrigerator for up to five days where they will retain their texture.

MELONS

These include sweet and juicy cantaloupe, charentais, watermelon and honeydew. Watermelons are very low in calories because of their high water content. Avoid buying ready-cut melons, as most of the vitamins will have been lost.

Buying and Storing: look for melons that feel heavy for their size and yield to firm pressure at the stem end. Store the fruit at room temperature.

FIGS

These delicate, thin-skinned fruits may be purple, brown or greenish-gold. Delicious raw, figs can also be poached or baked.

Buying and Storing: choose unbruised, ripe fruits that yield to gentle pressure, and eat on the day of purchase. If they are not too ripe, they can be kept in the refrigerator for a day or two.

DATES

Like figs, dates are one of the oldest cultivated fruits. Fresh dates are sweet and make a natural sweetener: purée the cooked fruit, then add to cake mixtures, or mix into natural (plain) yogurt with a few chopped almonds or walnuts as a quick, delicious and nutritious dessert.

Buying and Storing: dates should be plump and glossy. Medjool dates from the Middle East and California have a wrinkly skin and a uniquely perfumed flavour, but most other varieties are smooth skinned. They can be stored in the refrigerator for several weeks.

TROPICAL FRUIT

This exotic collection of fruits ranges from the familiar bananas and pineapples to the more unusual papayas and passion fruit. The diversity in colours, shapes and flavours is sure to excite the taste buds.

PINEAPPLES

These distinctive-looking fruits have a sweet, exceedingly juicy and golden flesh. Unlike most other fruits, pineapples do not ripen after picking, although leaving a slightly unripe fruit for a few days at room temperature may reduce its acidity.
Buying and Storing: choose pineapples that have fresh green spiky leaves, are heavy for their size, and are slightly soft to the touch. Store in the refrigerator when ripe.

PAPAYA

Also known as pawpaw, these pear-shaped fruits come from South America. When ripe, the green skin turns a speckled yellow and the pulp is a glorious orange-pink colour. The numerous edible, small black seeds taste peppery when dried. Peel off the skin using a sharp knife or a vegetable peeler before enjoying the creamy flesh, which has a lovely perfumed aroma and sweet flavour. Ripe papaya is best eaten raw, while unripe green fruit can be used in cooking and grated into salads.

MANGO

The skin of these luscious, fragrant fruits can range in colour from green to yellow, orange or red. Their shape varies tremendously, too. An entirely green skin is a sign of an unripe fruit, although in Asia, these are often used in salads. Ripe fruit should yield to gentle pressure and, when cut, it should reveal a juicy, orange flesh. Serve sliced, or purée and use as a base for ice creams and sorbets (sherbets).

BANANAS

A concentrated bundle of energy, bananas are also full of valuable nutrients. The soft and creamy flesh can be blended into smooth, sweet drinks, mashed and mixed with yogurt, or the fruits can be baked and cooked whole on a barbecue. Bananas also make an ideal weaning food for babies, as they rarely cause an allergic reaction.

Buying and Storing Papaya, Mango and Bananas

When buying, look for fruit that is heavy for its size. Mangoes and papayas should yield to gentle pressure. Avoid overly soft or bruised fruit, or those with any hard spots. Ripe mangoes and papayas are best kept in the refrigerator. If you wish to buy ripe bananas, choose yellow (or red) fruit that are patched with brown. Bananas with patches of green can be ripened at room temperature. Do not buy very green bananas as these rarely ripen. Store bananas at cool room temperature.

OTHER TROPICAL FRUIT

Kiwi fruit, which is also known as the Chinese gooseberry, has a brown, downy skin and vivid green flesh that is peppered with tiny black seeds.

Passion fruit is a dark purple, wrinkly, egg-shaped fruit, which hides a pulpy, golden flesh with edible black seeds. Cut in half and scoop out the inside with a spoon.

CEREAL GRAINS

G rains have been cultivated throughout the world for centuries. The seeds of cereal grasses are packed with concentrated goodness. The most popular types of grain, such as wheat, rice, oats, barley and corn or maize, come in various forms, from whole grains to flours. Inexpensive and readily available, grains are incredibly versatile and should form a major part of our diet.

WHEAT

The wheat kernel comprises three parts: bran, germ and endosperm. Wheat bran is the outer husk, while wheat germ is the nutritious seed from which the plant grows. Sprouted wheat is an excellent food, highly recommended in cancer-prevention diets. The endosperm, the inner part of the kernel, is full of starch and protein and forms the basis of wheat flour. In addition to flour, wheat comes in various other forms.

WHEAT BERRIES

These are whole wheat grains with the husks removed and they can be bought in health food stores. Wheat berries may be used to add a sweet, nutty flavour and chewy texture to breads, soups and stews, or can be combined with rice or other grains. They can also be added to salads. Wheat berries must be soaked overnight, then cooked in lightly salted boiling water until tender.

WHEAT BRAN

Wheat bran is the outer husk of the wheat kernel and is a by-product of white flour production. It is very high in soluble dietary fibre, which makes it nature's most effective laxative. Wheat bran makes a healthy addition to bread doughs, breakfast cereals, cakes, muffins and biscuits (cookies), and it can also be added to stews and bakes.

WHEAT FLAKES

Steamed and softened wheat berries that have been rolled and pressed are known as wheat flakes or rolled wheat. They are best used on their own or mixed with other flaked grains in porridge, as a base for muesli (granola), or to add nutrients and substance to breads and cakes. They become more digestible if eating raw in a muesli if they are soaked overnight.

WHEAT GERM

The nutritious heart of the whole wheat berry, wheat germ is a rich source of protein, vitamins B and E, and iron. It is used in much the same way as wheat bran and lends a pleasant, nutty flavour to breakfast cereals and porridge. It is available toasted or untoasted. Store wheat germ in an airtight container in the refrigerator, as it can become rancid if kept at room temperature.

CRACKED WHEAT

This is made from crushed wheat berries and retains all the nutrients of wholewheat. Often confused with bulgur wheat, cracked wheat can be used in the same way as wheat berries (although it cooks in much less time), or as an alternative to rice and other grains. When cooked, it has a slightly sticky texture and pleasant crunchiness. Serve it as an accompaniment, or use in salads and pilaffs.

BULGUR WHEAT

Unlike cracked wheat, this grain is made from cooked wheat berries, which have the bran removed, and are then dried and crushed. This light, nutty grain is simply soaked in water for 20 minutes, then drained – some manufacturers specify cold water, but boiling water produces a softer grain. It can also be cooked in boiling water until tender. It is the main ingredient in the Middle Eastern salad, tabbouleh, where it is combined with parsley, mint, tomatoes, cucumber and onion, and dressed with lemon juice and olive oil.

SEMOLINA

Made from the endosperm of durum wheat, semolina can be used to make a milk pudding or to give cakes, biscuits (cookies) and breads a grainy texture.

COUSCOUS

This is a form of pasta made by steaming and drying cracked durum wheat. It is popular in north Africa, where it forms the basis of a national dish of the same name. Grains are moistened by hand, passed through a sieve and then steamed in a couscousière, set over a bubbling vegetable stew, until light and fluffy. Nowadays, quick-cooking couscous, which simply needs soaking is available. Couscous has a fairly bland flavour, which makes it a good foil for spicy dishes.

WHEAT FLOUR

This is ground from the whole grain and may be wholemeal (whole-wheat) or white, depending on the degree of processing. Hard, or strong flour is high in a protein called gluten, which makes it ideal for bread making, while soft flour is lower in gluten but higher in starch and is better for light cakes and pastries. Durum wheat flour comes from one of the hardest varieties of wheat and is used to make pasta. Most commercial white flour is "all purpose" – a combination of soft and hard wheat.

Because the refining process robs many commercial flours of most of their nutrients, the lost vitamins and minerals are synthetically replaced. Look for brands that are unbleached and organically produced as these have fewer chemical additives. Nutritionally, stoneground wholewheat flour is the best buy because it is largely unprocessed and retains all the valuable nutrients. It produces slightly heavier breads, cakes and pastries than white flour, but can be combined with white flour to make lighter versions, although, of course, the nutritional value will not be so high.

Buying and Storing Wheat-based Foods

Obtain wheat-based foods from stores with a high turnover of stock. Wheat berries can be kept for about 6 months, but wholewheat flour should be used within 3 months, as its oils turn rancid. Always decant grains into airtight containers and store in a cool, dark place. Wheat germ should be stored in an airtight container in the refrigerator for no more than a month.

RICE

Throughout Asia, a meal – even breakfast – is considered incomplete without rice. It is a staple food for over half the world's population, and almost every culture has its own repertoire of rice dishes, ranging from Italian risottos to Middle Eastern pilaffs. What is more, this valuable food provides a good source of vitamins and minerals and contains some important proteins, as well as being a steady supply of energy.

LONG GRAIN RICE

The most widely used type of rice is long grain rice, where the grain is five times as long as it is wide. Long grain brown rice has had its outer husk removed, leaving the bran and germ intact, which gives it a chewy, nutty flavour. It takes longer to cook than white rice, but contains more fibre, vitamins and minerals. Long grain white rice has had its husk, bran and germ removed, taking most of the nutrients with them and leaving a bland-flavoured rice that is light and fluffy when cooked. It is often whitened with chalk, talc or other preservatives, so rinsing is essential. Easy-cook long grain white rice, sometimes called par-boiled or converted rice, has been steamed under pressure. This process hardens the grain and makes it difficult to overcook, and some nutrients are transferred from the bran and germ into the kernel during this process. Easy-cook brown rice cooks more quickly than normal brown rice.

JASMINE RICE

This rice has a soft, sticky texture and a delicious, mildly perfumed flavour – which accounts for its other name, fragrant rice. It is a long grain rice that is widely used in Thai cooking, where its delicate flavour tempers strongly spiced food.

BASMATI RICE

This is a slender, long grain rice, which is grown in the foothills of the Himalayas. It is aged for a year after harvest, a process that gives it a characteristic light, fluffy texture and aromatic flavour. In fact, its name means "fragrant".

Both white and brown types of basmati rice are available. Brown basmati contains more nutrients as the bran and germ have been retained. It has a slightly nuttier flavour and chewier texture than the white variety and cooks more rapidly than other types of brown rice, making it ideal for quick meals. Widely used in Indian cooking, basmati rice has a cooling effect on hot and spicy curries. It is also excellent for biryanis and for rice salads, when you want very light, fluffy separate grains.

RED RICE

This rice comes from the Camargue in France and has a distinctive chewy texture and a nutty flavour. It is an unusually hard grain, which although it takes about an hour to cook, retains its shape. Cooking intensifies its red colour, making it a distinctive addition to salads and stuffings. It is excellent for pilaffs and works particularly well with mushrooms.

WILD RICE

This is not a true rice but an aquatic grass grown in North America. It has dramatic, long, slender brown-black grains that have a nutty flavour and chewy texture. It takes longer to cook than most types of rice – 35–60 minutes, depending on whether you like it chewy or tender – but you can reduce the cooking time by soaking it in water overnight. Wild rice is extremely nutritious. It contains all eight essential amino acids and is particularly rich in lysine. It is a good source of fibre, low in calories and gluten free. Use in stuffings, serve plain or mix with other rices in pilaffs and rice salads.

VALENCIA RICE

Traditionally used for making Spanish paella, this short grain rice is not so sturdy as risotto rice and needs to be handled with care because it breaks down easily. The best way of cooking paella is to leave the rice unstirred once all the ingredients are in the pan. Valencia rice can be difficult to obtain outside Spain and risotto rice is often used as a substitute.

RISOTTO RICE

To make Italian risotto, it is essential that you use a special, fat, short grain rice. Arborio rice, which originates from the Po Valley region in Italy, is the most widely sold variety of risotto rice, but you may also find varieties such as Carnaroli and Vialone Nano in specialist stores. When cooked, most rice absorbs around three times its weight in water, but risotto rice can absorb nearly five times its weight, and the result is a creamy grain that still retains a slight bite.

PUDDING RICE

This rounded, short grain rice is suitable for milk puddings and rice desserts. The grains swell and absorb a great deal of milk during cooking, which gives the pudding a soft, creamy consistency. Brown pudding rice is also available.

GLUTINOUS RICE

This rice is almost round in shape and has a slightly sweet flavour. Despite its name, the rice is gluten-free. The grains stick together when cooked owing to their high starch content, making the rice easier to eat with chopsticks. Glutinous rice, which can be either white, black or purple, is used in many South-east Asian countries to make sticky, creamy puddings. In China, white glutinous rice is often wrapped in lotus leaves and steamed to make a popular dim sum dish.

JAPANESE SUSHI RICE

Similar to glutinous rice, this is mixed with rice vinegar to make sushi. Most sushi rice eaten in the West is grown in California.

Buying and Storing Rice

To ensure freshness, always buy rice from stores that have a regular turnover of stock. Store in an airtight container in a cool, dry, dark place to keep out moisture and insects. Wash before use to remove any impurities. Cooked rice should be cooled quickly, then chilled in the refrigerator and reheated thoroughly before serving.

BOILING RICE

The open pan method is the easiest way to cook rice. Bring a large pan of lightly salted water to the boil. Add the rice, bring back to the boil, stir once, then cook for about 15 minutes, depending on the variety. Make sure the water is boiling quite vigorously throughout to keep the grains separated. Drain, leave to stand for 5 minutes, then fluff up with a fork.

OTHER GRAINS

Wheat and rice are undoubtedly the most widely used grains, yet there are others, such as oats, rye, corn, barley, and quinoa, that should not be ignored because they provide variety in our diet and are packed with nutrients. Grains come in many different forms, from whole grains and flakes to flour and are used for baking, breakfast cereals and cooked dishes.

OATS

Available rolled, flaked, as oatmeal or oatbran, oats are warming and sustaining when cooked. Like rye, oats are a popular grain in northern Europe, particularly Scotland, where they are commonly turned into porridge, oatcakes and pancakes.

Whole oats are unprocessed with the nutritious bran and germ remaining intact. Oat groats are the hulled, whole kernel, while rolled oats are made from groats that have been heated and pressed flat. Quick-cooking rolled oats have been pre-cooked in water and then dried, which diminishes their nutritional value. Medium oatmeal is best in cakes and breads, while fine is ideal in pancakes, and fruit and milk drinks. Oat flour is gluten-free and has to be mixed with other flours that contain gluten to make leavened bread. Oat bran can be sprinkled over breakfast cereals and mixed into natural (plain) or fruit yogurt.

RYE

The most popular grain for bread-making in eastern Europe, Scandinavia and Russia, rye flour produces a dark, dense and dry loaf that keeps well. It is a hardy grain, which grows where most others fail – hence its popularity in colder climates. Rye is low in gluten and so rye flour is often mixed with high-gluten wheat flours to create lighter textured breads; the colour of which is sometimes intensified using molasses. The whole grain can be soaked overnight, then cooked in boiling water until tender, but the flour, with its robust, full flavour and greyish colour, is the most commonly used form. The flour ranges from dark to light, depending on whether the bran and germ have been removed.

CORN

Although we are most familiar with yellow corn or maize, blue, red, black and even multi-coloured varieties can also be found. Corn is an essential store-cupboard (pantry) ingredient in the USA, the Caribbean and Italy, and comes in many forms.

Cornmeal The main culinary uses for cornmeal are cornbread, a classic bread from the southern states of America, and polenta, which confusingly is both the Italian name for cornmeal as well as a dish made with the grain. Polenta (the cooked dish) is a thick, golden porridge, which is often flavoured with butter and cheese or chopped herbs. Once cooked, polenta can also be left to cool, then cut into slabs and fried, cooked on a barbecue or griddled until golden brown. Enjoy polenta with roasted Mediterranean vegetables or a tomato sauce. Ready-to-slice polenta is available from some supermarkets.

Polenta grain comes in various grades, ranging from fine to coarse. You can buy polenta that takes 40–45 minutes to cook or an "instant" part-cooked version that can be cooked in less than 5 minutes.

In the Caribbean, cornmeal is used to make puddings and dumplings.

Cornflour A fine white powder, cornflour (cornstarch) is a useful thickening agent for sauces and casseroles. It can also be added to cakes. It must be diluted with a little liquid before adding to a hot dish so that it will blend smoothly.

Popcorn This strain of corn is grown specifically to make the popular snack food. The kernel's hard outer casing explodes when heated. Popcorn can easily be made at home and flavoured to be sweet or savoury according to taste. There is a type suitable for the microwave. The store-bought types are often high in salt or sugar.

BARLEY

Believed to be the oldest cultivated grain, barley is still a fundamental part of the everyday diet in eastern Europe, the Middle East and Asia.

Pearl barley, the most usual form, is husked, steamed and then polished to give it its characteristic ivory-coloured appearance. It has a mild, sweet flavour and chewy texture, and can be added to soups, stews and baked dishes. It is also used to make old-fashioned barley water.

Pot barley is the whole grain with just the inedible outer husk removed. It takes much longer to cook than pearl barley. Barley flakes, which make a satisfying porridge, and barley flour are also available.

QUINOA

Hailed as the supergrain of the future, quinoa (pronounced "keen-wa") is really a grain of the past. It was called "the mother grain" by the Incas, who cultivated it for hundreds of years, high in the Andes, solely for their own use.

Nowadays, quinoa is widely available. The tiny, bead-shaped grains have a mild, slightly bitter taste and firm texture. It is cooked in the same way as rice, but the grains quadruple in size, becoming translucent with an unusual white outer ring. Quinoa is useful for making stuffings, pilaffs, baked dishes and breakfast cereals. It is gluten-free and contains a substantial amount of protein.

MILLET

This highly nutritious grain remains a staple ingredient in many parts of the world, including Africa, China and India. Its mild flavour makes it an ideal accompaniment to spicy stews and curries, and it can be used as a base for pilaffs or milk puddings. The tiny, firm grains can also be flaked or ground into flour. Millet is gluten-free, so it is a useful food for people with coeliac disease. The flour can be used for baking, but needs to be combined with high-gluten flours to make leavened bread.

BUCKWHEAT

In spite of its name, buckwheat is not a type of wheat, but is actually related to the rhubarb family. Available plain or toasted, it has a nutty, earthy flavour. It is a staple food in eastern Europe as well as Russia, where the triangular grain is milled into a speckled-grey flour and used to make blini. The flour is also used in Japan for soba noodles and in Italy for pasta. Buckwheat pancakes are popular in France. The whole grain, which is also known as kasha, makes a fine porridge.

Buying and Storing Other Grains

Always buy grains from a source with a regular turnover of stock and store in an airtight container in a cool, dry, dark place.

HOW TO COOK GRAINS

Grains can be simply boiled in water but, to enhance their flavour, first cook them in a little oil for a few minutes. When they are well coated, add two or three times their volume of water or stock with herbs or spices. Bring to the boil, then simmer, covered, until the water is absorbed and the grains are tender. Do not disturb the grains while they are cooking.

Legumes

Lentils, peas and pulses provide the cook with a diverse range of flavours and textures. They have long been a staple food in the Middle East, South America, India and the Mediterranean. Low in fat and high in complex carbohydrates, vitamins and minerals, legumes are also an important source of protein for vegetarians, matching animal-based sources when eaten with cereals.

LENTILS AND PEAS
The humble lentil is one of our oldest foods. Lentils are hard even when fresh, so they are always sold dried. Unlike virtually all other pulses, they do not need soaking before cooking.

RED LENTILS
Bright orange-coloured red split lentils, sometimes known as Egyptian lentils, are the most familiar variety. They cook in just 20 minutes, eventually disintegrating into a thick purée. They are ideal for thickening soups and casseroles and, when cooked with spices, make a delicious dhal. In the Middle East, red or yellow lentils are cooked and mixed with spices and vegetables to form balls known as kofte.

YELLOW LENTILS
Lesser-known yellow lentils taste very similar to the red variety and are used in much the same way.

GREEN AND BROWN LENTILS
Sometimes referred to as continental lentils, these disc-shaped pulses retain their shape when cooked. They take longer to cook than split lentils – about 40–45 minutes – and are ideal for adding to warm salads, casseroles and stuffings. Alternatively green and brown lentils can be cooked and blended with herbs or spices to make a nutritious pâté.

PUY LENTILS
These tiny, dark, blue-green, marbled lentils grow in the Auvergne region in central France. They are considered to be far superior in taste and texture than other varieties, and they retain their bead-like shape during cooking, which takes around 25–30 minutes. Puy lentils are a delicious addition to simple dishes, such as warm salads, and are also good braised in wine and flavoured with fresh herbs.

PEAS
Dried peas come from the field pea not the garden pea, which is eaten fresh. Unlike lentils, peas are soft when young and require drying. They are available whole or split; the latter have a sweeter flavour and cook more quickly. Like split lentils, split peas do not hold their shape when cooked, making them perfect for dhals, purées, casseroles and soups. They take about 45 minutes to cook. Marrowfat peas are larger in size and are used to make the traditional British dish "mushy" peas. Like other whole peas, they require soaking overnight before use.

Buying and Storing Lentils and Peas
Although lentils and peas can be kept for up to a year, they toughen with time. Buy from stores with a fast turnover of stock and store in airtight containers in a cool, dark place. Look for bright, unwrinkled pulses.

PULSES

The edible seeds from plants belonging to the legume family, pulses, which include chickpeas and a vast range of beans, are packed with protein, vitamins, minerals and fibre, and are extremely low in fat. For the cook, their ability to absorb the flavours of other foods means that pulses can be used as the base for an infinite number of dishes.

ADUKI BEANS

Also known as adzuki beans, these tiny, deep-red beans have a sweet, nutty flavour. In Chinese cooking, they form the base of red bean paste. Known as the "king of beans" in Japan, the aduki bean is reputed to be good for the liver and kidneys. They cook quickly and can be used in casseroles and bakes. They are also ground into flour for use in cakes, breads and pastries.

BLACK BEANS

These shiny, black, kidney-shaped beans are often used in Caribbean cooking. They have a sweetish flavour, and their distinctive colour adds a dramatic touch to soups, mixed bean salads or casseroles.

BLACK-EYED BEANS

Known as black-eye peas or cow peas in the USA, black-eyed beans are an essential ingredient in Creole cooking and some spicy Indian curries. The small, creamy-coloured bean is characterized by the black spot on its side where it was once attached to the pod. Good in soups and salads, they can also be added to savoury baked dishes and casseroles, and can be used in place of haricot (navy) or cannellini beans in a wide variety of dishes.

BORLOTTI BEANS

These oval beans have red-streaked, pinkish-brown skin and a bitter-sweet flavour. When cooked, they have a tender, moist texture, which is good in Italian bean and pasta soups, as well as hearty vegetable stews. In most recipes, they are interchangeable with red kidney beans.

BROAD BEANS

These large beans were first cultivated by the ancient Egyptians. Usually eaten in their fresh form, broad (fava) beans change in colour from green to brown when dried, making them difficult to recognize in their dried state. The outer skin can be very tough and chewy, and some people prefer to remove it after cooking. They can also be bought ready-skinned.

BUTTER BEANS AND LIMA BEANS

Similar in flavour and appearance, both butter beans and lima beans are characterized by their flattish, kidney shape

---

SOAKING BEANS

Most pulses require soaking in cold water for several hours or even overnight before use, so it is wise to plan ahead. If you are short of time, the long soaking process can be speeded up: first, cook the beans in boiling water for 2 minutes, then remove the pan from the heat. Cover and leave for 2 hours. Drain, rinse and cover with plenty of fresh cold water before cooking.

1–2 hours
Split peas, whole peas

3–4 hours
Aduki, black, borlotti, broad, butter, cannellini, flageolet, haricot, kidney, lima, mung, navy, pinto

5–8 hours
Chickpeas, ful medames, soya beans

and soft, floury texture. Cream-coloured butter beans are familiar in Britain and Greece, while lima beans are popular in many dishes in the USA.

In Greek cooking, butter beans are oven-baked with tomato, garlic and olive oil until tender and creamy. The pale-green lima bean is the main ingredient in succotash, an American dish that also includes corn kernels. Butter and lima beans are also good with creamy herb sauces. Care should be taken not to overcook both butter and lima beans as the texture becomes pulpy.

CANNELLINI BEANS

These small, white, kidney-shaped beans – sometimes called white kidney beans – have a soft, creamy texture when cooked and are popular in Italian cooking. They can be used in place of haricot beans and, when dressed with olive oil, lemon juice, garlic and parsley, make an excellent warm salad.

CHICKPEAS

Also known as garbanzo beans, robust and hearty chickpeas have a delicious nutty flavour and creamy texture. They need lengthy cooking and are much used in Mediterranean and Middle Eastern cooking. In India, they are known as gram and are ground into flour to make fritters and flat breads. Gram flour, also known as besan, can be found in health food stores and Asian grocery stores.

FLAGEOLET BEANS

These young haricot beans are removed from the pod before they are fully ripe, hence their fresh delicate flavour. A pretty, mint-green colour, they are the most expensive bean to buy and are best treated simply. Cook them until they are tender, then season and drizzle with a little olive oil and lemon juice to be eaten warm or at room temperature.

COOKING BEANS

Most types of beans, with the exception of mung and black-eyed beans, require soaking for 5–6 hours or overnight and then boiling rapidly for 10–15 minutes to remove any harmful toxins. This is particularly important for kidney beans, which can cause serious food poisoning if not treated in this way.

1 Wash the beans well, then place in a bowl that allows plenty of room for expansion. Cover with cold water and leave to soak overnight or for 8–12 hours, then drain and rinse.

2 Place the beans in a large pan and cover with fresh cold water. Bring to the boil and boil rapidly for 10–15 minutes, then reduce the heat and simmer gently for 1–1½ hours until tender. Drain and serve.

COOK'S TIPS

• *Cooking beans in a pressure cooker will reduce the cooking time by around three-quarters.*
• *Do not add salt to beans while they are cooking as this will cause the skins to toughen. Cook the beans first, then season with salt and pepper. Acid foods, such as tomatoes or lemons, or vinegar will also toughen beans, so only add these ingredients once the beans are soft.*

HARICOT BEANS

Most commonly used for canned baked beans, these versatile, ivory-coloured beans are small and oval in shape. Called navy or Boston beans in the USA, they suit slow-cooked dishes, such as casseroles. They also make delicious soups, such as minestrone.

PINTO BEANS

A smaller, paler version of the borlotti bean, the savoury-tasting pinto has an attractive speckled skin – it is aptly called the painted bean. One of the many relatives of the kidney bean, pinto beans feature extensively in Mexican cooking, most familiarly in refried beans, when they are cooked until tender and fried with garlic, chilli and tomatoes. While cooking, the beans are mashed, resulting in a wonderful, spicy, rough purée that is usually served with warm tortillas and salad. Sour cream, Tabasco and garlic-flavoured guacamole are good accompaniments.

RED KIDNEY BEANS

Glossy, mahogany-red kidney beans retain their colour and shape when cooked. They have a soft texture and are popular in South American cooking. An essential ingredient in spicy chillies, they can also be used to make Mexican refried beans (although this dish is traditionally made from pinto beans). Cooked kidney beans can also be used to make a variety of salads, but they are especially good combined with thinly sliced red onion and chopped flat leaf parsley and fresh mint, then tossed in an olive oil dressing.

It is essential to follow the cooking instructions when preparing kidney beans, as they contain a toxic substance that causes severe food poisoning if they are not pre-boiled vigorously for 10–15 minutes, uncovered, to destroy it.

SOYA BEANS

These small, oval beans vary in colour from creamy-yellow through brown to black. Soya beans contain all the nutritional properties of animal products but without the disadvantages. They are extremely dense and need to be soaked for up to 12 hours before cooking. They combine well with robust ingredients such as garlic, herbs and spices, and they make a healthy addition to soups, casseroles and salads.

Soya beans are also used to make tofu, tempeh, textured vegetable protein (TVP), flour and the different versions of soy sauce.

MUNG BEANS

Instantly recognizable in their sprouted form as beansprouts, mung or moong beans are small, olive-coloured beans native to India. They are soft and sweet when cooked, and are used in the spicy curry, moong dhal. Soaking is not essential, but if they are soaked overnight, this will reduce the usual 40 minutes cooking time by half.

Buying and Storing Pulses

Look for plump, shiny beans with unbroken skins. Beans toughen with age so, although they will keep for up to a year in a cool, dry place, it is best to buy them in small quantities from stores with a regular turnover of stock. Avoid any beans that look dusty or dirty or smell musty, and store them in an airtight container in a cool, dark and dry place.

SOYA BEAN PRODUCTS

These beans are incredibly versatile and are used to make an extensive array of by-products that can be used in cooking – tofu, tempeh, textured vegetable protein, flour, miso, and a variety of sauces. The soya bean is the most nutritious of all beans. Rich in high-quality protein, it is one of the few vegetarian foods that contains all eight essential amino acids that cannot be synthesized in the body.

TOFU

Also known as beancurd, tofu is made in a similar way to soft cheese. The beans are boiled, mashed and sieved to make soya "milk", and the "milk" is then curdled using a coagulant. The resulting curds are drained and pressed and there are several different types to choose from.

Firm Tofu This type of tofu is sold in blocks and can be cubed or sliced and used in vegetable stir-fries, kebabs, salads, soups and casseroles. Alternatively, firm tofu can be mashed and used in bake dishes and burgers. The bland flavour is improved by marinating, because the porous texture readily absorbs flavours.

Silken Tofu Soft with a smooth texture, this tofu is ideal for sauces, dressings, dips and soups. It is a useful dairy-free alternative to cream, soft cheese or yogurt.

Other Forms of Tofu Smoked, marinated and deep-fried tofu are all readily available in health food stores and Asian stores, as well as supermarkets.

Deep-fried tofu is fairly tasteless, but it has an interesting texture. It puffs up during cooking and, underneath the golden, crisp coating the tofu is white and soft, and easily absorbs the flavour of other ingredients. It can be used in much the same way as firm tofu and, as it has been fried in vegetable oil, it is suitable for vegetarian cooking.

Buying and Storing Tofu

All types of fresh tofu can be kept in the refrigerator for up to 1 week. Firm tofu should be kept covered in water, which must be changed regularly. It is also available in vacuum packs which have a longer storage period than fresh. Freezing is not recommended, because it alters the texture. Silken tofu, which is ideal for dips and desserts, is often available in long-life vacuum packs, which do not have to be kept in the refrigerator.

TEMPEH

This Indonesian speciality is made by fermenting cooked soya beans with a cultured starter. Tempeh has a firmer texture than tofu and has a nuttier, more savoury flavour. It can be used in the same way as firm tofu in stir-fries, kebabs or salads and also benefits from marinating. The firm texture of tempeh means that it can be used instead of meat products in pies and casseroles adding complete protein to the dish.

Buying and Storing: tempeh is available chilled or frozen in health food stores and Asian stores. It has usually been deep fried before being vacuum packed. Chilled tempeh can be stored in the refrigerator for up to a week. Frozen tempeh can be left in the freezer for 1 month; thaw before use.

TVP

Textured vegetable protein, or TVP, is a useful meat replacement and is usually bought in dry chunks or minced (ground). Made from processed soya beans, TVP is very versatile and readily absorbs the strong flavours of ingredients, such as herbs, spices and vegetable stock. It is inexpensive and is a convenient store-cupboard (pantry) item. TVP needs to be rehydrated in boiling water or vegetable stock, and can be used in stews and curries, or as a filling for pies.

SOYA FLOUR

This is a finely ground, high-protein flour, which is also gluten-free. It is often mixed with other flours in bread and pastries, adding a pleasant nuttiness, or it can be used as a thickener in sauces. Because it has no gluten it cannot be used alone for breadmaking.

Buying and Storing TVP and Soya Flour

Store TVP and soya flour in an airtight container in a cool, dry, dark place.

SOY SAUCE

This soya by-product originated over 2,000 years ago and the recipe has changed little since then. It is made by combining crushed soya beans with wheat, salt, water and a yeast-based culture called koji, and the mixture is left to ferment for between 6 months and 3 years.

There are two basic types of soy sauce: light and dark. Light soy sauce is slightly thinner in consistency and saltier. It is used in dressings and soups. Dark soy sauce is heavier and sweeter, with a more rounded flavour, and is used in marinades, stir-fries and sauces. Try to buy naturally brewed soy sauce, as many other kinds are now chemically prepared, and may contain flavourings and colourings.

SHOYU

Made in Japan, shoyu is aged for 1–2 years to produce a full-flavoured sauce that can be used in the same way as dark soy sauce. It is less salty than ordinary soy sauce. You can buy it in all health food stores and Asian supermarkets.

TAMARI

This form of soy sauce is a natural by-product of making miso, although it is often produced in the same way as soy sauce. Most tamari is made without wheat, which means that it is gluten-free. It is also much lower in salt than other soy sauces. It is brewed for up to 2 years giving it a rich, dark, robust flavour and is used in cooking or as a condiment.

Buying and Storing Soya Sauces

Keep soy sauce, shoyu and tamari in a cool, dark place. It will keep for some time but check the "best before" date on the bottle if you use it infrequently.

MISO

This thick paste is made from a mixture of cooked soya beans, rice, wheat or barley, salt and water. Miso is left to ferment for up to 3 years. It can be used to add a savoury flavour to soups, stocks, stir-fries and noodle dishes, and is a staple food in Asia. There are three main types: kome, or white miso, is the lightest and sweetest; medium-strength mugi miso, which has a mellow flavour and is usually preferred for everyday use; and hacho miso, which is a dark chocolate colour, and has a thick texture and a strong flavour. Thin with cooking liquid before adding, and do not boil.

Buying and Storing: miso keeps well and can be stored for several months, but should be kept in an airtight container in the refrigerator once it has been opened.

Dairy Foods & Other Options

While it would be foolish to advocate the consumption of vast quantities of high-fat milk, cream and cheese, a diet that includes small amounts of dairy products does provide valuable vitamins and minerals. There is little reason to reject dairy products as they can enrich vegetarian cooking. However, for those who choose to avoid dairy foods, there are plenty of alternatives.

Milk, Cream and Yogurt

This wide group of ingredients includes milk, cream and yogurt made from cow's, goat's and sheep's milk, as well as non-dairy products such as soya milk and cream.

Milk

This is one of our most widely used ingredients. Cow's milk remains the most popular type although, with the growing concern about saturated fat and cholesterol, semi-skimmed (low-fat) and skimmed milks now outsell the full-fat version. Skimmed milk contains half the calories of the full-fat type and only a fraction of the fat, but nutritionally it is on a par, retaining its vitamins and minerals.

Buy organic milk if you can, because it comes from cows that have been fed on a pesticide-free diet, and are not routinely treated with hormones, antibiotics, or BST (bovine somatotrophin), which is used to boost the milk yield from cows.

Goat's and sheep's milk These milks make useful alternatives for people who are intolerant to cow's milk. They are nutritionally similar to cow's milk, but are easier to digest. Goat's milk has a stronger musky flavour, while sheep's milk is a little creamier and richer with a less assuming flavour. They can now be obtained fresh or frozen from health food stores and some supermarkets. It is even possible to obtain semi-skimmed versions.

Buttermilk

Traditionally made from the milky liquid left over after butter making, buttermilk is now more likely to be made from skimmed milk, mixed with milk solids and then cultured with lactic acid. It has a creamy, mild, sour taste and makes a tangy and distinctive addition to desserts. It is a popular ingredient in Eastern European cooking where it is used in baking. Buttermilk gives cakes and soda bread a moist texture. It is low in fat, containing only 0.1 per cent.

Cream

The high fat content of cream means that it is not an ingredient to be eaten daily. Used with discretion, however, it lends a richness to soups, sauces, baked dishes and desserts.

The fat content of cream ranges widely: half-cream contains about 12 per cent, single (light) cream 18 per cent, double (heavy) cream 48 per cent, and clotted cream about 55 per cent.

Sour Cream

This thick-textured cream is treated with lactic acid, which gives it its characteristic tang. Full-fat sour cream contains about 20 per cent fat, although low- and non-fat versions are available. It can be used in the same way as cream. Care should be taken when cooking, as it can curdle if heated to too high a temperature.

CRÈME FRAÎCHE

A rich, cultured cream similar to sour cream, but its high fat content, at around 35 per cent, means that it does not curdle when gently cooked. Crème fraîche is delicious served with fresh fruit, such as ripe summer berries, puréed mangoes or sliced bananas.

SMETANA

This is made from skimmed milk and single cream with an added culture. It has a similar fat content to strained yogurt (about 10 per cent), and should be treated in the same way. Smetana can quickly curdle if it is overheated.

Buying and Storing Milk and Cream

When buying milk, cream and cream-related products, check the label. Manufacturers and retailers are obliged to give a "use by" date on the packet. The fat content, nutritional information and list of ingredients will also be detailed. Store dairy products in the refrigerator and consume within a few days of opening. Long-life cartons will keep indefinitely unopened.

SOYA SUBSTITUTES

Soya milk This is the most widely used alternative to cow's milk. Made from pulverized soya beans, it is suitable for both cooking and drinking and is used to make yogurt, cream and cheese. It is interchangeable with cow's milk, although it has a slightly thicker consistency and a nutty flavour. Fruit- and chocolate-flavoured soya milk, and fortified versions are available.

Soya cream This is a product made from a higher proportion of beans than that in soya "milk", which gives it a richer flavour and thicker texture. It has a similar consistency to single cream and can be used in the same ways.

Buying and Storing Soya Substitutes

Most soya milks and creams are sold in long-life cartons, which extend their shelf-life and means that they do not require refrigeration until opened. It may be sweetened or non-sweetened. Some retailers stock fresh soya milk and this should be treated in the same way as cow's milk.

YOGURT

Praised for its health-giving qualities, yogurt has earned a reputation as one of the most valuable health foods. The consistency may be thin or thick. Greek (US strained plain) yogurt, which is made from cow's or sheep's milk, is higher in fat than other types of yogurt, but contains less fat than cream and makes a healthier alternative. Lower fat yogurts can also be used instead of cream, but are best used in uncooked dishes unless mixed with a little diluted cornflour. Strained yogurt has its watery whey removed to make it thicker and richer, and has a similar fat content to Greek yogurts. When buying yogurt, look for "live" on the label. This signifies that it has been fermented with a starter culture bacteria, which is beneficial to health.

Buying and Storing: it is important to check the "best before" or "sell-by" date on the label or lid. Store all types of yogurt in the refrigerator.

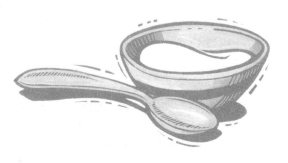

Soft and Hard Cheeses

The selection of cheeses in this section is a mere fraction of the extensive range that is available in good cheese stores and supermarkets. Some, like mozzarella and feta, are more often cooked in pies or on pizzas, or used in salads, while others, like the soft, white goat's cheeses, make a good addition to a cheese board.

Mozzarella

Delicate, silky-white mozzarella is usually made from cow's milk, although authentic mozzarella should be made from buffalo's milk. The sweet milky balls of cheese have excellent melting qualities, hence its use on pizzas and in baked dishes, but it is equally delicious served in salads. When combined with slices of avocado and tomato it makes the classic Italian three-colour salad.

Feta

Believed to be one of the first cheeses, feta is curdled naturally without the addition of rennet. Although it was once made with goat's or sheep's milk, it is now more often made with milk from cows. It is preserved in brine, hence its saltiness, and has a firm, crumbly texture. It is used in the classic Greek salad with cucumber, tomatoes and olives. To reduce the salty taste of feta, rinse it in water, then leave to soak in cold water for 10 minutes.

Goat's cheese

Indispensable for those intolerant or allergic to cow's milk, goat's cheese varieties range from soft and creamy in texture through a Camembert-type, which has a soft centre and downy rind, to the firm Cheddar-style alternative. Similarly, the flavour of goat's cheese spans from fresh, creamy and mild to sharp and pungent. It can be used in a wide variety of dishes.

Halloumi

This cheese is commonly sold in small blocks, and is often sprinkled with mint. Halloumi has a firm, rubbery texture and retains its shape when grilled (broiled) or fried. Some people consider it to be the vegetarian alternative to bacon.

Cheddar

Unfortunately, much of the Cheddar sold today is made in factories. Avoid these fairly tasteless, rubbery blocks and look for traditional farmhouse Cheddar, which is matured for between 9 and 24 months, and has a rich, strong, savoury flavour.

Parmesan

Allowed to mature for at least 18 months and up to four years, this richly flavoured cheese may be high in fat – though not as high as Cheddar – but a little goes a long way. Avoid ready-grated Parmesan and opt for a freshly cut chunk. Parmesan keeps for a long time in the refrigerator and is excellent grated and added to pasta and risottos or shaved over salads.

Buying and Storing Soft and Hard Cheeses

If possible, hard cheeses are best stored in a cool larder (pantry) If kept in the refrigerator, the cheese should be left at room temperature for at least an hour before eating. Cheese starts to dry out as soon as it is cut, so keep it loosely wrapped in foil or baking parchment.

FRESH UNRIPENED CHEESES

As their name suggests, fresh unripened cheeses are young and immature. They have a light, mild taste that readily accepts stronger-flavoured ingredients, such as fresh herbs and spices. They are lower in fat than mature hard cheeses. Fresh cheeses can be used in both savoury dishes and desserts.

FROMAGE FRAIS

This smooth, fresh cheese has the same consistency as thick yogurt, but is less acidic. It can be used in the same way as yogurt; mixed with fruit purée to make fools, combined with dried fruit, nuts and grains, or in sweet and savoury flans. The fat content varies from almost nothing to about 8 per cent. Full-fat fromage frais is the best choice for cooking, as it is less likely to separate when heated.

RICOTTA

A soft, low-fat unsalted cheese, which can be made from sheep's, goat's or cow's milk, ricotta has a slightly granular texture and is widely used in Italian cooking. Its mild, clean flavour means that it is incredibly versatile. It makes a neutral base for crêpe fillings, and can be used as a stuffing for pasta, when it is often combined with spinach. Ricotta is also good in tarts, cakes and cheesecakes, or it can be served simply on its own with fruit. Mixed with herbs it makes a tasty sandwich filling.

QUARK

This low-fat curd cheese is usually made with semi-skimmed (low-fat) or skimmed milk. Its mild, slightly tangy flavour and light, creamy texture make it perfect in cheesecakes and desserts, or it can be diluted with milk to make an alternative to cream. In northern European countries, it is used as a spread instead of butter.

COTTAGE CHEESE

Lower in fat than most other cheeses (between 2 and 5 per cent), cottage cheese is not usually used for cooking, but is good in salads, dips and baked potatoes. It makes a fine accompaniment to soft fruits and is best eaten as fresh as possible.

CREAM CHEESE

Commonly used in cheesecakes, dips and spreads, this cheese has a rich, velvety texture, mild flavour and a high fat content – about 35 per cent – although it is possible to buy lower-fat alternatives made from skimmed milk.

NON-DAIRY SOFT CHEESES

A wide range of soft, soya-based cheeses is available from health food stores. They are a valuable alternative for people who prefer not to buy dairy products.

Buying and Storing Fresh Cheeses

Fresh unripened cheeses do not keep for very long and are best bought in small quantities and eaten soon after purchase. Store in the refrigerator.

ALWAYS READ THE LABEL

Check the labels on low-fat yogurts and soft cheeses, as these products sometimes contain animal-derived gelatine, which is used as a setting agent. Until recently, the rennet used for cheese-making was invariably obtained from rennin, an enzyme found in the stomachs of animals. Nowadays, however, vegetarian rennet is more widely used. This is a coagulating agent obtained from plant sources or a genetically engineered rennet. It may not be mentioned on the pack that the cheese has been made using vegetarian rennet. If in doubt, check with the manufacturer.

EGGS

An inexpensive, self-contained source of nourishment, hen's eggs offer the cook tremendous scope, whether served simply solo or as part of a dish. There are several different types, but the best are organic, free-range eggs from a small producer.

Organic Free-range Eggs These eggs are from hens that are fed on a natural diet, which has not had hormones or artificial colorants added. The hens are able to roam on land that has not been treated with chemical fertilizers and is certified organic. Free-range hens have the same indoor conditions as barn hens but also have daytime access to the open air – although the term "access" has sometimes been open to abuse.

Organic, free-range hens are said to have better conditions than normal free-range hens, and are not routinely debeaked.

Battery Eggs Laid by hens that are kept in cages with a minimum amount of space in which to move. The hens are debeaked to prevent them pecking each other. These eggs are the cheapest to buy.

Barn or Perch Eggs These eggs are produced by hens that are kept indoors. Each hen can roam around in the barn, but they have no access to the outside. Barn or perch eggs are more expensive than battery eggs, but cheaper than eggs from hens reared in free-range conditions.

Fourgrain Eggs These eggs are produced by hens that are fed a diet based on barley, oats, wheat and rye. The hens have the same living conditions as barn or perch hens, in that they are kept indoors.

HEN'S EGGS

Graded according to their weight, hen's eggs range from small to extra large. Medium (US large) is the most popular size for most recipes. They are also graded according to quality and have a "best before" date stamped on the shell as well as printed on the box.

DUCK EGGS

Larger than hen's eggs and with a rich flavour, duck eggs are ideal for baking. They should always be well cooked and never eaten with a runny yolk. They are becoming more widely available.

QUAIL'S EGGS

These pretty speckled eggs are now widely available in supermarkets and may be eaten soft- or hard-boiled (hard-cooked), although they are tricky to shell when warm. They make wonderful canapés, traditionally served with celery salt, and they are very tasty with vegetarian olive tapenade. They are also useful for miniature appetizers, such as stuffed with a filling, tiny tartlets and eggs florentine.

MISLEADING LABELS

The labels on egg boxes often have phrases such as farm fresh, natural or country-fresh, which conjure up images of hens roaming around in the open, but they may well refer to eggs that are laid by birds reared in battery cages. It is advisable to avoid eggs that are labelled with such unlegislated claims.

Cooking with Eggs

Eggs can be cooked in myriad ways. Simply boiled, fried or poached, they make a wonderful breakfast dish. Lightly cooked poached eggs are also delicious served as a lunch dish with high-fibre lentils or beans. Eggs are delicious baked, either on their own, with a drizzle of cream, or broken into a nest of lightly cooked peppers or leeks. They make delicious omelettes, whether cooked undisturbed until just softly set, combined with tomatoes and peppers to make an Italian frittata, or cooked with diced potato and onions to make the classic Spanish omelette. They are also used as a filling for savoury tarts, flans and quiches.

Eggs are not, however, used only in savoury dishes. They are an essential ingredient in many sweet dishes, too. They are added to cake mixtures and batters for crêpes, pancakes and popovers, are crucial to meringues, whisked sponges, mousses and hot and cold soufflés, and are used in all manner of desserts, from ice creams and custards to rice pudding.

When separated, egg yolks are used to thicken sauces and soups, giving them a rich, smooth consistency, while egg whites can be whisked into peaks to make meringues and soufflés. It is important to use eggs at room temperature, so remember to remove them from the refrigerator about 30 minutes before cooking.

Buying and Storing Eggs

Freshness is paramount when buying eggs. Buy from a store that has a high turnover of stock. You should reject any eggs that have broken, dirty or damaged shells. Most eggs are date stamped, but you can easily check if an egg is fresh, by placing it in a bowl of cold water: if the egg sinks and lays flat it is fresh. The older the egg, the more it will stand on its end. A really old egg will actually float and should not be eaten. Store eggs in their box in the main part of the refrigerator and not in a rack in the door as this can expose them to damage. The shells are extremely porous, so eggs can be tainted by strong smells. Eggs should be stored large-end up for no longer than 3 weeks.

QUICK IDEAS FOR EGGS
- *Brush beaten egg on to pastries and bread before baking to give them a golden glaze.*
- *For a protein boost, top Thai- or Chinese-flavoured rice or noodle dishes with strips of thin omelette.*
- *Turn a mixed leaf salad into a light supper dish by adding a soft-boiled egg and some half-fat mayonnaise.*
- *For a simple dessert, make a soufflé omelette. Separate 2 eggs and whisk the whites and yolks separately. Fold together gently and add a little sugar. Cook in the same way as a savoury omelette and serve plain or fill with fruit conserve.*
- *Liven up poached eggs with a sauce made by combining 75ml/5 tbs natural (plain) yogurt, 75ml/5 tbsp mayonnaise, 30ml/2 tbsp wholegrain mustard and a pinch of cayenne pepper.*
- *Spice up scrambled eggs by first softening a small chopped onion in butter. Then stir in 5ml/1 tsp grated fresh root ginger and 1 finely chopped, seeded fresh chilli. Beat 6 eggs with 5ml/1 tsp ground turmeric, season with salt and scramble them in the same pan.*
- *For a classic hangover cure, blend 30ml/2 tbsp brandy, 15ml/1 tbsp wine vinegar, 15ml/1 tbsp Worcestershire sauce and a dash of tomato ketchup in a blender. Pour into a glass, break an egg into the mixture and sprinkle with cayenne pepper. Down the drink in one.*

THE PANTRY

In this section a diverse range of foods are featured that can enrich and add variety to a vegetarian diet. Some ingredients may be familiar, others less so, but all are useful to keep in the store cupboard and are generally easily available. Each of the foods mentioned comes with notes on choosing, storage and preparation, when necessary.

NUTS

With the exception of peanuts, nuts are the fruits of trees. The quality and availability of fresh nuts varies with the seasons, although most types are sold dried, either whole or prepared ready for use.

ALMONDS

There are two types of almond: sweet and bitter. The best sweet varieties are the flat and slender Jordan almonds from Spain. Heart-shaped Valencia almonds from Portugal and Spain, and the flatter Californian almonds are also widely available. For the best flavour, buy shelled almonds in their skins and blanch them yourself: cover with boiling water, leave for a few minutes, then drain and the skins will peel off easily. Almonds are available ready-blanched, flaked (sliced) and ground. The latter adds a richness to cakes, tarts, pastry and sauces. Bitter almonds are much smaller and are used in almond oil and essence. They should not be eaten raw.

BRAZIL NUTS

Brazil nuts have a sweet, milky taste and are used mainly as dessert nuts. They have a high fat content, so go rancid quickly.

CASHEW NUTS

These are the seeds of the "cashew apple" – an evergreen tree. Cashews have a sweet flavour and crumbly texture. They make delicious nut butters, or can be sprinkled into stir-fries or over salads. They are never sold in the shell and undergo a heating process to remove the seed from its casing.

CHESTNUTS

Most chestnuts are imported from France and Spain and they are excellent after roasting, which complements their soft, floury texture. Unlike other nuts, they contain very little fat. Out of season, chestnuts can be bought dried, canned or puréed. Add whole, cooked chestnuts to stews, soups, stuffings or pies. The sweetened purée is delicious in desserts and the flour makes a tasty pasta.

COCONUTS

This versatile nut grows all over the tropics. The white dense meat, or flesh, is made into desiccated (dry unsweetened shredded) coconut, blocks of creamed coconut (coconut cream) and a thick and creamy milk. A popular ingredient in Asian, African and South American cuisines, coconut lends a sweet, creamy flavour to desserts, curries, soups and casseroles. Use coconut in moderation, as it is particularly high in fat.

HAZELNUTS

Grown in the USA, Britain, Turkey, Italy and Spain, hazelnuts are usually sold dried, and can be bought whole, shelled and ground. They can be eaten raw and are very good toasted. They can be grated or chopped for use in cakes and desserts, but they are also tasty in salads and stir-fries.

MACADAMIA NUTS
This round nut, about the size of a large hazelnut, is native to Australia, but is now grown in California and South America. Macadamia nuts are commonly sold shelled. They have a crisp texture, a rich, buttery flavour and a high fat content.

PEANUTS
A member of the pulse family, peanuts are a staple food in many countries, and are widely used in South-east Asia, notably for satay sauce, and in African cuisines, where they are used as an ingredient in stews.

PECAN NUTS
A glossy, reddish-brown, oval-shaped shell encloses the pecan kernel, which looks like an elongated walnut, but has a sweeter, milder flavour. This native American nut is a favourite in sweet pies, but is also good eaten on its own, or added to salads. However, pecan nuts should be eaten only as an occasional treat, because they have the highest fat and calorific content of any nut.

PINE NUTS
These tiny, cream-coloured nuts are the fruit of the Mediterranean stone pine tree. They have a rich flavour, which lends itself to toasting. Buy in small quantities as their high oil content quickly turns them rancid.

Pine nuts are a key ingredient in pesto sauce, where they are pounded with garlic, olive oil and basil, and in the Middle Eastern sauce, tarator, in which toasted pine nuts are combined with bread, garlic, milk and olive oil to make a creamy paste.

PISTACHIO NUTS
These nuts have pale-green flesh and thin, reddish-purple skin. Sold shelled or in a split shell, they are often used chopped as a colourful garnish, sprinkled over both sweet and savoury foods. They have a wonderful flavour, and unsalted nuts are good in all manner of desserts, such as ice cream.

WALNUTS
This versatile nut has been around for hundreds of years. When picked young, walnuts are referred to as "wet" and have fresh, milky-white kernels, which can be eaten raw, but are often pickled.

Dried walnuts have a delicious bitter-sweet flavour and can be bought shelled, chopped or ground. They can be used to make excellent cakes and biscuits (cookies) as well as rich pie fillings, but are also tasty added to savoury dishes, such as stir-fries and salads.

Buying and Storing Nuts
Always buy nuts in small quantities from a store with a high turnover of stock. Nuts in their shells should feel heavy for their size. Store in airtight containers in a cool, dark place or in the freezer and they should keep fresh for at least 3 months. When buying a coconut, make sure that there is no sign of mould or a rancid smell. Give it a shake – it should be full of liquid. Keep coconut milk in the refrigerator or freezer once opened. Desiccated coconut can be stored in an airtight container, but do not keep it too long as it is prone to rancidity.

Seeds

They may look very small and unassuming, but seeds are nutritional powerhouses, packed with vitamins and minerals, as well as beneficial oils and protein. They can be used in a huge array of sweet and savoury dishes, and will add an instant, healthy boost, pleasant crunch and nutty flavour to rice and pasta, salads, stir-fries and soups.

Sesame Seeds

These tiny, white or black seeds are a feature of Middle Eastern and Asian cooking. In the Middle East they are ground into tahini, a thick paste that is a key component of hummus. Sesame seeds are also ground to make halva, a sweet confection from Greece, Israel and Turkey. Gomasio, or gomashio, is the name of a crushed sesame seed condiment used in Japan instead of salt. It can easily be made at home: toast the seeds, then crush with a little sea salt in a mortar using a pestle.

The flavour of sesame seeds is improved by roasting them in a dry frying pan; it gives them a distinctive nuttiness. The toasted seeds make a good addition to salads and noodle dishes. Unroasted seeds can be used as a topping for breads, cakes and biscuits, and they can be added to pastry dough.

Sunflower Seeds

Rich in vitamin E, these pale-green, tear-drop-shaped seeds have a semi-crunchy texture and an oily taste that is much improved by dry-roasting. Sprinkle them over salads, rice pilaffs and couscous, or use in bread dough, muffins, casseroles and baked dishes.

Poppy Seeds

These are the seeds of the opium poppy but without any of the habit-forming alkaloids. Poppy seeds can be blue (usually described as black) or white. The black variety looks good sprinkled over cakes and breads, adding a pleasant crunch. Black poppy seeds can be used to make delicious seed cakes and teabreads, and they are used in German and Eastern European pastries, strudels and tarts. In India, the ground white seeds are used to thicken sauces, adding a nutty flavour.

Pumpkin Seeds

These seeds make a nutritious snack eaten on their own. They are also delicious lightly toasted, tossed in a little toasted sesame seed oil or soy sauce, and stirred into a mixed leaf or rice salad. They are widely used in South American cooking where they are generally roasted and ground to make into rich sauces.

Hemp Seeds

The cultivation of hemp has a long history but for various reasons it fell out of fashion. Today, hemp is making a comeback as a food. Hemp seeds are best roasted and they can be used in sweet and savoury dishes.

Linseeds

The oil from linseeds has long been used to embellish wooden furniture. However, the golden seed, also known as flaxseed, is a rich source of polyunsaturated fat, including the essential fatty acid, linoleic acid. Linseeds can be added to breakfast cereals, bread dough or over salads.

Buying and Storing Seeds

Seeds are best bought in small quantities from stores with a high turnover of stock. Purchase whole seeds and store them in a cool, dark place as they are prone to turning rancid. After opening the packet, decant the seeds into an airtight container and use them within three months.

SPICES

Highly revered for thousands of years, spices – the seeds, fruit, pods, bark and buds of plants – add flavour, colour and interest to the most unassuming of ingredients, while the evocative aroma of spices stimulates the appetite.

ALLSPICE

These small, dried berries have a sweet, warming flavour reminiscent of a blend of cloves, cinnamon and nutmeg. Although allspice is available ready-ground, it is best to buy the spice whole to retain its flavour, and grind just before use in cakes and biscuits (cookies). The whole berries can be added to marinades or mulled wine.

CARAWAY

An important flavouring in eastern European, Austrian and German cooking, caraway seeds are sprinkled over rye bread, cakes and biscuits. They have a distinctive, sweet, aniseed flavour, which is also a welcome addition to potato- and cheese-based dishes or braised cabbage.

CARDAMOM

Often used in Middle Eastern and Indian cooking, cardamom is best bought whole in its pod, as it soon loses its aromatic flavour when ground. The pod can be used whole, slightly crushed, or for a more intense flavour, the seeds can be removed and ground. Cardamom is superb in both sweet and savoury dishes. It can be infused (steeped) in milk used to flavour rice pudding or ice cream, and is often added to curries and other Indian dishes.

CAYENNE

This fiery, reddish-brown powder adds colour and heat, rather than flavour, to curries, soups and stews. It comes from the ground pod and seeds of a very pungent variety of chilli, *Capsicum frutescens*, and is sometimes referred to as red pepper.

CELERY SEEDS

These tiny brown seeds have a similar flavour to celery, but are more highly aromatic. It is important to grind or crush them before use to avoid any bitterness. They can be used in almost any dish that calls for celery, and add a pungent flavour to baked dishes, stews, soups, sauces and egg dishes. Celery salt is a mixture of ground celery seeds, salt and herbs.

CHILLIES

Fresh chillies are covered in the vegetable section, but this versatile spice is also sold in dried, powdered and flaked form. Dried chillies tend to be hotter than fresh, and this is certainly true of chilli flakes, which contain both the seeds and the flesh. The best pure chilli powders do not contain added ingredients, such as onion and garlic.

CINNAMON

This warm, comforting spice is available in sticks and ground. As the bark is difficult to grind, it is useful to keep both forms in the store cupboard (pantry). Cinnamon can enhance both sweet and savoury dishes. Use the sticks to flavour pilaffs, curries, couscous and dried fruit compotes, but remove before serving. Ground cinnamon adds a pleasing fragrance to cakes, biscuits and fruit.

CLOVES

The unopened bud of an evergreen tree from South-east Asia, this spice is often used in combination with cinnamon to flavour desserts, cakes and biscuits. Cloves are often used to flavour the syrup when poaching oranges, but they are also delicious with cooked apples. Cloves are also used in some savoury dishes and in relishes.

CORIANDER

Alongside cumin, ground coriander is a key ingredient in Indian curry powders and garam masala, and in northern Europe the ivory-coloured seeds are used as a pickling spice. Coriander seeds have a sweet, earthy, burnt-orange flavour that is more pronounced than the fresh leaves. The ready-ground powder rapidly loses its flavour and aroma, so it is best to buy whole seeds, which are easily ground in a mortar using a pestle, or in a coffee grinder. Before grinding, lightly dry-roast the seeds in a frying pan to enhance their flavour.

CUMIN

Extensively used in Indian curries, cumin is also a familiar component of Mexican, North African and Middle Eastern cooking. The seeds have a robust aroma and slightly bitter taste, which is tempered by dry-roasting. Black cumin seeds are milder and sweeter. Ground cumin can be harsh, so it is best to buy the whole seeds and grind them just before use to be sure of a fresh flavour. Cumin is good used in tomato- or grain-based dishes.

FENUGREEK

This spice is commonly used in commercial curry powders, along with cumin and coriander. On its own though, fenugreek should be used in moderation because its bitter-sweet flavour, which is mellowed by

dry-frying, can be quite overpowering. The seeds have a hard shell and are difficult to grind, but they can be sprouted and make a good addition to mixed leaf and bean salads, as well as sandwich fillings.

GINGER

Fresh ginger root, which is spicy, peppery and fragrant, is good in both sweet and savoury dishes, adding a hot, yet refreshing, flavour to marinades, stir-fries, soups, curries, grains and fresh vegetables. It also adds warmth to poached fruit and cakes.

Ground ginger is the usual choice for flavouring cakes, biscuits and other baked goods, but finely grated fresh ginger can also be used and is equally good.

Pink Pickled Ginger This pretty, finely sliced ginger pickle is served as an accompaniment to Japanese food and is used to flavour sushi rice.

Stem Ginger Preserved in a thick sugar syrup and sold in jars, this sweet ginger can be chopped and used in desserts, or added to cake mixtures, steamed puddings, shortbread and muffins.

Buying and Storing Ginger
Fresh root ginger should look firm, thin-skinned and unblemished. Avoid withered, woody looking roots. Store in the refrigerator. Ground ginger should smell aromatic; keep in a cool, dark place. Freeze peeled ginger and grate frozen.

LEMON GRASS

This long fibrous stalk has a fragrant citrus aroma and flavour when cut and is a familiar part of South-east Asian cooking. To use, remove the tough, woody outer layers, trim the root, then cut off the lower 5cm/2in and slice or pound in a mortar using a pestle. Bottled, chopped lemon grass and lemon grass purée are also available.

GALANGAL

Closely related to ginger, fresh galangal looks similar but has a reddish-brown or cream-coloured skin. Its fragrant, slightly peppery taste can be overpowering if used in excess. Prepare the root in the same way as ginger.

MUSTARD

There are three different types of mustard seed, white, brown, and black. The flavour and aroma are only apparent when the seeds are crushed or mixed with liquid. If fried in a little oil before use, the flavour is improved. As the intensity of mustard diminishes with time and cooking; it is best added to dishes towards the end of cooking.

NUTMEG AND MACE

The nutmeg seed is surrounded by a lacy membrane called mace. Both are dried and used as spices. They taste similar, and their warm, sweet flavour enlivens white sauces, cheese-based dishes and vegetables, as well as custards, cakes and biscuits. Grate nutmeg freshly for the best flavour.

PEPPER

Undoubtedly the oldest, most widely used spice in the world, pepper is a very useful seasoning, because it not only adds flavour of its own to a dish, but also brings out the flavour of the other ingredients.

Black Peppercorns These dried green berries of the vine pepper are relatively mild. Black peppercorns are best when freshly ground as needed using a mill.

White Pepper This is less aromatic than black pepper and is used in white sauces and other pale-coloured dishes.

Green Peppercorns These unripened berries have a milder flavour than black or white peppercorns and may be dried or preserved in brine.

Pink Peppercorns These pretty berries are not a true pepper and should be used in small amounts in pâtés.

PAPRIKA

This is a milder relative of cayenne and can be used more liberally, adding flavour as well as heat.

SAFFRON

Only a tiny amount of this costly bright-orange spice is needed to add a wonderful colour and delicate bitter-sweet flavour to rice, stews, soups and milky puddings.

TURMERIC

Sometimes used as an alternative to saffron, turmeric delivers a similar yellow colour, but has a very different flavour.

VANILLA

These slender, chocolate-brown pods (beans) have a fragrant, exotic aroma and luscious, almost creamy flavour. They can be used more than once; simply rinse and dry before storing in an airtight jar.

Buying and Storing Spices

Always buy spices in small quantities from a store with a regular turnover of stock. Aroma is the best indication of freshness. Store in airtight jars in a cool place away from direct light.

Pasta

This versatile food is now recognized as an important part of a healthy diet. The variety of shapes is almost endless, from the myriad tiny soup pastas to huge shells used for stuffing. Pasta can be plain, made with egg or flavoured and coloured with ingredients such as tomato, beetroot (beet) or spinach. It is available fresh or dried with both types needing minimal cooking. It is best served *al dente* – with a little bite. Low in fat and high in a range of complex carbohydrates, it provides plenty of long-term energy. Corn and buckwheat varieties are also available, as is wholewheat, which is high in fibre.

Durum Wheat Pasta

This is the most readily available type of pasta and can be made with or without egg. Plain wheat pasta is used for straight long shapes, such as spaghetti and fettuccine, while long shapes made with egg pasta, because it is more delicate, are traditionally packed in nests or compressed into waves. Lasagne can be made with either plain or egg pasta. At one time, almost all short pasta shapes were made from plain pasta, but shapes made with egg pasta are becoming increasingly available. Pasta made with egg has several advantages over plain pasta: it is more nutritious, many people consider it to have a superior flavour, and it is more difficult to overcook, so you are unlikely to spoil the texture.

Coloured and Flavoured Pasta

A variety of ingredients can be added to the pasta dough to give it both flavour and colour. The most common additions are tomato and spinach, but beetroot, saffron, fresh herbs, such as basil, and even chocolate are used. Mixed bags of pasta are also available – the traditional combination of plain and spinach-flavoured pasta is called paglia e fieno, which means straw and hay. But there are many other mixtures, some having as many as seven different flavours and colours of pasta. Black pasta is coloured with squid or cuttlefish ink and is, therefore, not suitable for vegetarians.

Wholewheat Pasta

This substantial pasta is made using wholemeal (whole-wheat) flour and it contains more fibre than plain durum wheat pasta. It has a slightly chewy texture and nutty flavour and takes longer to cook. Wholewheat spaghetti (bigoli), a traditional Italian variety that comes from the area around Venice, can be found in good Italian delicatessens, and in health food stores and supermarkets. There is an increasing range of wholewheat shapes, from tiny soup pastas to rotelle (wheels) and lasagne.

Buckwheat Pasta

Pasta made from buckwheat flour has a nutty taste and is darker in colour than wholewheat pasta. Pizzoccheri from Lombardy is the classic shape. These thin, flat noodles are traditionally sold in nests like tagliatelle (although pizzoccheri are about half the length), but they are also available cut into short strips.

Buckwheat pasta is gluten-free and suitable for people who are intolerant to gluten or wheat. It is also very nutritious, containing all eight amino acids, calcium, zinc and B vitamins.

CORN PASTA

This pasta, made with corn or maize flour, is gluten-free. It is made in a wide range of shapes, including spaghetti, fusilli (spirals) and conchiglie (shells). Plain corn pasta is sunshine-yellow in colour, and may be flavoured with spinach or tomato. It is cooked and used in the same way as wheat pasta and is available from many health food stores and supermarkets.

PASTA SHAPES

Long Pasta   Dried long pasta in the form of spaghetti is probably the best known, but there are many other varieties, from fine vermicelli to pappardelle – broad ribbon noodles. Tagliatelle, the most common form of ribbon noodles, is usually sold coiled into nests. Long pasta is best served with a thin sauce, made with olive oil, butter, cream, eggs, grated cheese, tomatoes or chopped fresh herbs. When vegetables are added to the sauce, they should be finely chopped to fit on a fork.

Short Pasta   There are hundreds of different types of short dried pasta shapes. They are often sold fresh because most shapes are difficult to produce, but you may find one or two dried versions in Italian delicatessens and larger supermarkets.

Conchiglie (shells) are one of the most useful shapes because they are concave and trap virtually any sauce. Fusilli (spirals) are good with tomato-based sauces and farfalle (butterflies) can be served with creamy sauces, but are versatile and also work well with tomato- or olive oil-based sauces. Macaroni used to be the most common short shape, and being hollow, it is good for most sauces and baked dishes. However, penne (quills) have become more popular and are available either smooth or rigate – ridged. They are good with chunky vegetable sauces or baked with cheese sauce.

Flat Pasta   Lasagne is designed to be baked between layers of sauce, or cooked in boiling water, then layered or rolled around a filling to make cannelloni. Lasagne is made from plain or egg pasta and both fresh and dried versions are available in different flavours such as spinach.

Stuffed Pasta   The most common stuffed pasta shapes are ravioli, tortellini (little pies) and cappelletti (little hats). Plain, spinach and tomato doughs are the most usual, and there is a wide range of vegetarian fillings including mixed mushroom or spinach with sharp ricotta.

Pasta for Soup   These tiny shapes are mostly made from plain durum wheat pasta, although you may find them with egg. There are hundreds of different ones, from tiny risi, which look like grains of rice, to alfabeti (alphabet shapes). Slightly larger shapes, such as farfalline (little bows) and tubetti (little tubes), are used in thicker soups such as minestrone.

Buying and Storing Pasta

The quality of pasta varies tremendously – choose good-quality Italian brands made from 100 per cent durum wheat, and buy fresh pasta from an Italian delicatessen rather than pre-packed pasta from the supermarket. Dried pasta will keep almost indefinitely, but if you keep it in a storage jar, it is a good idea to use it all up before adding any from a new packet. Fresh pasta from a delicatessen is usually sold loose and is best cooked the same day, but can be kept in the refrigerator for a day or two. Fresh pasta from a supermarket is likely to be packed in plastic packs and bags and will keep for 3–4 days in the refrigerator. Fresh pasta freezes well and should be cooked from frozen. Convenient packs of super-market pasta have the advantage of being easy to store in the freezer.

NOODLES

The fast food of the East, noodles can be made from wheat flour, rice, buckwheat flour or mung bean flour. Both fresh and dried noodles are readily available in health food stores and Asian stores as well as most supermarkets.

WHEAT NOODLES

There are two main types of noodle: plain and egg. Plain noodles are made from strong flour and water, they can be flat or round and come in various thicknesses.

Udon Noodles These thick Japanese noodles can be round or flat and are available fresh, pre-cooked or dried. Wholewheat udon noodles have a more robust flavour.

Somen Noodles Usually sold in bundles, these thin, white noodles are often used in Japanese soups.

Egg Noodles Far more common than the plain wheat variety, egg noodles are sold both fresh and dried. The Chinese type are available in various thicknesses. Very fine egg noodles, which resemble vermicelli, are usually sold in individual coils. More substantial wholewheat egg noodles are widely available from larger supermarkets.

Ramen Noodles These coiled Japanese egg noodles are often cooked and served with broth.

RICE NOODLES

These fine, delicate noodles are made from rice and are opaque-white in colour. They come in various widths, from the very thin strands known as rice vermicelli, which are popular in Thailand and southern China, to the thicker rice sticks, which are used in Vietnam and Malaysia. A huge range of rice noodles is available dried in Asian grocers and fresh ones are occasionally found in the chiller cabinets. Since all rice noodles are

pre-cooked, they need only to be softened in hot water for a few minutes before use in stir-fries and salads.

CELLOPHANE VERMICELLI AND NOODLES

Made from mung bean starch, these translucent noodles, also known as bean thread vermicelli and glass noodles, come in a variety of thicknesses and are only available dried. Although very fine, the strands are firm and fairly tough. Cellophane noodles do not need to be boiled, and are simply soaked in boiling water for 10–15 minutes. They have a fantastic texture, which they retain when cooked, never becoming soggy. Cellophane noodles are almost tasteless unless combined with other strongly flavoured foods and seasonings. They are never eaten on their own, but used as an ingredient. They are good in vegetarian dishes, and as an ingredient in spring rolls.

BUCKWHEAT NOODLES

Soba are the best-known type of buckwheat noodles. They are a much darker colour than wheat noodles – almost brownish grey. In Japan, soba noodles are traditionally served in soups or stir-fries.

Buying and Storing Noodles

Packets of fresh noodles are found in the chiller cabinets of Asian stores. They usually carry a use-by date and must be stored in the refrigerator or freezer. Dried noodles will keep for many months in an airtight container in a cool, dry place.

VINEGARS

One of our oldest condiments, vinegar is made by acetic fermentation, a process that occurs when a liquid containing less than 18 per cent alcohol is exposed to the air. Most countries produce their own type of vinegar, usually based on their most popular alcoholic drink – wine in France and Italy; sherry in Spain; rice wine in Asia; and beer and cider in Great Britain. Commonly used as a preservative in pickles and chutneys, it is also an ingredient in marinades and salad dressings and can add flavour to cooked dishes and sauces.

WINE VINEGARS

These can be made from white, red or rosé wine, and the quality will depend on the quality of the original ingredient. The finest wine vinegars are made by the slow and costly Orleans method. Cheaper and faster methods of fermentation involve heating, which produces a harsher vinegar that lacks the complexities of the original wine. Use in dressings, mayonnaise, sauces or to add flavour to stews and soups.

BALSAMIC VINEGAR

This is a rich, dark, mellow vinegar. Made in Modena in northern Italy, balsamic vinegar is made from grape juice, which is fermented in wooden barrels for at least four to five years and up to 40 or more years, resulting in an intensely rich vinegar with a concentrated flavour. Balsamic vinegar is delicious in dressings or sprinkled over roasted vegetables.

SHERRY VINEGAR

This vinegar can be just as costly as balsamic vinegar and, if left to mature in wooden barrels, can be equally good. Sweet and mellow in flavour, sherry vinegar is caramel in colour and can be used in the same way as balsamic vinegar – in dressings, sprinkled over roasted vegetables or added to sauces and stews.

RASPBERRY VINEGAR

Any soft fruit can be used to enhance the flavour of white wine vinegar but raspberries are the most popular. Raspberry vinegar can be made at home by macerating fresh raspberries in good-quality wine vinegar for two to three weeks. Once the mixture is strained, the vinegar is delicious as part of a salad dressing, or in sauces.

MALT VINEGAR

Made from soured beer, malt vinegar is used in Britain and other northern European countries for pickling onions and other vegetables. It can be clear, but is often sold coloured with caramel. Malt vinegar has a robust, harsh flavour and it is not suitable for salad dressings.

RICE VINEGAR

There are two kinds of rice vinegar: the type from Japan is mellow and sweet and is most often used to flavour sushi rice, but it can also be added to dressings, stir-fries and sauces; Chinese rice vinegar is much sharper in taste. It is usually a pale-brown colour, but it can also be inky-black, red or white.

CIDER VINEGAR

Made from cider and praised for its health-giving properties, cider vinegar is made in the same way as wine vinegar. It is a clear, pale brown colour and has a slight apple flavour, but it is too strong and sharp to use in the same ways as wine vinegar. It can be used for salad dressings, but it is perhaps best kept for pickling fruits, such as pears. Cider vinegar can be served as a soothing drink, mixed with honey, lemon juice and hot water, as a remedy for colds and flu.

OILS

There is a wide variety of cooking oils and they are produced from a number of different sources: from cereals such as corn; from fruits such as olives; from nuts such as walnuts, almonds and hazelnuts; and from seeds such as safflower and sunflower. Virgin oils, which are obtained from the first cold pressing of the olives, nuts or seeds, are sold unrefined, and have the most characteristic flavour. They are also the most expensive.

OLIVE OIL

This varies in flavour and colour, depending on how it is made and where it comes from. Olive oils from southern Italy, Greece, Syria and Spain have a stronger flavour and a darker colour than those from the rest of Italy and France.

Extra Virgin Olive Oil This premium olive oil has a superior flavour. It comes from the first cold pressing of the olives and has a low acidity – less than 1 per cent. It is not recommended for frying, as heat impairs its flavour, but it is good in salad dressings. Extra virgin olive oil is delicious as a sauce on its own, stirred into pasta with chopped garlic and black pepper, or drizzled over steamed vegetables.

Virgin Olive Oil Also a first-pressed oil, this has a slightly higher level of acidity than extra virgin olive oil, and can be used in the same way.

Pure Olive Oil Refined and blended to remove impurities, this type of olive oil has a much lighter flavour than virgin or extra virgin olive oil and is suitable for all types of cooking. It can be used for shallow frying.

OTHER OILS

There is a wide range of light, processed oils on the market, which are all relatively taste-free and have a variety of culinary uses.

Corn Oil One of the most economical and widely used vegetable oils, corn oil has a deep golden colour and a fairly strong flavour. It is suitable for cooking and frying, but should not be used for salad dressings. Corn is rich in omega-6 (linoleic) fatty acids, which are believed to reduce harmful cholesterol in the body.

Safflower Oil This is a light, all-purpose oil, which comes from the seeds of the safflower. It can be used in place of sunflower and groundnut (peanut) oils, but is a little thicker and has a slightly stronger flavour. It is suitable for deep-frying, but is best used with other more strongly flavoured ingredients, and is ideal for cooking spicy foods. Safflower oil contains a higher proportion of polyunsaturated fat than any other type of oil and it is low in saturated fat. Try to find unrefined, cold pressed oil for the highest quality.

Sunflower Oil Perhaps the best all-purpose oil, sunflower oil is very light and almost tasteless. It is very versatile, and can be used for frying and in cooking, or to make salad dressings, when it can be combined with a stronger flavoured oil, such as olive oil or walnut oil. It can also be used in some cakes. Sunflower oil is extracted from the seeds of the sunflower.

Soya Oil This light neutral-flavoured, all-purpose oil, which is extracted from soya beans, is probably the most widely used oil in the world. It is useful for frying because it has a high smoking point, and remains stable at high temperatures.

Groundnut Oil Also known as peanut oil, this relatively tasteless oil is useful for frying, cooking and dressing salads. Chinese peanut oil is darker in colour than groundnut oil and has a more distinctive nutty flavour. It is good in Asian salads and cooking stir-fries.

Rapeseed Oil This bland-tasting, all-purpose oil, also known as canola, can be used for frying, cooking and in salad dressings instead of olive oil.

Grapeseed Oil A delicate, mild flavoured oil, grapeseed oil is pressed from grape seeds left over from wine-making. It is good in cooking and for frying, and can be used to make salad dressings, especially when combined with a stronger flavoured nut or olive oil.

SPECIALITY OILS

As well as the light, all-purpose oils that are used for everyday cooking, there are several richly flavoured oils that are used in small quantities, often as a flavouring ingredient in salad dressings and marinades.

Sesame Oil There are two types of sesame oil – the pale and light version that is pressed from untoasted seeds, and the rich, dark, toasted oil that is used in Asian cuisines. The lighter oil, popular in India and the Middle East, has a mild flavour and a high smoking point and is useful for cooking. Dark sesame oil, which has a wonderfully nutty aroma and taste, is useful for flavouring marinades and stir-fries. Heating helps to intensify the aroma of toasted sesame oil, but it should never be heated for too long.

Walnut Oil This is an intensely flavoured oil that is delicious in salad dressings and marinades, but should not be used for frying as heat diminishes its rich taste. The French, unrefined, cold pressed type is reputed to have the best flavour. Drizzle a little of the oil over roasted or steamed vegetables, use it to make a simple sauce for pasta, or stir into freshly cooked noodles just before serving. It can be used in small quantities, in place of some of the fat or oil in a recipe, to add flavour to cakes and biscuits (cookies), especially those that contain walnuts. It is a rich source of essential fatty acids.

Hazelnut Oil This fine, fragrant oil has a rich brown colour and a delicious, roasted hazelnut flavour. It is quite expensive to buy but, because it has such a strong flavour, only a little is needed. It works well combined with less strongly flavoured oils such as sunflower or groundnut, for salad dressings and sauces, and can be used to add a nutty flavour to teabreads, cakes, biscuits and pastry.

Almond Oil This pale, delicate oil is mainly used in confectionery and desserts. It has a subtle, sweet flavour of almonds, although it is not pronounced enough to give an almond flavour to baked goods, such as cakes and biscuits. It is often found in sweet recipes from the Middle East.

Buying and Storing Oils

Cooking oils such as sunflower, soya and safflower are more stable than nut or seed oils and will not burn at high temperatures. They also have longer keeping properties. To keep them at their peak, store in a cool, dark place away from direct sunlight. Nut and seed oils including sesame walnut and hazelnut are more volatile and turn rancid quickly and should always be kept in the refrigerator after opening.

TEAS AND TISANES

A popular reviving drink for centuries tea comes in many different forms, from traditional ones, such as green tea, oolong tea and black tea, to fragrant fruit infusions and healing herbal tisanes.

GREEN TEA

This tea is popular with the Chinese and Japanese who enjoy its light, slightly bitter but nevertheless refreshing flavour. It is produced from leaves that are steamed and dried but not fermented, a process that retains their green colour.

OOLONG TEA

The leaves are partially fermented to produce a tea that falls between the green and black varieties in strength and colour. It is particularly fragrant.

BLACK TEA

This is the most widely available tea and is made by fermenting withered tea leaves, then drying them. It produces a dark brown brew that has a more assertive taste than green tea. Darjeeling and English breakfast tea are two examples.

SMOKED TEA

Sometimes known as tarry tea, this is fermented black tea that has been smoke-dried. It is always drunk without milk, sugar or lemon. Lapsang souchong is the best-known variety.

FRUIT TEAS

These are made from a blend of fruit flavours, such as rosehip, strawberry, orange, raspberry and lemon, along with fruit pieces and sometimes herbs or real tea. It is a good idea to check the packaging to make sure the tea is naturally, rather than artificially, flavoured. Fruit teas make refreshing caffeine-free drinks, which are almost calorie-free. They are an ideal drink for pregnant women and, because of their low-sugar content, they are also suitable for diabetics. They are good served iced.

HERBAL TISANES

These teas (made from the leaves, seeds and flowers of herbs) are generally mild and good, healthy, caffeine-free drinks. Even so, some varieties are not recommended for young children and pregnant women and so it is advisable to check the packaging. The most popular types of herbal teas are listed below.

Peppermint tea is recommended as a digestive to be drunk after a meal. It is also effective in settling other stomach problems and for treating colds. **Camomile tea** soothes and calms the nerves and can induce sleep. **Raspberry leaf tea** prepares the uterus for birth and is said to reduce labour pains, but it is not recommended in early pregnancy. It can also relieve period pains. **Rosehip tea** is high in vitamin C and may help to ward off colds and flu. **Dandelion and lemon verbena** teas are effective diuretics. **Rosemary tea** can stimulate the brain and improve concentration. **Thyme tea** can boost the immune system and fight viral, bacterial and fungal infections. **Elderflower tea** is calming and can ease painful sinuses and bronchial conditions.

SWEETENERS

Nutritionists have diverse opinions on sugar and sugar alternatives. Some maintain that these products cause hyperactivity in children, while others believe that sugars can induce relaxation and sleep. Many recipes from breads to desserts contain different types of sugar and/or sugar substitutes, such as molasses, honey, malt and grain syrups, as well as dried fruit, and would not be palatable without them. So, provided that a diet is well balanced and varied, a moderate amount of sugar is considered nutritionally acceptable.

MOLASSES

This rich, syrupy liquid is a by-product of sugar refining and ranges in quality and colour. The most nutritionally valuable type is thick and very dark blackstrap molasses, which contains less sugar than lighter alternatives and is richer in minerals. However, it may be better to choose organically produced molasses.

HONEY

The colour, flavour, consistency and quality of honey depends on the source of nectar as well as the method of production. In general, the darker the colour, the stronger the flavour. From the point of view of both flavour and health, it is best to buy raw unfiltered honey from a single flower source. Nutritionally, honey offers few benefits, but as it is much sweeter than sugar, less is needed.

MAPLE SYRUP

This is made from the sap of the maple tree. Look for pure varieties rather than maple-flavoured syrup, which contains additives. There are various grades, the highest being the sweetest and the lowest having the strongest maple taste. Maple syrup has a rich, distinctive flavour and is sweeter than ordinary sugar.

CAROB

This caffeine-free alternative to chocolate is made from the aromatic, fleshy bean pod of a Mediterranean tree. Carob powder (flour) looks and tastes similar to cocoa powder (unsweetened) and can be used to replace it in hot drinks, confectionery and baked goods. It is naturally sweeter and lower in fat than cocoa powder. It is also available as bars to be used in the same way as melted chocolate in cakes or desserts.

GRAIN SYRUPS

Corn, barley, wheat and rice can be transformed into syrups that are used in place of sugar in baked goods and sauces. Grain syrups tend to be easier to digest and enter the bloodstream more slowly than other forms of refined sugar, which cause swings in blood sugar levels. Grain syrups are not so sweet as sugar and have a mild, subtle flavour. Malt extract, a by-product of barley, has a more intense flavour and is good in breads and other baked goods.

FRUIT JUICE

Freshly squeezed fruit juice is a useful alternative to sugar in baked goods, sauces, pies and ice cream. Fruit juice concentrates such as apple, pear and grape, which have no added sugar or preservatives, are available from health food stores. They can be diluted or used in concentrated form in cakes, pies and puddings.

SOUPS

Homemade soup is always a special treat, yet it is extremely easy to prepare. The range of ingredients is almost limitless and vegetables may be used in combination, as in the warming and nourishing Pea, Leek & Broccoli Soup, or a single type can take a starring role, as in the classic French Onion Soup. Chilled soups, such as Gazpacho, are wonderfully refreshing on a hot, summer's day, while robust and filling dishes, such as Roasted Vegetable Soup, help keep out the winter's cold. A delicately flavoured, light soup makes a perfect first course for a dinner party, while more substantial broths provide a complete meal in a bowl.

CHILLED LEEK & POTATO SOUP

This creamy-smooth soup is served with a tangy yogurt topping that beautifully complements its subtle but distinctive flavour.

SERVES 4

INGREDIENTS
25g/1oz/2 tbsp butter
15ml/1 tbsp vegetable oil
1 small onion, chopped
3 leeks, sliced
2 medium floury potatoes, diced
about 600ml/1 pint/2½ cups vegetable stock
about 300ml/½ pint/1¼ cups milk
45ml/3 tbsp single (light) cream
salt and ground black pepper
60ml/4 tbsp natural (plain) yogurt and fried chopped leeks, to serve

1 Heat the butter and oil in a large, heavy pan and add the onion, leeks and potatoes. Cover and cook over a low heat, stirring occasionally, for 15 minutes, until the vegetables have softened and the onion is golden. Stir in the stock and milk. Bring to the boil, lower the heat, cover and simmer for 10 minutes.

2 Allow to cool slightly, then process the mixture, in batches if necessary, in a blender or a food processor to a purée. Pour the soup into a bowl, stir in the cream and season generously with salt and pepper.

3 Set the soup aside to cool, then cover and chill in the refrigerator for 3–4 hours. You may need to add a little extra milk or vegetable stock to thin the soup before serving, as it will thicken slightly as it cools. Ladle the soup into chilled soup bowls and top each with a spoonful of yogurt and a sprinkling of fried leeks.

COOK'S TIP
You will need two thin young leeks for the garnish. Clean and slice them into rounds. Fry in a mixture of butter and olive oil until they are crisp-tender.

CHILLED COCONUT SOUP

Refreshing, cooling and not too filling, this soup makes an excellent summer
appetizer, but it could also be served after a spicy curry, to refresh the palate.

SERVES 6

INGREDIENTS
1.2 litres/2 pints/5 cups milk
225g/8oz/2⅔ cups unsweetened desiccated (dry unsweetened
  shredded) coconut
400ml/14fl oz/1⅔ cups coconut milk from a can or carton
400ml/14fl oz/1⅔ cups vegetable stock
200ml/7fl oz/scant 1 cup double (heavy) cream
2.5ml/½ tsp salt
2.5ml/½ tsp ground white pepper
5ml/1 tsp caster (superfine) sugar
small bunch of fresh coriander (cilantro)

1 Bring the milk to the boil in a large pan. Stir in the coconut, lower the heat and simmer, stirring occasionally, for 30 minutes. Spoon the mixture into a food processor and process until smooth. This may take a while – up to 5 minutes – so pause frequently and scrape down the sides of the bowl.

2 Rinse the pan to remove any traces of coconut, pour in the processed mixture and add the coconut milk. Stir in the stock, cream, salt, pepper and sugar. Bring to the boil, stirring occasionally, then lower the heat and cook for 10 minutes.

3 Reserve a few coriander leaves for the garnish, then chop the rest finely and stir them into the soup. Pour the soup into a large bowl, let it cool, then cover and chill in the refrigerator.

4 Just before serving, taste the soup and adjust the seasoning if necessary, as chilling will have altered the taste. Serve in chilled bowls, garnished with the reserved coriander leaves.

Cold Cucumber & Yogurt Soup with Walnuts

Walnuts make an interesting addition to this refreshing cold soup. You could also use almonds and almond oil as an alternative.

SERVES 5–6

INGREDIENTS
1 cucumber
4 garlic cloves, peeled
2.5ml/½ tsp salt
75g/3oz/¾ cup walnut pieces
40g/1½oz day-old white bread, torn into pieces
30ml/2 tbsp walnut oil
400ml/14fl oz/1⅔ cups natural (plain) yogurt
120ml/4fl oz/½ cup chilled still mineral water
5–10ml/1–2 tsp lemon juice

FOR THE GARNISH
40g/1½ oz/scant ½ cup walnuts, coarsely chopped
25ml/1½ tbsp olive oil
fresh dill sprigs

1 Cut the cucumber in half lengthways. Peel one half. Dice both halves, so that you have a mixture of peeled and unpeeled pieces of cucumber. Set aside.

2 Crush the garlic and salt together in a mortar with a pestle. Add the walnuts and crush them into the mixture, then work in the bread. When the mixture is smooth, gradually add the walnut oil, using the pestle to make sure that the ingredients are thoroughly combined.

3 Scrape the mixture into a large bowl. Beat in the yogurt and diced cucumber, then beat in the mineral water and lemon juice to taste. Process in a food processor or blender if you want a smooth soup. Chill the soup if time permits.

4 Pour the soup into chilled soup bowls. Sprinkle the coarsely chopped walnuts on top, drizzle a little olive oil over the nuts, then garnish with dill.

CHILLED ALMOND SOUP WITH GRAPES

Unless you want to spend time pounding the ingredients for this refreshing Spanish soup by hand, a food processor is an essential kitchen tool.

SERVES 6

INGREDIENTS
4 slices day-old fresh white bread, crusts removed
750ml/1¼ pints/3 cups chilled water
115g/4oz/1 cup blanched almonds
2 garlic cloves, sliced
75ml/5 tbsp olive oil
25ml/1½ tbsp sherry vinegar
salt and ground black pepper
toasted flaked (sliced) almonds and skinned seedless grapes, to garnish

1 Break the bread into a bowl and pour over 150ml/¼ pint/⅔ cup of the chilled water. Leave for 5 minutes. Meanwhile, put the almonds and garlic in a blender or food processor and process until very finely ground. Add the soaked white bread and process until smooth.

2 With the motor running, gradually add the oil through the lid or feeder tube until the mixture forms a smooth paste. Add the sherry vinegar and remaining chilled water and process until smooth and thoroughly combined.

3 Scrape the mixture into a bowl and season, adding a little more water if the soup is very thick. Chill in the refrigerator for at least 3 hours. Ladle the soup into chilled bowls and sprinkle with the toasted almonds and skinned grapes.

COOK'S TIP
To blanch almonds, put the kernels in a bowl, pour over boiling water and leave for about 5 minutes. Drain, then rub off the skins with the palms of your hands.

GAZPACHO

A colourful and flavour-packed combination of tomatoes, cucumber and peppers forms the basis of this classic, Spanish chilled soup.

SERVES 4

INGREDIENTS
2 slices day-old white bread
600ml/1 pint/2½ cups chilled water
1kg/2¼lb tomatoes
1 cucumber
1 red (bell) pepper, halved, seeded and chopped
1 fresh green chilli, seeded and chopped
2 garlic cloves, chopped
30ml/2 tbsp extra virgin olive oil
juice of 1 lime
juice of 1 lemon
a few drops of Tabasco sauce
salt and ground black pepper
a handful of fresh basil leaves, to garnish
ice cubes, to serve

FOR THE GARLIC CROÛTONS
2 slices day-old white bread, crusts removed
1 garlic clove, halved
15ml/1 tbsp olive oil

> COOK'S TIP
> *For the best, sweetest flavour, use sun-ripened or vine-ripened tomatoes.*

1 Soak the bread in 150ml/¼ pint/⅔ cup of the chilled water for 5 minutes. Meanwhile, place the tomatoes in a bowl and pour over boiling water to cover. Leave for 30 seconds, then drain, peel, seed and chop the flesh.

2 Peel the cucumber thinly, then cut it in half lengthways and scoop out the seeds with a teaspoon. Discard the seeds and chop the flesh.

3 Place the soaked bread, tomatoes, cucumber, red pepper, chilli, garlic, olive oil, lime juice, lemon juice and Tabasco sauce in a food processor or blender, with the remaining chilled water. Process until thoroughly combined, but still chunky.

4 Pour the blended soup into a large bowl, season to taste with plenty of salt and freshly ground pepper. Cover and chill in the refrigerator for 2–3 hours.

5 Make the croûtons. Rub the surface of the bread slices with the cut garlic clove. Cube the bread and toss with the olive oil until evenly coated. Heat a large non-stick frying pan and fry the croûtons over a medium heat until crisp and golden. Drain on kitchen paper.

6 When ready to serve, ladle the soup into chilled bowls and add two ice cubes to each portion. Garnish with the fresh basil leaves and serve immediately. Hand round the croûtons separately.

FRENCH ONION SOUP

This classic French soup is popular the world over. It is always served with a slightly chewy topping of melted Gruyère or Emmenthal cheese.

SERVES 4

INGREDIENTS

50g/2oz/¼ cup butter
2 onions, about 250g/9oz total weight, sliced
10ml/2 tsp plain (all-purpose) flour
1 litre/1¾ pints/4 cups vegetable stock
60ml/4 tbsp dry white wine or 30ml/2 tbsp dry sherry
4 slices crusty white bread
150g/5oz/1¼ cups grated Gruyère or Emmenthal cheese
salt and ground black pepper

1 Melt the butter in a large, heavy pan. Add the sliced onions and cook over a moderately low heat, stirring occasionally, for about 12 minutes, or until lightly browned. Stir in the plain flour and continue to cook, stirring constantly, until the flour turns a light sandy colour.

2 Pour in the stock and wine or sherry, then bring to the boil, stirring constantly. Season to taste with salt and pepper, cover and simmer for 15 minutes.

3 Spread out the slices of bread in a grill (broiler) pan and toast them lightly. Divide the grated cheese among them. Return to the grill and heat until the cheese is bubbling. Place the cheese toasts in four warmed, heatproof bowls.

4 Using a slotted spoon, scoop out the onions from the soup and divide them equally among the heated bowls. Pour the soup over them and serve.

COOK'S TIP
To give the soup a good, rich colour, make sure the sliced onions are lightly browned before you add the vegetable stock.

CREAM OF COURGETTE SOUP

The joys of this soup are its delicate colour, creamy texture and subtle taste. It is the perfect start to a summer meal.

SERVES 4–6

INGREDIENTS
30ml/2 tbsp olive oil
15g/½oz/1 tbsp butter
1 medium onion, coarsely chopped
900g/2lb courgettes (zucchini), trimmed and sliced
5ml/1 tsp dried oregano
about 600ml/1 pint/2½ cups vegetable stock
115g/4oz Dolcelatte cheese, rind removed, diced
300ml/½ pint/1¼ cups single (light) cream
salt and ground black pepper
fresh oregano and extra Dolcelatte, to garnish

1 Heat the oil and butter in a large pan over a medium heat until foaming. Add the onion and cook gently, stirring frequently, for about 5 minutes, or until softened, but not brown.

2 Add the sliced courgettes and dried oregano and season with salt and pepper to taste. Cook over a medium heat, stirring frequently, for 10 minutes.

3 Pour in the stock and bring to the boil, stirring constantly. Lower the heat and partially cover the pan. Simmer gently, stirring occasionally, for about 30 minutes. Stir in the diced Dolcelatte until melted.

4 Pour the mixture into a blender or food processor. Process until smooth, then press through a sieve into a clean pan.

5 Add two-thirds of the cream. Stir over a low heat until hot, but not boiling. Check the consistency and add more stock if the soup is too thick. Taste for seasoning, then pour into heated bowls. Swirl in the remaining cream. Garnish with fresh oregano and extra cheese and serve immediately.

Asparagus Soup

Home-made asparagus soup has a delicate flavour, quite unlike that from a can.
Use young asparagus, which is tender and easy to blend.

SERVES 4

INGREDIENTS
450g/1lb young asparagus
40g/1½oz/3 tbsp butter
6 shallots, sliced
15g/½oz/2 tbsp plain (all-purpose) flour
600ml/1 pint/2½ cups vegetable stock
15ml/1 tbsp lemon juice
250ml/8fl oz/1 cup milk
120ml/4fl oz/½ cup single (light) cream
salt and ground black pepper
10ml/2 tsp chopped fresh chervil, to garnish

COOK'S TIP
The thinnings or first pickings of fresh asparagus are
known as sprue and these are usually less expensive
than thicker stalks but still have a good flavour.

1 Trim the stalks of the asparagus if necessary. Cut 4cm/1½in off the tops of half the asparagus and set aside for a garnish. Slice the remaining asparagus.

2 Melt 25g/1oz/2 tbsp of the butter in a large, heavy pan. Add the sliced shallots and cook over a low heat, stirring occasionally, for 2–3 minutes, until softened and translucent, but not brown.

3 Add the sliced asparagus and cook over a gentle heat for about 1 minute. Stir in the plain flour and cook, stirring constantly, for 1 minute. Stir in the vegetable stock and lemon juice and season to taste with salt and pepper. Bring to the boil, then lower the heat and simmer, partially covered, for 15–20 minutes, until the asparagus is very tender.

4 Cool the soup slightly, then process the mixture with the milk in a blender or food processor until smooth. Press the purée through a sieve into a clean pan using a wooden spoon or ladle.

5 Melt the remaining butter in a frying pan over a low heat. Add the reserved asparagus tips and cook gently for 3–4 minutes, until softened but still fairly firm and not browned.

6 Heat the soup gently for 3–4 minutes. Stir in the single cream and the cooked asparagus tips. Ladle into heated bowls, sprinkle with the chopped fresh chervil and serve immediately.

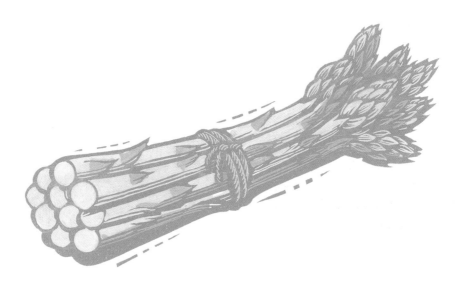

Tomato & Fresh Basil Soup

This is the perfect choice for late summer, when fresh tomatoes are at their most flavoursome and sweet. It can also be served chilled.

SERVES 4–6

INGREDIENTS
15ml/1 tbsp olive oil
25g/1oz/2 tbsp butter
1 medium onion, finely chopped
900g/2lb ripe Italian plum tomatoes, coarsely chopped
1 garlic clove, coarsely chopped
about 750ml/1¼ pints/3 cups vegetable stock
120ml/4fl oz/½ cup dry white wine
30ml/2 tbsp sun-dried tomato purée (paste)
30ml/2 tbsp shredded fresh basil, plus a few whole leaves, to garnish
150ml/¼ pint/⅔ cup double (heavy) cream
salt and ground black pepper

1 Heat the oil and butter in a large, heavy pan. Add the chopped onion and cook over a low heat, stirring occasionally, for about 5 minutes, until softened and translucent but not browned.

2 Stir in the chopped tomatoes and garlic, then add the vegetable stock, white wine and sun-dried tomato paste and season with salt and pepper to taste. Bring to the boil, then lower the heat, partially cover the pan and simmer gently for 20 minutes, stirring occasionally.

3 Process the soup with the shredded basil in a blender or food processor until smooth, then press through a fine sieve into a clean pan, pushing the purée through with a ladle or wooden spoon.

4 Stir in the double cream and heat through, stirring constantly. Do not allow the soup to approach boiling point. Check the consistency and flavour. Add more stock and seasoning if necessary. Pour into heated bowls and garnish with whole basil leaves. Serve immediately.

Garlic & Coriander Soup

This simple soup should be made with the best ingredients – plump garlic, fresh coriander, high-quality, crusty country bread and extra virgin olive oil.

Serves 6

Ingredients
25g/1oz/1 cup fresh coriander (cilantro), leaves and stalks chopped separately
1.5 litres/2½ pints/6¼ cups vegetable stock
5–6 plump garlic cloves, peeled
6 eggs
3 slices day-old white bread, crusts removed and torn into bitesize pieces
90ml/6 tbsp extra virgin olive oil, plus extra to serve
salt and ground black pepper

1 Place the coriander stalks in a pan. Add the vegetable stock and bring to the boil over a medium heat. Lower the heat and simmer for 10 minutes. Cool slightly, then process the mixture in a blender or food processor. Press through a sieve into a clean pan. Heat gently.

2 Crush the garlic with 5ml/1 tsp salt, then stir in 120ml/4fl oz/½ cup of the hot coriander stock. Return the mixture to the pan. Bring the soup to the boil and season to taste with salt and pepper. Leave over a low heat. Poach the eggs.

3 Divide the pieces of bread among six soup plates or bowls and drizzle the olive oil over it. Stir the chopped coriander leaves into the soup, then ladle it over the bread. Stir each portion once, then carefully add a poached egg to each bowl. Serve immediately, offering more olive oil at the table so that it can be drizzled over the soup to taste.

Cook's Tip
The olive oil is traditionally used to moisten the bread and flavour the soup, but you can use less than the recommended quantity if you like.

WILD MUSHROOM SOUP

*Dried porcini mushrooms have an intense flavour, so a small quantity is sufficient
to give this soup a truly superb, robust taste.*

SERVES 4

INGREDIENTS
25g/1oz/½ cup dried porcini mushrooms
250ml/8fl oz/1 cup warm water
30ml/2 tbsp olive oil
15g/½oz/1 tbsp butter
2 leeks, thinly sliced
2 shallots, coarsely chopped
1 garlic clove, coarsely chopped
225g/8oz/3¼ cups fresh wild mushrooms
about 1.2 litres/2 pints/5 cups vegetable stock
2.5ml/½ tsp dried thyme
150ml/¼ pint/⅔ cup double (heavy) cream
salt and ground black pepper
fresh thyme sprigs, to garnish

1 Soak the dried porcini in the warm water for 20–30 minutes. Lift out of the
liquid and squeeze out as much of the liquid as possible. Strain all the liquid and
reserve. Chop the mushrooms.

2 Heat the oil and butter in a large pan and cook the leeks, shallots and garlic
gently for about 5 minutes, stirring frequently.

3 Slice the fresh mushrooms and add them to the pan. Stir over a medium heat
until they begin to soften, then pour in the vegetable stock and bring to the boil.
Add the porcini, soaking liquid and dried thyme and season to taste with salt and
pepper. Lower the heat, partially cover the pan and simmer gently for 30 minutes,
stirring occasionally.

4 Process three-quarters of the soup in a blender or food processor until smooth.
Return it to the pan, stir in the cream and heat through. Add more stock if the
soup is too thick. Taste and adjust the seasoning, if necessary. Serve hot, garnished
with the thyme sprigs.

ROASTED VEGETABLE SOUP

Root vegetables roasted with herbs gives this winter soup a wonderful depth of flavour. You could vary the vegetables depending on availability.

SERVES 6

INGREDIENTS
60ml/4 tbsp olive oil
1 small butternut squash, peeled, seeded and cubed
2 carrots, cut into thick rounds
1 large parsnip, cubed
1 small swede (rutabaga), cubed
2 leeks, thickly sliced
1 onion, quartered
3 bay leaves
4 fresh thyme sprigs, plus extra to garnish
3 fresh rosemary sprigs
1.2 litres/2 pints/5 cups vegetable stock
salt and ground black pepper
sour cream, to serve

1 Preheat the oven to 200°C/400°F/Gas 6. Put the olive oil into a large bowl. Add the vegetables and toss until well coated.

2 Spread out the vegetables in a single layer on one large or two small baking sheets. Tuck the bay leaves and herb sprigs among the vegetables.

3 Roast the vegetables for about 50 minutes, or until tender, turning them occasionally. Remove the baking sheets from the oven, discard the thyme and rosemary sprigs and transfer the vegetables to a large pan.

4 Pour the stock into the pan and bring to the boil. Lower the heat, season to taste with salt and pepper, then simmer for 10 minutes. Transfer the soup to a food processor or blender and process for a few minutes until thick and smooth.

5 Return the soup to the pan and heat through. Season well with salt and pepper. Serve in heated bowls, adding a swirl of sour cream to each portion. Garnish with the extra thyme sprigs.

PEA, LEEK & BROCCOLI SOUP

A delicious and nutritious soup, ideal for a family supper to warm those chilly winter evenings. It can also be made in advance and frozen.

SERVES 4–6

INGREDIENTS
1 onion, chopped
225g/8oz/2 cups sliced leeks
225g/8oz unpeeled potatoes, diced
900ml/1½ pints/3¾ cups vegetable stock
1 bay leaf
225g/8oz/2 cups broccoli florets
175g/6oz/1½ cups frozen peas
30–45ml/2–3 tbsp chopped fresh parsley
salt and ground black pepper
fresh parsley leaves, to garnish

1 Put the onion, leeks, potatoes, stock and bay leaf in a large, heavy pan and mix together well. Cover and bring to the boil over a medium heat. Lower the heat and simmer, stirring frequently, for 10 minutes.

2 Add the broccoli and peas, cover and return to the boil. Lower the heat and simmer, stirring occasionally, for a further 10 minutes. Set aside to cool slightly.

3 Remove and discard the bay leaf. Process the soup in a blender or food processor, in batches if necessary, to a smooth purée. Add the parsley, season to taste with salt and pepper and process again briefly. Return to the pan and reheat gently until piping hot. Ladle into heated soup bowls and garnish with parsley leaves. Serve immediately.

VARIATIONS
- *If you like, cut the vegetables finely and leave the cooked soup chunky rather than puréeing it.*
- *Substitute frozen or drained, canned corn kernels for the frozen peas.*

Spiced Indian Cauliflower Soup

Light and tasty, this creamy, mildly spicy soup makes a wonderfully warming first course. It would also make a delicious light lunch with some Indian bread.

Serves 4–6

Ingredients

1 large potato, diced
1 small cauliflower, chopped
1 onion, chopped
15ml/1 tbsp sunflower oil
45ml/3 tbsp water
1 garlic clove, crushed
15ml/1 tbsp grated fresh root ginger
10ml/2 tsp ground turmeric
5ml/1 tsp cumin seeds
5ml/1 tsp black mustard seeds
10ml/2 tsp ground coriander
1 litre/1¾ pints/4 cups vegetable stock
300ml/½ pint/1¼ cups natural (plain) yogurt
salt and ground black pepper
fresh coriander (cilantro) or parsley sprigs, to garnish

1 Put the potato, cauliflower and onion into a large, heavy pan with the oil and water. Cook over a medium heat until hot and bubbling, then cover and lower the heat. Continue cooking the mixture for about 10 minutes.

2 Add the garlic, ginger, turmeric, cumin seeds, mustard seeds and ground coriander. Stir well and cook for a further 2 minutes, stirring occasionally.

3 Pour the stock into the pan and season to taste with salt and pepper. Bring to the boil, then lower the heat, cover and simmer for about 20 minutes.

4 Stir in the yogurt, then taste and adjust the seasoning, if necessary. Ladle the soup into heated soup bowls, garnish with fresh coriander or parsley sprigs and serve immediately.

SPICED LENTIL SOUP

A subtle blend of spices takes this warming soup to new heights. Serve it with warm crusty bread for a satisfying lunch.

SERVES 6

INGREDIENTS
2 onions, finely chopped
2 garlic cloves, crushed
4 tomatoes, coarsely chopped
2.5ml/½ tsp ground turmeric
5ml/1 tsp ground cumin
6 cardamom pods
½ cinnamon stick
225g/8oz/1 cup red lentils
900ml/1½ pints/3¾ cups water
400g/14oz can coconut milk
15ml/1 tbsp fresh lime juice
salt and ground black pepper
cumin seeds, to garnish

1 Put the onions, garlic, tomatoes, turmeric, cumin, cardamoms, cinnamon and lentils into a pan. Pour in the water. Bring to the boil, lower the heat, cover and simmer gently for about 20 minutes, or until the lentils are soft.

2 Remove and discard the cardamoms and cinnamon stick. Process the mixture in a blender or food processor to a smooth purée. Press the soup through a sieve, then return it to a clean pan.

3 Reserve a little of the coconut milk for the garnish and add the remainder to the pan, together with the lime juice. Stir well. Season to taste with salt and pepper. Reheat the soup gently without boiling. Ladle into heated bowls, swirl in the reserved coconut milk, garnish with the cumin seeds and serve.

VARIATION
You could also make this soup with green or yellow split peas instead of lentils for a heartier version.

North African Spiced Soup

Warm, aromatic spices, such as cinnamon and ginger, give this thick vegetable and chickpea soup an unforgettable flavour.

SERVES 6

INGREDIENTS
1 large onion, chopped
1.2 litres/2 pints/5 cups vegetable stock
5ml/1 tsp ground cinnamon
5ml/1 tsp ground turmeric
15ml/1 tbsp grated fresh root ginger
pinch of cayenne pepper
2 carrots, diced
2 celery sticks, diced
400g/14oz can chopped tomatoes
450g/1lb floury potatoes, diced
5 saffron threads
400g/14oz can chickpeas, drained
30ml/2 tbsp chopped fresh coriander (cilantro)
15ml/1 tbsp lemon juice
salt and ground black pepper
fried lemon wedges, to serve

1 Place the onion in a large pan with 300ml/½ pint/1¼ cups of the vegetable stock. Bring to the boil, lower the heat and simmer gently for about 10 minutes.

2 Meanwhile, spoon the cinnamon, turmeric, ginger and cayenne pepper into a bowl. Stir in 30ml/2 tbsp of the remaining stock to form a thick paste. Stir the spice paste into the onion mixture, together with the diced carrots and celery. Pour in the rest of the stock. Bring the mixture to the boil, lower the heat, then cover and simmer gently for 5 minutes.

3 Stir in the chopped tomatoes and diced potatoes. Cover and simmer gently for 20 minutes. Add the saffron threads, chickpeas, fresh coriander and lemon juice. Season to taste with salt and pepper. When piping hot, serve in heated bowls with fried lemon wedges.

JERUSALEM ARTICHOKE SOUP

Thanks to their mild, nutty flavour, Jerusalem artichokes make a remarkably good, creamy soup. Look for the smoothest ones if they are to be peeled.

SERVES 4

INGREDIENTS
30ml/2 tbsp olive oil
1 large onion, chopped
1 garlic clove, chopped
1 celery stick, chopped
675g/1½lb Jerusalem artichokes, peeled or scrubbed and chopped
1.2 litres/2 pints/5 cups vegetable stock
300ml/½ pint/1¼ cups milk
8 slices French bread
115g/4oz/1 cup grated Gruyère cheese
salt and ground black pepper

1 Heat the oil in a large pan and cook the onion, garlic and celery over a medium heat, stirring occasionally, for about 5 minutes, or until softened. Add the Jerusalem artichokes and cook for 5 minutes more.

2 Add the stock and season with salt and pepper to taste. Bring to the boil, lower the heat and simmer, stirring occasionally, for 20–25 minutes, or until the artichokes are tender.

3 Transfer the soup to a food processor or blender and process. Return the soup to the pan, stir in the milk and heat through gently for 2 minutes.

4 To make Gruyère toasts, spread out the slices of French bread in a grill (broiler) pan and toast them lightly on one side under a hot grill. Turn the slices of bread over and sprinkle the untoasted side of each with the grated Gruyère. Grill (broil) until the cheese melts and is golden. Ladle the soup into bowls and top with Gruyère toasts and ground black pepper.

Spinach & Rice Soup

Use young spinach leaves to prepare this light and fresh-tasting soup. Use arborio, Vialone Nano or carnaroli rice for the rice soup.

Serves 4

Ingredients
675g/1½lb fresh young spinach, washed
45ml/3 tbsp extra virgin olive oil
1 small onion, finely chopped
2 garlic cloves, finely chopped
1 small fresh red chilli, seeded and finely chopped
200g/7oz/1 cup risotto rice
1.2 litres/2 pints/5 cups vegetable stock
salt and ground black pepper
60ml/4 tbsp grated Pecorino cheese, to serve

1 Place the spinach in a large pan with just the water that clings to its leaves after washing. Add a large pinch of salt. Heat gently until the spinach has just wilted, then remove from the heat and drain, reserving any liquid.

2 Either chop the spinach finely using a large knife or place it in a food processor and process to a fairly coarse purée.

3 Heat the oil in a large, heavy pan. Add the onion, garlic and chilli and cook over a low heat, stirring occasionally, for 4–5 minutes, or until softened.

4 Add the rice and stir until all the grains are well coated, then pour in the stock and reserved spinach liquid. Bring to the boil over a medium heat, then lower the heat and simmer for about 10 minutes.

5 Add the spinach to the pan and season with salt and pepper to taste. Cook for 5–7 minutes more, until the rice is tender. Check the seasoning and serve in warmed soup plates with the grated Pecorino cheese.

RIBOLLITA

This Italian soup is rather like minestrone, but with beans instead of pasta.
It is traditionally served ladled over bread and a rich green vegetable.

SERVES 6–8

INGREDIENTS
45ml/3 tbsp olive oil
2 onions, chopped
2 carrots, sliced
4 garlic cloves, crushed
2 celery sticks, thinly sliced
1 fennel bulb, trimmed and chopped
2 large courgettes (zucchini), thinly sliced
400g/14oz can chopped tomatoes
30ml/2 tbsp home-made or ready-made pesto
900ml/1½ pints/3¾ cups vegetable stock
400g/14oz can haricot (navy) or borlotti beans, drained
salt and ground black pepper

TO FINISH
15ml/1 tbsp extra virgin olive oil, plus extra for drizzling
450g/1lb fresh young spinach or Swiss chard
6–8 slices white bread

1 Heat the oil in a large pan. Add the chopped onions, carrots, garlic, celery and fennel and cook gently for 10 minutes without allowing to brown. Add the courgettes and cook for 2 minutes more.

2 Stir in the chopped tomatoes, pesto, stock and beans and bring to the boil. Lower the heat, cover and simmer gently for 25–30 minutes, or until the vegetables are completely tender. Season with salt and pepper to taste.

3 To serve, heat the oil in a heavy frying pan and cook the spinach or chard for 2 minutes, or until wilted. Put a slice of bread in each heated soup bowl, spoon the spinach or chard on top, then ladle the soup over the it. Offer extra olive oil at the table, so that guests can drizzle it on to the soup. Freshly ground black pepper can be sprinkled on top.

BORLOTTI BEAN & PASTA SOUP

A complete meal in a bowl, this is based on a classic Italian soup. Traditionally, the person who finds the bay leaf is honoured with a kiss from the cook.

SERVES 4

INGREDIENTS
75ml/5 tbsp olive oil
1 onion, chopped
1 celery stick, chopped
2 carrots, chopped
1 bay leaf
1.2 litres/2 pints/5 cups vegetable stock
400g/14oz can chopped tomatoes
175g/6oz/1½ cups dried pasta shapes
400g/14oz can borlotti beans, drained
250g/9oz fresh young spinach
salt and ground black pepper
50g/2oz/⅔ cup freshly grated Parmesan cheese, to serve

1 Heat the olive oil in a large, heavy pan and add the chopped onion, celery and carrots. Cook over a medium heat, stirring occasionally, for 5 minutes, or until the vegetables soften and the onion is translucent. Add the bay leaf, stock and tomatoes and bring to the boil. Lower the heat and simmer for about 10 minutes, until the vegetables are just tender.

2 Bring the soup back to the boil, add the pasta and beans and simmer for 8 minutes, until the pasta is *al dente*. Stir the soup frequently to prevent the pasta from sticking to the base of the pan.

3 Season to taste with salt and pepper, add the spinach and cook for 2 minutes more. Serve in heated bowls, sprinkled with the grated Parmesan.

VARIATIONS
- *Add a glass of white wine with the stock.*
- *Substitute two shallots for the onion and ½ small fennel bulb for the celery.*

APPETIZERS

Vegetarian ingredients, from cheese to mushrooms and from vegetables to eggs, are the perfect choice for appetizers, canapés and snacks. Refreshing salads, such as Dressed Salad of Fresh Ceps, delicious dips, such as Hummus with Crudités, melt-in-the-mouth pastries, such as Brandied Roquefort Tarts, and a superb collection of marinated, stuffed and roasted vegetables appeal to the eye and tempt the appetite. As well as serving these versatile dishes as appetizers – whether for a dinner party or a family gathering – you can also combine many of them for a spectacular party buffet table or even serve them as a light lunch.

Pear & Parmesan Salad with Poppy Seed Dressing

This is a good appetizer when pears are at their seasonal best. Drizzle them with a poppy-seed dressing and top them with shavings of Parmesan cheese.

SERVES 4

INGREDIENTS
4 just-ripe pears
50g/2oz piece of Parmesan cheese
watercress or American cress, to garnish
water biscuits (crackers) or rye bread, to serve (optional)

FOR THE DRESSING
30ml/2 tbsp cider vinegar
2.5ml/½ tsp soft light brown sugar
good pinch of dried thyme
30ml/2 tbsp extra virgin olive oil
15ml/1 tbsp sunflower oil
15ml/1 tbsp poppy seeds
salt and ground black pepper

1 Peel the pears if you wish, although they look more attractive with the skin on. Cut them in quarters and remove the cores.

2 Cut each pear quarter in half lengthways and arrange them attractively on four small serving plates.

3 Make the dressing. Mix the vinegar, sugar and thyme in a jug (pitcher). Gradually whisk in the olive oil, then the sunflower oil. Season with salt and pepper to taste, then tip in the poppy seeds.

4 Trickle the dressing over the pears slices. Shave Parmesan over the top and garnish with watercress or American cress. Serve with water biscuits or thinly sliced rye bread, if you like.

DRESSED SALAD OF FRESH CEPS

Mushrooms make a marvellous salad, especially if you are able to obtain fresh ceps or bay boletus. Any wild or cultivated mushrooms can be used.

SERVES 4

INGREDIENTS
350g/12oz/4 cups fresh ceps or bay boletus, thinly sliced
175g/6oz ready-to-serve mixed salad leaves
50g/2oz/½ cup broken walnut pieces, toasted
50g/2oz piece of Parmesan cheese
salt and ground black pepper

FOR THE DRESSING
2 egg yolks (optional, see Watchpoint)
2.5ml/½ tsp French mustard
75ml/5 tbsp groundnut (peanut) oil
45ml/3 tbsp walnut oil
30ml/2 tbsp lemon juice
30ml/2 tbsp chopped fresh parsley
pinch of caster (superfine) sugar

1 Make the dressing. Place the egg yolks in a small screw-top jar with the French mustard, groundnut oil, walnut oil, lemon juice, parsley and caster sugar. Close the jar tightly and shake well.

2 Place the mushrooms in a bowl and pour the dressing over them. Toss to coat, then set aside for 10–15 minutes. Add the salad leaves to the mushrooms and toss. Season well. Divide the salad among four large plates. Sprinkle each portion with walnuts and shavings of Parmesan cheese.

WATCHPOINT
Expectant mothers, young children and the elderly are advised to avoid raw egg yolks. Be sure to use only the freshest eggs from a reputable supplier.

ASPARAGUS IN EGG
& LEMON SAUCE

As an appetizer or light lunch, fresh asparagus is a special treat, especially when topped with a tangy, fresh-tasting sauce.

SERVES 4

INGREDIENTS
675g/1½lb asparagus
15ml/1 tbsp cornflour (cornstarch)
about 10ml/2 tsp sugar
2 egg yolks
juice of 1½ lemons
salt

1 Trim the asparagus stalks, discarding the tough ends, then tie them in a bundle with kitchen string. Cook in a tall pan of lightly salted boiling water over a medium heat for 7–10 minutes.

2 Drain well, reserving 200ml/7fl oz/scant 1 cup of the cooking liquid. Untie the asparagus stems and arrange them in a shallow serving dish.

3 Put the cornflour in a small pan. Stir in enough of the reserved cooking liquid to form a smooth paste, then stir in the remaining cooking liquid. Slowly bring to the boil, stirring constantly, and cook over a low heat until the sauce has thickened slightly. Stir in the sugar, then remove the pan from the heat. Set the sauce aside to cool slightly.

4 Beat the egg yolks with the lemon juice. Gradually stir the mixture into the cooled sauce with a wooden spoon. Cook over a very low heat, stirring constantly, until the sauce is fairly thick. Immediately remove the pan from the heat. Continue stirring for 1 minute.

5 Taste the sauce and add salt or sugar if needed. Let it cool slightly, then pour a little over the cooked asparagus. Cover and chill for at least 2 hours before serving with the rest of the sauce.

Baby Onions & Mushrooms à la Grecque

There are many variations of this classic dish. The mushrooms may be omitted, but they add immeasurably to the flavour and texture.

SERVES 4

INGREDIENTS
2 carrots
350g/12oz baby (pearl) onions
60ml/4 tbsp olive oil
120ml/4fl oz/½ cup dry white wine
5ml/1 tsp coriander seeds, lightly crushed
2 bay leaves
pinch of cayenne pepper
1 garlic clove, crushed
350g/12oz/4½ cups button (white) mushrooms
3 tomatoes, peeled, seeded and quartered
salt and ground black pepper
45ml/3 tbsp chopped fresh parsley, to garnish
crusty bread, to serve

1 Peel the carrots and cut them into small dice. Peel the baby onions and trim the tops and roots.

2 Heat 45ml/3 tbsp of the olive oil in a deep frying pan. Add the carrots and onions and cook, stirring occasionally, for about 20 minutes, or until the vegetables have browned lightly.

3 Add the white wine, coriander seeds, bay leaves, cayenne, garlic, mushrooms and tomatoes and season with salt and pepper to taste. Cook, uncovered, for 20–30 minutes, or until the vegetables are soft and the sauce has thickened.

4 Transfer the mixture to a serving dish and leave to cool. Cover and chill until needed. Before serving, pour over the remaining olive oil and sprinkle with the chopped parsley. Serve with crusty bread.

Marinated Vegetable Antipasti

If you ever want to prove just how delectable vegetables can be, serve this sensational selection of Italian-style appetizers. It is perfect for an al fresco *lunch or an informal dinner party. You could use a selection of mushrooms for a contrasting flavour and texture, if you like.*

SERVES 4

INGREDIENTS
FOR THE PEPPERS
3 red (bell) peppers, halved and seeded
3 yellow (bell) peppers, halved and seeded
4 garlic cloves, sliced
a handful of fresh basil leaves, plus extra to garnish
extra virgin olive oil
salt

FOR THE MUSHROOMS
450g/1lb/6 cups open cap mushrooms
60ml/4 tbsp extra virgin olive oil
1 large garlic clove, crushed
15ml/1 tbsp chopped fresh rosemary
250ml/8fl oz/1 cup dry white wine
salt and ground black pepper
fresh rosemary sprigs, to garnish

FOR THE OLIVES
120ml/4fl oz/½ cup extra virgin olive oil
1 dried red chilli
grated rind of 1 lemon
225g/8oz/1⅓ cups Italian black olives
30ml/2 tbsp chopped fresh flat leaf parsley
1 lemon wedge, to serve

1 Place the pepper halves, skin-side up, on a grill (broiler) rack and cook until the skins have charred. Transfer to a bowl and cover with crumpled kitchen paper or clear film (plastic wrap). Leave to cool slightly.

2 When the pepper halves are cool enough to handle, peel off their skins, then cut the flesh into strips. Place the strips in a bowl and add the sliced garlic and basil leaves. Sprinkle with salt to taste, cover with olive oil and set aside to marinate for 3–4 hours, tossing occasionally. Chill in the refrigerator.

3 Slice the mushrooms thickly and place them in a large heatproof bowl. Heat the oil in a small pan and add the garlic and rosemary. Pour in the wine. Bring the mixture to the boil, then lower the heat and simmer for 3 minutes. Season with salt and ground black pepper to taste.

4 Pour the mixture over the mushrooms. Mix thoroughly and set aside until cool, stirring occasionally. Cover and leave to marinate overnight in the refrigerator.

5 Prepare the olives. Place the oil in a small pan and crumble in the chilli. Add the lemon rind. Heat gently for about 3 minutes. Add the olives and heat for 1 minute more. Tip into a bowl and leave to cool. Set aside to marinate overnight.

6 Let the marinated mushrooms come to room temperature before serving. Garnish them with rosemary sprigs. Garnish the chilled peppers with basil leaves. Sprinkle the olives with parsley and serve with the lemon wedge.

AUBERGINE & SPINACH TERRINES

These individual terrines make a strong visual impact with their different layers of pale and dark green vegetables.

SERVES 4

INGREDIENTS

1 aubergine (eggplant)
30ml/2 tbsp extra virgin olive oil
2 courgettes (zucchini), thinly sliced
leaves from 1 small fresh thyme sprig
4 firm tomatoes, peeled and seeded
4 fresh basil leaves, finely sliced
275g/10oz fresh baby spinach leaves
1 garlic clove, crushed
15g/½oz/1 tbsp butter
pinch of freshly grated nutmeg
salt and ground black pepper
½ roasted red (bell) pepper, peeled and chopped, plus a little
  balsamic vinegar, to serve

COOK'S TIP
There are two grades of balsamic vinegar. The commercial kind is labelled industriale, *while* naturale *is still made by the traditional method and aged for about twenty years.*

1 Preheat the oven to 190°C/375°F/Gas 5. Seal four 6cm/2½in diameter metal muffin rings at one end with clear film (plastic wrap).

2 Slice the aubergine into four rounds of equal size. Heat half the oil in a frying pan and cook the aubergine slices on both sides until brown. Place them on a baking sheet and cook in the oven for 10 minutes. Transfer to a plate lined with kitchen paper.

3 Heat half the remaining oil in the same pan and cook the courgettes for 2 minutes, then drain on the kitchen paper. Season and sprinkle with thyme.

Place the tomatoes, basil and remaining olive oil in a heavy frying pan and cook
for 5–8 minutes. Cook the spinach, garlic and butter in a pan, allowing all the
water to evaporate. Drain thoroughly, add the nutmeg, then season to taste with
salt and pepper.

Line the base and 1cm/½ in of the sides of the muffin rings with the spinach
leaves, leaving no gaps. Place courgette slices around the edges of each ring,
overlapping them slightly. Divide the tomato mixture equally among the rings,
pressing it down well. Place the aubergines on the top, trimming the edges to fit.

Seal the top with clear film and pierce the base to allow any liquid to escape.
Chill overnight. Remove from the rings and serve with roasted pepper, drizzled
with balsamic vinegar.

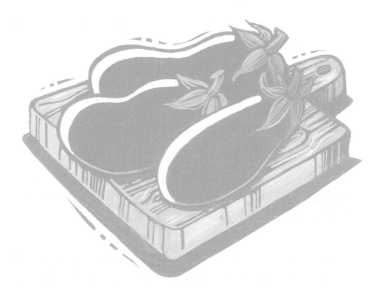

STUFFED VINE LEAVES

Whether you serve these as part of a meze or as a solo appetizer, they are certain to prove popular with your guests.

MAKES ABOUT 40

INGREDIENTS
40 fresh vine leaves or two packets of vine leaves
  preserved in brine, rinsed well
60ml/4 tbsp olive oil
lemon wedges and a crisp salad, to serve

FOR THE STUFFING
150g/5oz/³⁄4 cup long grain rice, rinsed
2 bunches spring onions (scallions), finely chopped
40g/1½oz/scant ½ cup pine nuts
45ml/3 tbsp seedless raisins
30ml/2 tbsp chopped fresh mint leaves
60ml/4 tbsp chopped fresh parsley
4ml/³⁄4 tsp ground black pepper
salt

1 Using a knife or a pair of scissors, snip out the thick, coarse stems from the vine leaves. Blanch the leaves in a large pan of salted boiling water until they just begin to change colour. Drain, refresh in cold water, then drain again.

2 To make the stuffing, mix all the ingredients together in a bowl and season to taste with salt. Open out the vine leaves, ribbed side uppermost. Place a heaped teaspoonful of the stuffing on each.

3 Fold over the two outer edges to secure the stuffing, then roll up each vine leaf from the stem end to form a neat roll. Arrange the stuffed vine leaves neatly in a steamer and sprinkle over the olive oil. Steam over boiling water for 50–60 minutes, or until the rice is completely cooked. Serve cold, but not chilled, with lemon wedges and a salad.

CHILLED STUFFED COURGETTES

Full of flavour but low in calories and fat, this makes a superb summer appetizer. Use a mixture of yellow and green courgettes for visual appeal.

SERVES 4

INGREDIENTS

6 courgettes (zucchini), trimmed
1 Spanish (Bermuda) onion, very finely chopped
1 garlic clove, crushed
60–90ml/4–6 tbsp well-flavoured French dressing
1 green (bell) pepper, seeded and diced
3 tomatoes, peeled, seeded and diced
15ml/1 tbsp drained and chopped rinsed capers
5ml/1 tsp chopped fresh parsley
5ml/1 tsp chopped fresh basil
salt and ground black pepper
fresh parsley sprigs, to garnish

1 Bring a large shallow pan of lightly salted water to the boil. Add the courgettes and simmer for 2–3 minutes, or until they are lightly cooked. Drain well.

2 Cut the courgettes in half lengthways. Carefully scoop out the flesh, leaving the courgette shells intact. Chop the flesh into small cubes. Place in a bowl and cover with half the chopped onion. Dot with the crushed garlic. Drizzle 30ml/2 tbsp of the dressing over, cover and marinate for 2–3 hours. Wrap the courgette shells tightly in clear film (plastic wrap) and chill them until needed.

3 Stir the pepper, tomatoes and capers into the courgette mixture, with the remaining onion and the herbs. Season to taste with salt and pepper. Pour over enough of the remaining dressing to moisten the mixture, toss well and chill.

4 Spoon the filling into the courgette shells, arrange on a platter and serve garnished with fresh parsley.

MALFATTI WITH ROASTED PEPPER SAUCE

Deliciously light spinach and ricotta dumplings are wonderful when served with a smoky pepper and tomato sauce.

SERVES 5

INGREDIENTS
500g/1¼lb fresh leaf spinach
1 onion, finely chopped
1 garlic clove, crushed
15ml/1 tbsp extra virgin olive oil
350g/12oz/1½ cups ricotta cheese
3 eggs, beaten
50g/2oz/¾ cup natural-coloured dried breadcrumbs
50g/2oz/½ cup plain (all-purpose) flour
50g/2oz/⅔ cup freshly grated Parmesan cheese
freshly grated nutmeg
25g/1oz/2 tbsp butter, melted
salt and ground black pepper

FOR THE SAUCE
2 red (bell) peppers, quartered and seeded
30ml/2 tbsp extra virgin olive oil
1 onion, chopped
400g/14oz can chopped tomatoes
150ml/¼ pint/⅔ cup water

COOK'S TIP
Drain the blanched spinach well, squeeze out as much water as possible, then spread out on a clean dishtowel, roll it up and wring out any liquid.

1 Make the sauce. Grill (broil) the peppers, skin-side up, until the skins have charred. Place in a bowl, cover with crumpled kitchen paper and leave to cool. Peel off the skins and chop the flesh.

Heat the oil in a pan and sauté the onion and peppers for 5 minutes. Add the tomatoes and water and season to taste with salt and pepper. Bring to the boil, lower the heat and simmer for 15 minutes. Process in a food processor or blender, then return to the clean pan.

Trim any thick stalks from the spinach, then blanch in a pan of boiling water for about 1 minute. Drain, refresh under cold water and drain again. Squeeze dry, then chop finely. Put the onion, garlic, oil, ricotta, eggs, breadcrumbs and spinach in a bowl. Mix well, then stir in the flour and 5ml/1 tsp salt. Add half the Parmesan, then season to taste with pepper and nutmeg. Roll the mixture into 15 small logs and chill lightly.

Bring a large pan of water to the boil. Cook the malfatti, in batches, for 5 minutes. Remove them with a slotted spoon and toss them with the melted butter. To serve, reheat the sauce and divide it among five plates. Arrange three malfatti on each and sprinkle over the remaining Parmesan. Serve immediately.

VEGETABLE TEMPURA

These deep-fried fritters are based on Kaki-age, *a popular Japanese dish. They are ideal for an informal gathering as they are fun to make.*

MAKES 8

INGREDIENTS
2 medium courgettes (zucchini)
½ medium aubergine (eggplant)
1 large carrot
½ small Spanish (Bermuda) onion
vegetable oil, for deep-frying
salt and ground black pepper
sea salt flakes, lemon slices and Japanese soy sauce, to serve

FOR THE BATTER
1 egg
120ml/4fl oz/½ cup iced water
115g/4oz/1 cup plain (all-purpose) flour

VARIATION
You could substitute or add other vegetables to the mixture, such as small cauliflower florets, baby corn, button (white) mushrooms or broccoli and red or yellow (bell) pepper cut into thin batons.

1 Using a vegetable peeler, pare strips of peel from the courgettes and aubergine to give a stripy effect. Cut the courgettes, aubergine and carrot into strips about 7.5–10cm/3–4in long and 3mm/⅛in wide and put them in a colander.

2 Sprinkle the vegetable strips liberally with salt. Leave for about 30 minutes, then rinse thoroughly under cold running water. Drain well.

3 Thinly slice the Spanish onion from top to base, discarding the plump pieces in the middle. Separate the layers so that there are lots of fine long strips. Mix all the vegetables together and season to taste with salt and pepper.

4 Make the batter immediately before frying: mix the egg and iced water in a bowl, then sift in the flour. Mix very briefly with a fork or chopsticks – the batter should remain lumpy. Add the vegetables to the batter and mix to combine.

5 Half-fill a wok with oil and heat to 180°C/350°F, or until a cube of day-old bread browns in 60 seconds. Scoop up one heaped tablespoon of the mixture at a time and carefully lower it into the oil to make a fritter. Deep-fry in batches for about 3 minutes, or until golden brown and crisp.

6 Drain the cooked fritters on kitchen paper, and serve immediately, offering each diner sea salt flakes, lemon slices and a tiny individual bowl of Japanese soy sauce for dipping.

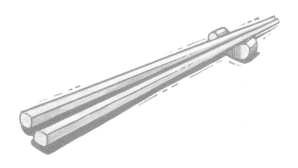

Eggs Benedict with Quick Hollandaise

This classic American brunch dish originated in New York, and is ideal for serving on a special occasion, such as a birthday treat or New Year's day.

SERVES 4

INGREDIENTS
4 large (US extra large) eggs, plus 2 egg yolks
5ml/1 tsp dry mustard
15ml/1 tbsp white wine vinegar or lemon juice
175g/6oz/³⁄4 cup butter, plus extra for spreading
4 muffins, split
30ml/2 tbsp rinsed capers
salt and ground black pepper
a little chopped fresh parsley, to garnish

> VARIATION
> *Instead of the toasted muffins, you could make more of a main meal by serving the poached eggs and sauce on a bed of well-drained lightly steamed or blanched spinach.*

1 Put the egg yolks in a blender or food processor. Add the dry mustard and a pinch of salt and ground pepper and process for a few seconds. Add the vinegar or lemon juice and process again.

2 Heat the butter until it is on the point of bubbling, then, with the motor running, slowly pour it through the lid or feeder tube. When the mixture is thick and creamy, switch off the blender or food processor and set the sauce aside.

3 Toast the split muffins under a hot grill (broiler). Cut four of the halves in half again and butter them lightly. Place the four uncut halves on warmed plates and set aside without buttering them.

4 Poach the eggs either in gently simmering water or in an egg poacher. Drain well and slip carefully on to the muffin halves. Spoon the hollandaise sauce over the muffins, then sprinkle with capers and parsley. Serve immediately with the buttered muffin quarters.

Twice Baked Gruyère & Potato Soufflés

Soufflés were all the rage a few years ago and should not be forgotten as they are delicious. Easily prepared in advance, they are perfect for entertaining.

SERVES 4

INGREDIENTS
butter, for greasing
225g/8oz floury potatoes
2 eggs, separated
175g/6oz/1½ cups grated Gruyère cheese
50g/2oz/½ cup self-raising (self-rising) flour
50g/2oz fresh young spinach leaves, finely chopped
salt and ground black pepper
salad leaves, to serve

1 Preheat the oven to 200°C/400°F/Gas 6. Grease four large ramekins. Cook the potatoes in lightly salted boiling water for 20 minutes, until very tender. Drain thoroughly and mash with the egg yolks. Stir in half the Gruyère cheese and all the flour. Season to taste with salt and pepper, then fold in the spinach.

2 Whisk the egg whites until they form soft peaks. Stir a little of the egg white into the spinach mixture to loosen it slightly, then fold in the rest.

3 Place the ramekins on a baking sheet. Divide the mixture among them. Bake for 20 minutes. Remove from the oven and leave to cool.

4 Reheat the oven to 200°C/400°F/Gas 6. Carefully invert the soufflés on a baking sheet and sprinkle with the remaining Gruyère cheese. Bake for 5 minutes. Serve immediately with salad leaves.

VARIATION
For a different flavouring, try replacing the Gruyère with a crumbled blue cheese, such as Stilton.

COURGETTE FRITTERS WITH CHILLI JAM

Rather like a thick chutney, chilli jam is hot, sweet and sticky. It adds a piquancy to these light courgette fritters but is also delicious with pies or a chunk of cheese.

MAKES 12 FRITTERS

INGREDIENTS
450g/1lb courgettes (zucchini)
50g/2oz/⅔ cup freshly grated Parmesan cheese
2 eggs, beaten
60ml/4 tbsp unbleached plain (all-purpose) flour
vegetable oil, for frying
salt and ground black pepper

FOR THE CHILLI JAM
75ml/5 tbsp olive oil
4 large onions, diced
4 garlic cloves, chopped
1–2 fresh Thai chillies, seeded and sliced
25g/1oz/2 tbsp soft dark brown sugar
a few thin slices of fresh red chilli, to garnish

1 First make the chilli jam. Heat the oil in a frying pan and cook the onions and garlic, stirring frequently, for 20 minutes, until the onions are very soft. Set aside to cool, then put into a food processor or blender. Add the Thai chillies and sugar and process until smooth, then return to the pan. Cook over a low heat, stirring frequently, for 10 minutes, or until the liquid has evaporated. Cool slightly.

2 To make the fritters, coarsely grate the courgettes on to a clean dishtowel, then gather up the sides and squeeze tightly to remove any excess moisture. Tip into a bowl and stir in the Parmesan, eggs and flour, and season with salt and pepper.

3 Heat enough oil to cover the base of a large frying pan. Add 30ml/2 tbsp of the mixture for each fritter and cook three fritters at a time for 2–3 minutes on each side, until golden. Keep warm while you cook the remaining fritters. Drain on kitchen paper and serve with a spoonful of the chilli jam, garnished with chilli.

FALAFEL

In North Africa and parts of the Middle East, these spicy fritters are made using dried broad (fava) beans, but chickpeas are easier to buy. They are lovely served as a snack with creamy yogurt or stuffed into warmed pitta bread pockets. Falafel are ideal hot snacks to serve at parties and can be prepared in advance and frozen.

SERVES 4

INGREDIENTS
150g/5oz/⅔ cup dried chickpeas
1 large onion, coarsely chopped
2 garlic cloves, coarsely chopped
60ml/4 tbsp coarsely chopped parsley
5ml/1 tsp cumin seeds, crushed
5ml/1 tsp coriander seeds, crushed
2.5ml/½ tsp baking powder
vegetable oil, for deep-frying
salt and ground black pepper

TO SERVE
pitta bread
salad
natural (plain) yogurt

VARIATION
For additional flavour and colour, add 30 ml/2 tbsp chopped fresh mint and 30 ml/2 tbsp chopped fresh coriander (cilantro) with the parsley in step 3.

1 Put the chickpeas in a bowl and add sufficient cold water to cover well. Leave to soak overnight.

2 Drain the chickpeas and put them in a large pan. Pour over enough water to cover them by at least 5cm/2in. Bring to the boil, then lower the heat and simmer for 1–1½ hours, or until soft.

3 Drain the chickpeas and place them in a food processor. Add the onion, garlic, parsley, cumin seeds, coriander seeds and baking powder. Season with salt and pepper to taste. Process until the mixture forms a fine paste.

4 As soon as the paste is cool enough to handle, shape it into walnut-size balls, flattening them slightly.

5 Pour oil to a depth of 5cm/2in into a deep frying pan. Heat until a little of the falafel mixture added to the hot oil sizzles on the surface.

6 Fry the falafel, in batches, until golden. Drain on kitchen paper and keep hot while frying the remainder. Serve warm in pitta bread, with salad and yogurt.

THAI TEMPEH CAKES WITH SWEET DIPPING SAUCE

Made from soya beans, tempeh is similar to tofu, but has a nuttier taste. Here, it is combined with spices and formed into small patties.

MAKES 8 CAKES

INGREDIENTS

1 lemon grass stalk, outer leaves removed, coarsely chopped
2 garlic cloves, chopped
2 spring onions (scallions), finely chopped
2 shallots, coarsely chopped
2 fresh chillies, seeded and coarsely chopped
2.5cm/1in piece of fresh root ginger, finely chopped
60ml/4 tbsp chopped fresh coriander (cilantro), plus extra to garnish
250g/9oz tempeh, thawed if frozen, sliced
15ml/1 tbsp freshly squeezed lime juice
5ml/1 tsp caster (superfine) sugar
45ml/3 tbsp plain (all-purpose) flour
1 large (US extra large) egg, lightly beaten
vegetable oil, for frying
salt and ground black pepper

FOR THE DIPPING SAUCE
45ml/3 tbsp mirin
45ml/3 tbsp white wine vinegar
2 spring onions (scallions), thinly sliced
15ml/1 tbsp sugar
2 fresh red chillies, chopped
30ml/2 tbsp chopped fresh coriander

1 To make the dipping sauce, mix the mirin, vinegar, spring onions, sugar, chillies, coriander and a large pinch of salt in a small bowl and set aside.

2 Place the lemon grass, garlic, spring onions, shallots, chillies, ginger and coriander in a food processor or blender and process to a coarse paste.

3 Add the tempeh, lime juice and sugar, then process until thoroughly combined. Add the flour and egg and season with plenty of salt and pepper. Process again until the mixture forms a coarse, sticky paste.

4 Using a tablespoon, scoop up a generous quantity of the tempeh mixture. Dampen your hands, then shape the mixture to a round, slightly flattened cake. Make seven more tempeh cakes in the same way.

5 Heat enough oil to cover the base of a large frying pan. Fry the tempeh cakes, in batches, for 5–6 minutes, turning once, until golden. Drain on kitchen paper and keep warm while cooking the remainder. Serve warm with the dipping sauce, garnished with coriander.

COOK'S TIP
Use red or green chillies, choosing a variety with the degree of fieriness you require. In general, dark green chillies tend to be hotter than pale green ones, which, in turn, are hotter than red chillies. (As the chillies ripen, they become red and relatively sweeter.) Also, the small, pointed chillies tend to be fiercer than the larger, rounder ones. However, there are always exceptions and even different pods from the same plant can vary in their level of spiciness. Err on the side of caution, if in doubt.

SPICED SWEET POTATO TURNOVERS

A subtle hint of sweetness underscores the spicy flavour of these turnovers. Use sweet potatoes with an orange flesh as they have a better flavour.

SERVES 4

INGREDIENTS
15ml/1 tbsp olive oil
1 small egg
150ml/¼ pint/⅔ cup natural (plain) yogurt
115g/4oz/½ cup butter, melted
1.5ml/¼ tsp bicarbonate of soda (baking soda)
275g/10oz/2½ cups plain (all-purpose) flour
10ml/2 tsp paprika
beaten egg, to glaze
salt and ground black pepper
fresh mint sprigs, to garnish

FOR THE FILLING
1 sweet potato, about 225g/8oz
30ml/2 tbsp vegetable oil
2 shallots, finely chopped
10ml/2 tsp coriander seeds, crushed
5ml/1 tsp ground cumin
5ml/1 tsp garam masala
115g/4oz/1 cup frozen petits pois, thawed
15ml/1 tbsp chopped fresh mint

1 To make the filling, cook the sweet potato in lightly salted boiling water for 15–20 minutes, until tender. Drain and leave to cool, then peel the potato and cut into 1cm/½in cubes.

2 Heat the vegetable oil in a frying pan and cook the shallots until softened. Add the potato and cook until it browns at the edges. Sprinkle over the spices and cook, stirring, for a few seconds. Remove the pan from the heat and add the peas and mint, and season with salt and pepper to taste. Leave to cool.

3 Preheat the oven to 200°C/400°F/Gas 6. Grease a baking sheet. To make the pastry, whisk together the olive oil and egg, stir in the yogurt, then add the melted butter. Sift the bicarbonate of soda, flour, paprika and 5ml/1 tsp salt into a bowl, then stir into the yogurt mixture to form a soft dough.

4 Turn out the dough, and knead gently. Roll it out, then stamp out 10cm/4in rounds. Spoon 10ml/2 tsp of the filling on to one side of each round, fold over and seal the edges. Re-roll the trimmings and stamp out more rounds until the filling is used.

5 Arrange the turnovers on the baking sheet and brush with beaten egg. Bake for 20 minutes, until crisp. Garnish with mint sprigs and serve immediately.

COOK'S TIP
If you like, you can prepare garam masala yourself. Dry-fry 10 dried red chillies, 2 curry leaves and 3 cinnamon sticks in a heavy pan for 2 minutes. Add 30ml/2 tbsp each coriander and cumin seeds and 5 ml/1 tsp each black mustard seeds, black peppercorns, fenugreek seeds and cloves, and dry-fry, shaking the pan frequently, for 8–10 minutes more. Leave to cool slightly, then grind in a spice mill, coffee grinder or mortar. Stir in 1.5 ml/¼ tsp chilli powder and transfer to an airtight container. The garam masala will keep for up to 4 months.

Cheese & Pesto Turnovers

Dispense with a formal appetizer and serve these with drinks instead. They are also perfect for parties as they can be made in advance.

SERVES 8

INGREDIENTS
225g/8oz packet frozen chopped spinach
30ml/2 tbsp pine nuts
60ml/4 tbsp pesto sauce
115g/4oz/1 cup grated Gruyère cheese
50g/2oz/⅔ cup freshly grated Parmesan cheese
2 × 275g/10oz packets frozen filo pastry, thawed
30ml/2 tbsp olive oil
salt and ground black pepper

1 Preheat the oven to 190°C/375°F/Gas 5. Prepare the filling. Put the frozen spinach into a pan. Heat it gently, breaking it up as it thaws. Increase the heat to drive off any excess moisture. Transfer to a bowl and cool.

2 Spread out the pine nuts in a frying pan and stir over a very low heat until they are lightly toasted. Chop them and add them to the spinach, with the pesto. Stir in the Gruyère and Parmesan cheeses. Season to taste with salt and pepper.

3 Keep the filo pastry covered with clear film (plastic wrap) or a damp dishtowel, removing only one sheet at a time. Cut one sheet into 5cm/2in wide strips. Brush each strip with oil. Put a teaspoon of filling on one end of a strip of pastry. Fold the end over in a triangle, enclosing the filling.

4 Continue to fold the triangle over and over again until the end of the strip is reached. Repeat with the other strips, until all the filling has been used up.

5 Place the turnovers on baking sheets, brush them with olive oil and bake for 20–25 minutes, or until golden brown and crisp. Cool slightly on a wire rack. Serve the turnovers warm.

BRANDIED ROQUEFORT TARTS

*Light puff pastry rounds are topped with the irresistible combination of brandy and
Roquefort cheese. The walnuts give extra flavour and crunch.*

MAKES 6

INGREDIENTS
150g/5oz Roquefort cheese
30ml/2 tbsp brandy
30ml/2 tbsp olive oil
2 red onions (total weight about 225g/8oz), thinly sliced
225g/8oz puff pastry, thawed if frozen
plain (all-purpose) flour, for dusting
beaten egg or milk, to glaze
6 walnut halves, chopped
30ml/2 tbsp chopped fresh chives
salt and ground black pepper
chopped chives, to garnish
salad leaves, diced cucumber and thin tomato wedges, to serve

1 Crumble the Roquefort into a small bowl, pour the brandy over and leave to marinate for 1 hour. Meanwhile, heat the oil in a frying pan and cook the onions gently for 20 minutes, stirring occasionally. Set the pan aside.

2 Preheat the oven to 220°C/425°F/Gas 7. Grease a baking sheet. Roll out the pastry on a floured surface to a 5mm/¼in thickness and stamp out six rounds with a 10cm/4in fluted cutter. Put them on the baking sheet and prick with a fork.

3 Brush the edges of the pastry with a little beaten egg or milk. Add the walnuts and chives to the onion mixture and season with salt and pepper to taste. Divide the mixture among the pastry shapes, leaving the edges clear.

4 Spoon the brandied cheese mixture on top of the pastries and bake for 12–15 minutes, until golden. Serve warm, garnished with chives, on a bed of salad leaves, diced cucumber and thin tomato wedges.

BUTTERNUT SQUASH DIP

One of the most tasty squashes, butternut has a rich, nutty flavour. It makes an unusual but very tasty dip, which is best served warm.

SERVES 4

INGREDIENTS

1 butternut squash
15g/½oz/1 tbsp butter
4 garlic cloves, unpeeled
30ml/2 tbsp freshly grated Parmesan cheese
45–75ml/3–5 tbsp double (heavy) cream
salt and ground black pepper
Melba toast, cheese straws or crudités, to serve

1 Preheat the oven to 200°C/400°F/Gas 6. Cut the butternut squash in half lengthways, then scoop out and discard the seeds.

2 Use a small, sharp knife to score the flesh deeply in a criss-cross pattern; cut as close to the skin as possible, but take care not to cut through it. Arrange both halves in a small roasting pan and dot them with the butter. Sprinkle with salt and pepper to taste and roast for 20 minutes. Tuck the garlic cloves around the squash in the roasting pan and roast for 20 minutes more, until the flesh of the squash is tender and softened.

3 Scoop the flesh out of the squash shells and place it in a blender or food processor. Slip the garlic cloves out of their skins and add the pulp to the squash. Process until smooth.

4 With the motor running, add half the grated Parmesan cheese, then add the double cream. Check and adjust the seasoning, if necessary. Spoon the dip into a serving bowl, sprinkle the reserved cheese over the top and serve warm with Melba toast, cheese straws or crudités.

SPICED CARROT DIP

This is a delicious low-fat dip with a sweet and spicy flavour. Serve with wheat crackers or tortilla chips.

SERVES 4

INGREDIENTS
1 onion
4 carrots
grated rind and juice of 2 oranges
15ml/1 tbsp hot curry paste
150ml/¼ pint/⅔ cup low-fat natural (plain) yogurt
a handful of fresh basil leaves
15–30ml/1–2 tbsp fresh lemon juice, to taste
Tabasco sauce, to taste
salt and ground black pepper

1 Chop the onion finely. Peel and grate the carrots. Place three-quarters of the grated carrot in a small pan and add the onion, orange rind and juice, and curry paste. Stir well to mix. Bring to the boil, lower the heat, cover and simmer gently for 10 minutes, or until tender.

2 Leave the carrot mixture to cool slightly, then process in a blender or food processor until smooth. Scrape into a bowl and leave to cool completely.

3 Stir the yogurt into the cooled carrot mixture, a little at a time. Tear the basil leaves into small pieces and stir them in. Season with lemon juice, Tabasco, salt and pepper to taste. Mix well. Serve at room temperature within a few hours of making. Garnish with the remaining grated carrot.

VARIATION
Greek (US strained plain) yogurt or sour cream can be used instead of natural yogurt to make a richer, creamier dip.

Butterbean & Herb Dip

A refreshing dip that is especially good served with crudités and breadsticks. It is ideal for a picnic or al fresco lunch.

Serves 4–6

Ingredients
225g/8oz/1 cup plain cottage cheese
400g/14oz can butter (lima) beans, drained and rinsed
1 bunch spring onions (scallions), chopped
50g/2oz watercress or American cress, chopped
60ml/4 tbsp mayonnaise
45ml/3 tbsp chopped fresh mixed herbs
salt and ground black pepper
watercress or American cress sprigs, to garnish
crudités and breadsticks, to serve

1 Put the cottage cheese, butter beans, spring onions, watercress or American cress, mayonnaise and herbs in a blender or food processor and process to a coarse purée.

2 Spoon the mixture into a dish, season to taste with salt and pepper and cover tightly with clear film (plastic wrap). Chill in the refrigerator for several hours.

3 Transfer to a serving dish (or individual dishes) and garnish with watercress or American cress sprigs. Serve with crudités and breadsticks.

Variation
Substitute flageolet, cannellini or haricot beans (navy beans) for the butter beans and rocket (arugula) for the watercress.

Hummus with Crudités

Always a great family favourite and popular party dish, hummus can be made quickly at home with the help of a blender.

SERVES 2–3

INGREDIENTS
400g/14oz can chickpeas
30ml/2 tbsp tahini
30ml/2 tbsp lemon juice
1 garlic clove, crushed
salt and ground black pepper
olive oil and paprika, to garnish

TO SERVE
whole baby carrots and radishes
strips of green and red (bell) pepper, chicory (Belgian endive), celery and cucumber
bitesize chunks of bread, pitta or grissini sticks

1 Drain the chickpeas and put them in a blender or food processor. Add the tahini, lemon juice and garlic. Process to a smooth paste.

2 Season the hummus with plenty of salt and pepper. Spoon it into a bowl and swirl the top with the back of a spoon. Trickle over a little olive oil and sprinkle with paprika.

3 Arrange the baby carrots, radishes and the strips of salad vegetables around the rim of a large plate.

4 Add chunks of bread, pieces of pitta or grissini. Place the bowl of hummus in the centre. Serve immediately.

Tzatziki

Cool, creamy and refreshing, tzatziki is wonderfully easy to make and even easier to eat. Serve this classic Greek dip with pitta bread, potato wedges or a selection of chargrilled vegetables. It is best eaten on the day it is made.

SERVES 4

INGREDIENTS
1 mini cucumber, trimmed
4 spring onions (scallions)
1 garlic clove
200ml/7fl oz/scant 1 cup Greek (US strained plain) yogurt
45ml/3 tbsp chopped fresh mint
salt and ground black pepper
fresh mint sprig, to garnish
toasted mini pitta breads, to serve

1 Cut the cucumber into 5mm/¼in dice. Trim the spring onions and garlic, then chop both very finely. Beat the yogurt until smooth, if necessary, then gently stir in the cucumber, onions, garlic and mint.

2 Scrape the mixture into an attractive serving bowl and season with salt and plenty of ground black pepper to taste. Cover with clear film (plastic wrap) and chill in the refrigerator until needed. Garnish with a small mint sprig and serve with toasted mini pitta breads.

COOK'S TIP
Choose Greek yogurt for this dip, as it has a higher fat content than most yogurts, which gives it a deliciously rich, creamy texture.

AUBERGINE & PEPPER SPREAD

With its rich colour and robust texture, this mixture makes an excellent contrast to a creamy cheese dip. It goes especially well with black olives and is delicious with any kind of rustic bread, such as olive bread or ciabatta.

SERVES 6–8

INGREDIENTS
2 aubergines (eggplant), total weight about 675g/1½lb, halved lengthways
2 green (bell) peppers, seeded and quartered
45ml/3 tbsp olive oil
2 firm ripe tomatoes, halved, seeded and finely chopped
45ml/3 tbsp chopped fresh parsley or coriander
2 garlic cloves, crushed
30ml/2 tbsp red wine vinegar
lemon juice, to taste
salt and ground black pepper
fresh parsley or coriander (cilantro) sprigs, to garnish
dark rye bread, lemon wedges and black olives, to serve

1 Place the aubergines and pepper quarters, skin-side up, on a grill (broiler) rack and grill (broil) until the skins have blistered and charred. Turn the vegetables over and cook for 3 minutes more. Transfer to a bowl, cover with crumpled kitchen paper and leave to cool for about 10 minutes.

2 Peel off the blackened skin. Place the aubergine and pepper flesh in a food processor and process to a purée.

3 With the motor running, pour in the olive oil in a continuous stream through the lid or feeder tube and process until smooth and thoroughly combined.

4 Scrape the mixture into a serving bowl and stir in the chopped tomatoes, parsley or coriander, garlic, vinegar and lemon juice. Season to taste with salt and pepper, garnish with the parsley or coriander sprigs and serve with dark rye bread, wedges of lemon and black olives.

CHILLI BEAN DIP

This creamy bean dip is best served warm with warm pitta bread. It will keep in the refrigerator for 2–3 days where its flavour will develop.

SERVES 4

INGREDIENTS
30ml/2 tbsp vegetable oil
2 garlic cloves, crushed
1 onion, finely chopped
2 fresh green chillies, seeded and finely chopped
5–10ml/1–2 tsp hot chilli powder
400g/14oz can kidney beans
75g/3oz/³⁄₄ cup grated mature (sharp) Cheddar cheese, plus extra to garnish
1 fresh red chilli, seeded
salt and ground black pepper
fresh green chillies, to garnish
triangles of grilled (broiled) pitta bread, to serve

1 Heat the vegetable oil in a deep, heavy frying pan. Add the crushed garlic, chopped onion, green chillies and hot chilli powder, and cook over a low heat, stirring frequently, for about 5 minutes, or until the onions are softened and transparent, but not browned.

2 Drain the kidney beans, reserving the can juices. Set aside 30ml/2 tbsp of the beans and put the remainder in a food processor. Process to a purée. If you like a coarser dip, mash the beans with a potato masher.

3 Add the puréed beans to the onion mixture and moisten with 30–45ml/ 2–3 tbsp of the reserved can juices. Heat gently, stirring to mix well.

4 Stir in the reserved whole kidney beans and the grated Cheddar. Cook over a low heat, stirring constantly, for 2–3 minutes, until the cheese has melted. Season to taste with salt and pepper.

5 Cut the red chilli into thin strips. Spoon the dip into four individual serving bowls and sprinkle the chilli strips and extra cheese over the top. Serve warm, with the pitta triangles, garnished with green chillies.

NUTTY MUSHROOM PÂTÉ

Spread this delicious, medium-textured pâté on chunks of crusty French bread and eat with crisp lettuce leaves and sweet cherry tomatoes.

SERVES 4–6

INGREDIENTS
15ml/1 tbsp sunflower oil
1 onion, chopped
1 garlic clove, crushed
30ml/2 tbsp water
15ml/1 tbsp dry sherry
225g/8oz/3 cups button (white) mushrooms, chopped
75g/3oz/³⁄₄ cup cashew nuts or walnuts, chopped
150g/5oz/²⁄₃ cup low-fat soft cheese
15ml/1 tbsp soy sauce
few dashes of vegetarian Worcestershire sauce
salt and ground black pepper
fresh parsley, chopped, and a little paprika, to garnish

1 Heat the oil in a pan. Add the onion and garlic and cook over a medium heat, stirring occasionally, for 3 minutes. Stir in the water, sherry and mushrooms. Cook, stirring constantly, for about 5 minutes. Season to taste with salt and pepper. Remove the pan from the heat and leave to cool a little.

2 Put the mixture into a food processor and add the cashew nuts or walnuts, cheese, soy sauce and Worcestershire sauce. Process to a coarse purée – do not allow the mixture to become too smooth.

3 Check and adjust the seasoning, if necessary, then scrape the pâté into a serving dish. Swirl the top and chill lightly in the refrigerator. Serve the pâté sprinkled with parsley and paprika.

COOK'S TIP
Conventional bottled Worcestershire sauce contains anchovies. Look out for the vegetarian version in health-food stores.

LUNCHES
& SUPPERS

The range of main-course vegetarian dishes is vast – omelettes, pasta, risottos, baked dishes and gratins, pies and quiches, stews, casseroles, curries and more. Choose from quick and easy family suppers, such as Indian Stir-fried Vegetables with Cashews, hearty and filling dishes, such as Vegetable Crumble, treats for the barbecue or picnic, such as Red Bean & Mushroom Burgers and Cheese & Onion Quiche, or more elaborate dishes for informal entertaining, such as Stuffed Mushrooms with Pine Nut Tarator. From comfortable, familiar favourites to new and adventurous innovations, there is a perfect vegetarian dish.

SOUFFLÉ OMELETTE WITH MUSHROOMS

A soufflé omelette makes an ideal meal for one, especially with this delicious filling.
For a special treat use wild mushrooms, such as chanterelles or ceps.

SERVES 1

INGREDIENTS
2 eggs, separated
15ml/1 tbsp water
15g/½oz/1 tbsp butter
fresh flat leaf parsley or coriander (cilantro) leaves, to garnish

FOR THE MUSHROOM SAUCE
15g/½oz/1 tbsp butter
75g/3oz/generous 1 cup chestnut mushrooms, thinly sliced
15ml/1 tbsp plain (all-purpose) flour
90–120ml/3–4fl oz/⅓–½ cup milk
5ml/1 tsp chopped fresh parsley (optional)
salt and ground black pepper

1 Make the sauce. Melt the butter in a pan. Add the mushrooms and cook gently, stirring occasionally, for 4–5 minutes, until tender. Add the flour and cook, stirring constantly, for 1 minute, then gradually add the milk, stirring constantly until the sauce boils and thickens. Add the parsley, if using, and season. Keep the sauce hot while you make the omelette.

2 Beat the egg yolks with the water and season. Whisk the egg whites until stiff, then gently fold them into the egg yolks. Preheat the grill (broiler).

3 Melt the butter in a heavy frying pan that can be used under the grill. Pour in the egg mixture. Cook over a gentle heat for 2–4 minutes, then place the frying pan under the grill and cook for 3–4 minutes more, until the top is golden brown. Slide on to a warmed plate, pour the mushroom sauce over the top and fold in half. Garnish with parsley or coriander leaves and serve.

Sweet Pepper & Courgette Frittata

Eggs, cheese and vegetables form the basis of this excellent supper dish. Served cold in wedges, it is easily transportable and makes tasty picnic fare too.

SERVES 4

INGREDIENTS
45ml/3 tbsp olive oil
1 red onion, thinly sliced
1 large red (bell) pepper, seeded and thinly sliced
1 large yellow (bell) pepper, seeded and thinly sliced
2 garlic cloves, crushed
1 medium courgette (zucchini), thinly sliced
6 eggs
150g/5oz/1¼ cups grated Italian cheese, such as Fontina, Provolone or Taleggio
salt and ground black pepper
dressed mixed salad leaves, to serve

1 Heat 30ml/2 tbsp of the olive oil in a large, heavy frying pan that can safely be used under the grill (broiler). (Cover a wooden handle with foil to protect it.) Add the onion and red and yellow pepper slices and cook over a low heat, stirring occasionally, for about 10 minutes, or until softened.

2 Add the remaining oil to the pan. When it is hot, add the garlic and the courgette slices. Cook over a low heat, stirring constantly, for 5 minutes.

3 Beat the eggs with salt and pepper to taste. Stir in the grated cheese. Pour the mixture over the vegetables, stirring lightly to mix and covering the base of the pan evenly. Cook over a low heat until the mixture is just set.

4 Meanwhile, preheat the grill. When it is hot, slide the pan underneath and brown the top of the frittata lightly. Let the frittata stand in the pan for about 5 minutes before cutting into wedges. Serve hot or cold, with the salad.

INDIAN STIR-FRIED VEGETABLES WITH CASHEWS

This versatile stir-fry recipe will accommodate most combinations of vegetables – you do not have to use the selection suggested here.

SERVES 4

INGREDIENTS
2 medium carrots
1 medium red (bell) pepper, seeded
1 medium green (bell) pepper, seeded
2 courgettes (zucchini)
115g/4oz green beans
1 medium bunch of spring onions (scallions)
15ml/1 tbsp sunflower oil
4–6 curry leaves
2.5ml/½ tsp white cumin seeds
4 dried red chillies
10–12 cashew nuts
5ml/1 tsp salt
30ml/2 tbsp lemon juice
fresh mint leaves, to garnish

1 Prepare the vegetables: cut the carrots, peppers and courgettes into thin batons, halve the beans and chop the spring onions. Set aside.

2 Heat the oil in a wok and stir-fry the curry leaves, cumin seeds and dried chillies for 1 minute.

3 Add the vegetables and nuts and toss them over the heat for 3–4 minutes. Add the salt and lemon juice. Continue to stir and toss over the heat for 2 minutes more, or until the vegetables are crisp-tender.

4 Transfer to a warmed serving dish. Remove the dried chillies, if you like. Serve immediately, garnished with mint leaves.

SPICED TOFU STIR-FRY

Like Quorn, firm tofu is a boon to the vegetarian cook, as it readily absorbs the flavours of the other ingredients.

SERVES 4

INGREDIENTS
10ml/2 tsp ground cumin
15ml/1 tbsp paprika
5ml/1 tsp ground ginger
good pinch of cayenne pepper
15ml/1 tbsp caster (superfine) sugar
275g/10oz firm tofu, cubed
30ml/2 tbsp vegetable oil
2 garlic cloves, crushed
1 bunch spring onions (scallions), sliced
1 red (bell) pepper, seeded and sliced
1 yellow (bell) pepper, seeded and sliced
225g/8oz/generous 3 cups brown cap mushrooms, halved or quartered, if necessary
1 large courgette (zucchini), sliced
115g/4oz/scant 1 cup fine green beans, halved
15g/¹⁄₂oz/2 tbsp arame, soaked in warm water for 10 minutes and drained
50g/2oz/¹⁄₂ cup pine nuts
15ml/1 tbsp freshly squeezed lime juice
15ml/1 tbsp clear honey
salt and ground black pepper

1 Mix the spices and sugar in a bowl and add plenty of salt and pepper. Coat the tofu cubes in the spice mixture. Heat 15ml/1 tbsp of the oil in a wok or large frying pan and cook the tofu cubes over a high heat for 3–4 minutes, turning occasionally and taking care not to break them up too much. Remove with a draining spoon. Wipe out the pan with kitchen paper and return it to the heat.

2 Heat the remaining oil in the wok and stir-fry the garlic and spring onions for 3 minutes. Add the peppers, mushrooms, courgette, arame and beans and toss over a medium heat for about 6 minutes, or until beginning to soften and turn golden. Season well. Return the tofu cubes to the wok and add the pine nuts, lime juice and honey. Heat through, lightly stirring occasionally, then serve immediately.

PENNE RIGATE WITH MIXED VEGETABLE SAUCE

Strictly speaking, this is not a sauced dish, but a colourful medley of vegetables and pasta tossed in butter and oil. Vary the vegetables if you like.

SERVES 4

INGREDIENTS
25g/1oz/2 tbsp butter
45ml/3 tbsp extra virgin olive oil
1 small leek, thinly sliced
2 carrots, diced
2.5ml/½ tsp sugar
1 courgette (zucchini), diced
75g/3oz/½ cup green beans, cut in short lengths
115g/4oz/1 cup frozen peas
450g/1lb/4 cups dried penne rigate or other pasta shapes
a handful of fresh flat leaf parsley, chopped, plus extra, deep-fried, to garnish
2 ripe Italian plum tomatoes, peeled and diced
salt and ground black pepper

1 Melt the butter in the olive oil in a pan. When the mixture sizzles, add the sliced leek and carrots. Sprinkle the sugar over them and cook, stirring frequently, for about 5 minutes.

2 Stir in the courgette, green beans and peas and season to taste with salt and pepper. Cover and cook over a low heat, stirring occasionally, for about 10 minutes, or until the vegetables are tender.

3 Meanwhile, bring a large pan of lightly salted water to the boil and cook the pasta until it is *al dente*.

4 Drain the pasta and return it to the pan. Stir the parsley and tomatoes into the sauce. Taste and adjust the seasoning, if necessary. Pour the sauce over the pasta, toss to mix, then serve, garnished with the deep-fried parsley.

PASTA WITH SUGOCASA & CHILLI

This is a quick version of a popular Italian dish, pasta arrabbiata. *The name literally translates as "furious pasta", a reference to the heat generated by the chilli.*

SERVES 4

INGREDIENTS
475ml/16fl oz/2 cups bottled sugocasa (see Cook's Tip)
2 garlic cloves, crushed
150ml/¼ pint/⅔ cup dry white wine
15ml/1 tbsp sun-dried tomato paste
1 fresh red chilli
300g/11oz/2⅔ cups dried penne or other pasta shapes
60ml/4 tbsp finely chopped fresh flat leaf parsley
salt and ground black pepper
freshly grated Pecorino cheese, to serve

1 Put the sugocasa, garlic, wine, sun-dried tomato paste and chilli in a heavy pan and bring to the boil. Lower the heat, cover and simmer gently for about 15 minutes, or until thick.

2 Meanwhile, bring a large pan of lightly salted water to the boil. Add the pasta shapes and cook for 10–12 minutes, or until they are *al dente.*

3 Using tongs, remove the chilli from the sauce. Taste for seasoning. If you like a hotter taste, chop some or all of the chilli and return it to the sauce.

4 Drain the pasta and tip it into a large bowl. Stir half the parsley into the sauce, then pour the sauce over the pasta and toss to mix. Serve immediately, sprinkled with grated Pecorino and the remaining parsley.

COOK'S TIP
Bottles of sugocasa are often labelled "crushed Italian tomatoes". It is finer than canned chopped tomatoes and coarser than passata (bottled strained tomatoes), and so is ideal for pasta sauces and stews.

Rustic Buckwheat Pasta Bake

A spicy combination of nutty-flavoured buckwheat pasta, vegetables and creamy Fontina cheese, this makes a wonderful family supper.

Serves 6

Ingredients

45ml/3 tbsp olive oil, plus extra for greasing
2 potatoes, peeled and cubed
225g/8oz/2 cups dried buckwheat pasta shapes
275g/10oz/2½ cups shredded Savoy cabbage
1 onion, chopped
2 leeks, sliced
2 garlic cloves, chopped
175g/6oz/2½ cups brown cap mushrooms, sliced
5ml/1 tsp caraway seeds
5ml/1 tsp cumin seeds
150ml/¼ pint/⅔ cup vegetable stock
150g/5oz Fontina cheese, diced
25g/1oz/¼ cup walnuts, coarsely chopped
salt and ground black pepper

Cook's Tip

For perfect pasta, start timing from the moment the water returns to the boil after you have added the pasta to the pan. Dried pasta takes 8–10 minutes to cook, so start testing its texture after 8 minutes by removing a small piece and biting it between your front teeth. When it feels tender, but still firm to the bite – al dente *– it is ready.*

---

1 Preheat the oven to 200°C/400°F/Gas 6. Grease a deep, ovenproof dish with oil. Cook the cubed potatoes in a pan of lightly salted boiling water for 8–10 minutes, or until tender, then drain and set aside.

2 Meanwhile, bring a large pan of lightly salted water to the boil. Add the pasta and cook until it is *al dente*. Add the cabbage in the last minute of cooking time. Drain, then rinse under cold running water.

3 Heat the olive oil in a large heavy pan and cook the onion and leeks over a medium heat, stirring occasionally, for 5 minutes, or until softened.

4 Add the garlic and mushrooms and cook, stirring occasionally, for 3 minutes more, until tender. Stir in the caraway seeds and cumin seeds and cook, stirring constantly, for 1 minute.

5 Stir in the cooked potatoes, pasta and cabbage. Season well with salt and pepper. Spoon the mixture into the prepared dish. Pour the stock over the mixture, then sprinkle with the cheese and walnuts. Bake for 15 minutes, or until the cheese is melted and bubbling. Serve immediately.

FIVE-SPICE VEGETABLE NOODLES

*Vary this stir-fry by substituting mushrooms, bamboo shoots, beansprouts,
mangetouts (snowpeas) or water chestnuts for some or all of the vegetables.*

SERVES 2–3

INGREDIENTS
225g/8oz dried egg noodles
30ml/2 tbsp sesame oil
2 carrots
1 celery stick
1 small fennel bulb
2 courgettes (zucchini), halved lengthways and sliced
1 fresh red chilli
2.5cm/1in piece of fresh root ginger, grated
1 garlic clove, crushed
7.5ml/1½ tsp Chinese five-spice powder
2.5ml/½ tsp ground cinnamon
4 spring onions (scallions), sliced
salt

COOK'S TIP
*Chinese five-spice powder is a mixture of Sichuan
pepper, star anise, fennel, cloves and cinnamon. It is
quite different from Indian five-spice powder, so
make sure that you buy the right flavouring.*

1 Bring a large pan of salted water to the boil. Add the noodles and cook for
2–3 minutes, until they are just tender. Drain the noodles, return them to the
pan and toss them with a little of the oil. Set aside.

2 Cut the carrots and celery into thin batons. Cut the fennel bulb in half and cut
out the hard core. Cut into slices, then cut the slices into thin batons.

3 Heat the remaining oil in a wok until very hot. Add the carrots, celery, fennel
and courgettes and stir-fry over a medium heat for 7–8 minutes.

4 Cut half the chilli into rings, discarding any seeds, and set aside. Chop the rest of the chilli and add it to the wok.

5 Add the ginger and garlic and stir-fry for 2 minutes, then add the Chinese five-spice powder and cinnamon. Stir-fry for 1 minute, then toss in the spring onions and stir-fry for a further minute.

6 Pour in 60ml/4 tbsp warm water and cook for 1 minute. Stir in the noodles and toss over the heat until they have warmed through. Transfer to a warmed serving dish and serve sprinkled with the reserved sliced red chilli.

FRESH HERB PIZZA

Sometimes it is the simplest ideas that prove to be the most successful. This pizza is the perfect excuse to raid your herb garden for a delectable summer dish.

SERVES 2–3

INGREDIENTS
115g/4oz/about 3 cups mixed fresh herbs, such as parsley, basil and oregano
3 garlic cloves, crushed
120ml/4fl oz/½ cup double (heavy) cream
1 pizza base, 25–30cm/10–12in in diameter
15ml/1 tbsp garlic oil (see Cook's Tip)
115g/4oz/1⅓ cups grated Pecorino cheese
salt and ground black pepper

1 Preheat the oven to 220°C/425°F/Gas 7. Chop the herbs by hand or in a food processor, then tip them into a bowl. Stir in the garlic and cream. Season with plenty of salt and pepper.

2 Support the pizza base on a baking sheet. Brush it with the garlic oil, then spread the herb mixture over the surface, leaving a 1cm/½in rim all around.

3 Sprinkle over the Pecorino. Bake the pizza for 15–20 minutes, until the crust is crisp and golden, but the topping is still moist. Cut into thin wedges and serve.

COOK'S TIP
To make garlic oil, peel four garlic cloves, put them in a small jar or bottle and pour over about 120ml/4fl oz/½ cup olive oil. Cover and keep in the refrigerator for up to 1 month.

New Potato, Rosemary & Garlic Pizza

Smoked mozzarella cheese, new potatoes, fresh rosemary and garlic make the flavour of this pizza uniquely delicious.

SERVES 2–3

INGREDIENTS
350g/12oz new potatoes
45ml/3 tbsp olive oil
2 garlic cloves, crushed
1 pizza base, 25–30cm/10–12in in diameter
1 red onion, very thinly sliced
150g/5oz/1¼ cups grated smoked mozzarella cheese
10ml/2 tsp chopped fresh rosemary
salt and ground black pepper
30ml/2 tbsp freshly grated Parmesan cheese, to garnish

1 Preheat the oven to 220°C/425°F/Gas 7. Bring a large pan of lightly salted water to the boil and cook the potatoes for 5 minutes. Drain well. When cool, peel the potatoes and slice them thinly.

2 Heat 30ml/2 tbsp of the olive oil in a frying pan. Add the potato slices and crushed garlic and cook over a medium heat, stirring occasionally, for 5–8 minutes, or until tender but not browned.

3 Brush the pizza base with the remaining oil. Sprinkle over the onion, then arrange the potatoes on top. Sprinkle over the mozzarella and rosemary. Grind over plenty of black pepper. Bake for 15–20 minutes until the crust is crisp and golden. Sprinkle over the grated Parmesan and serve immediately.

Leek, Mushroom & Lemon Risotto

Fresh-tasting lemon and leeks go together beautifully in this light risotto, while mushrooms add texture and extra flavour.

SERVES 4

INGREDIENTS
30ml/2 tbsp olive oil
3 garlic cloves, crushed
225g/8oz trimmed leeks, sliced
225g/8oz/2–3 cups brown cap mushrooms, sliced
75g/3oz/6 tbsp butter
1 large onion, coarsely chopped
350g/12oz/1¾ cups risotto rice
1.2 litres/2 pints/5 cups simmering vegetable stock
grated rind of 1 lemon
45ml/3 tbsp lemon juice
50g/2oz/⅔ cup freshly grated Parmesan cheese
60ml/4 tbsp mixed chopped fresh chives and flat leaf parsley
salt and ground black pepper

1 Heat the olive oil in a large pan and cook the garlic for 1 minute. Add the leeks and mushrooms and season to taste with salt and pepper. Cook over a low heat, stirring occasionally, for about 10 minutes, or until the leeks have softened and browned. Spoon the mixture into a bowl and set aside.

2 Melt 25g/1oz/2 tbsp of the butter in the pan and cook the onion, stirring occasionally, for 5 minutes, until it has softened and is golden. Stir in the rice until coated, then add a ladleful of hot stock. Cook gently, stirring frequently, until all the liquid has been absorbed. Continue to add the remaining stock, a little at a time, and stirring constantly. After about 25–30 minutes, the rice will have absorbed all the stock and the risotto will be moist and creamy.

3 Add the leeks and mushrooms, with the remaining butter. Stir in the lemon rind and juice, then the grated Parmesan and the herbs. Adjust the seasoning, if necessary, spoon into a bowl and serve.

TOMATO BREAD & BUTTER PUDDING

This is a great family dish and is ideal when you do not have time to cook on the day, because it can be prepared in advance and reheated.

SERVES 4

INGREDIENTS
50g/2oz/¼ cup butter, softened
15ml/1 tbsp red pesto sauce
1 garlic and herb focaccia
150g/5oz mozzarella cheese, thinly sliced
2 large ripe tomatoes, sliced
300ml/½ pint/1¼ cups milk
3 large (US extra large) eggs
5ml/1 tsp fresh chopped oregano, plus extra leaves to garnish
50g/2oz/⅔ cup grated Pecorino cheese
salt and ground black pepper

1 Preheat the oven to 180°C/350°F/Gas 4. Mix the butter and pesto sauce in a small bowl. Slice the herb bread and spread one side of each slice with the pesto mixture.

2 In an oval ovenproof dish, layer the slices of herb bread with the mozzarella and tomatoes, overlapping each new layer with the next.

3 Beat the milk, eggs and oregano in a jug (pitcher), season well with salt and pepper and pour over the bread. Leave to stand for at least 5 minutes.

4 Sprinkle over the grated Pecorino cheese and bake the pudding for 40 minutes, or until golden brown and just set. Sprinkle with whole oregano leaves and serve immediately.

COOK'S TIP
The longer this stands before baking, the better it will be. Try to leave it for at least half an hour before baking, if you have time.

STUFFED MUSHROOMS WITH PINE NUT TARATOR

Field mushrooms have a rich flavour and a meaty texture. They go well with this fragrant and tasty herb and lemon stuffing.

SERVES 4–6

INGREDIENTS
45ml/3 tbsp olive oil, plus extra for brushing
1 onion, finely chopped
2 garlic cloves, crushed
30ml/2 tbsp chopped fresh thyme or 5ml/1 tsp dried thyme
8 field or portabello mushrooms, stalks removed and finely chopped
400g/14oz can aduki beans, drained and rinsed
50g/2oz/1 cup fresh wholemeal (whole-wheat) breadcrumbs
juice of 1 lemon
185g/6½oz goat's cheese, crumbled
salt and ground black pepper

FOR THE PINE NUT TARATOR
50g/2oz/½ cup pine nuts, toasted
50g/2oz/1 cup cubed white bread
2 garlic cloves, chopped
200ml/7fl oz/scant 1 cup milk
45ml/3 tbsp olive oil

1 Preheat the oven to 200°C/400°F/Gas 6. Heat the oil in a large, heavy frying pan. Add the onion and garlic and cook over a low heat, stirring occasionally, for 5 minutes, until softened. Add the thyme and the mushroom stalks and cook for 3 minutes more, stirring occasionally, until tender.

2 Stir the aduki beans into the mixture with the breadcrumbs and lemon juice, season well with salt and pepper, then cook for 2 minutes, until heated through.

3 Remove the pan from the heat and, using a fork or potato masher, mash the mixture until about two-thirds of the aduki beans are broken up, leaving the remaining beans whole.

4 Brush an ovenproof dish and the tops and sides of the mushroom caps with oil. Place them, gills uppermost, in the dish and top each one with a spoonful of the bean mixture. Cover with foil and bake for 20 minutes.

5 Remove and discard the foil. Top each mushroom with crumbled goat's cheese and bake for 15 minutes more, or until the cheese has melted and the mushrooms are tender.

6 Meanwhile, make the pine nut tarator. Put the pine nuts, bread and garlic in a food processor and process briefly. Add the milk and olive oil and process until creamy. Serve the tarator with the mushrooms.

COOK'S TIP
You can use 200g/7oz/1 cup dried beans if you like. Prepare, using the overnight or fast soaking method and then cook gently for 40 minutes in fresh water.

CHEESE & LEEK SAUSAGES WITH SPICY TOMATO SAUCE

These are based on Glamorgan sausages, which are traditionally made using white or wholemeal breadcrumbs alone. However, adding a little mashed potato lightens the sausages and makes them much easier to handle.

SERVES 4

INGREDIENTS
25g/1oz/2 tbsp butter
175g/6oz leeks, finely chopped
90ml/6 tbsp cold mashed potato
115g/4oz/2 cups fresh white breadcrumbs
150g/5oz/1¼ cups grated Caerphilly or other crumbly white cheese
30ml/2 tbsp chopped fresh parsley
5ml/1 tsp chopped fresh sage
2 large (US extra large) eggs, beaten
cayenne pepper
65g/2½oz/1 cup dry white breadcrumbs
oil, for shallow frying
salt and ground black pepper

FOR THE SAUCE
30ml/2 tbsp olive oil
2 garlic cloves, thinly sliced
1 fresh red chilli, seeded and finely chopped
1 small onion, finely chopped
500g/1¼lb tomatoes, peeled, seeded and chopped
2–3 fresh thyme sprigs
10ml/2 tsp balsamic vinegar
pinch of light muscovado (brown) sugar
15–30ml/1–2 tbsp chopped fresh marjoram

1 Melt the butter in a frying pan. Add the leeks and cook over a low heat, stirring occasionally, for 4–5 minutes, or until softened but not browned.

2 Mix the leeks with the mashed potato, fresh breadcrumbs, grated cheese, parsley and sage. Add about two-thirds of the beaten eggs to bind the mixture. Season well with salt and pepper and add a good pinch of cayenne.

3 Shape the mixture into 12 sausages. Put the remaining egg in a shallow dish and the dry breadcrumbs in another shallow dish. Dip the sausages first in egg, then in the dry breadcrumbs, shaking off any excess. Place the coated sausages on a plate, cover and chill in the refrigerator.

4 To make the sauce, heat the olive oil over a low heat. Add the garlic, chilli and onion and cook, stirring occasionally, for 3–4 minutes. Add the tomatoes, thyme and vinegar. Season to taste with salt, pepper and sugar.

5 Cook the sauce for 40–50 minutes, until much reduced. Remove and discard the thyme and process the sauce in a blender to a purée. Return to the clean pan and add the marjoram. Reheat gently, then taste and adjust the seasoning, adding more sugar, if necessary.

6 Fry the sausages in shallow oil until golden brown on all sides. Drain on kitchen paper and serve with the sauce.

CHEESE & ONION QUICHE

Perfect for picnics, parties and family suppers, this classic quiche celebrates a timeless combination of ingredients.

SERVES 6–8

INGREDIENTS
200g/7oz/1¾ cups plain (all-purpose) flour
2.5ml/½ tsp salt
90g/3½oz/scant ½ cup butter
about 60ml/4 tbsp iced water

FOR THE FILLING
25g/1oz/2 tbsp butter
1 large onion, thinly sliced
3 eggs
300ml/½ pint/1¼ cups single (light) cream
1.5ml/¼ tsp freshly grated nutmeg
90g/3½oz/scant 1 cup grated hard cheese, such as mature (sharp) Cheddar, Gruyère
* or Manchego*
salt and ground black pepper

COOK'S TIP
When baking blind – partially cooking a pastry case (pie shell) – baking beans are used to prevent the base from puffing up. Edible dried beans, such as kidney beans, may be used – keep them specifically for this purpose. Otherwise, metal or ceramic baking beans are available from cookware stores.

1 To make the pastry, sift the flour and salt into a bowl. Rub in the butter with your fingertips, then add enough iced water to make a firm dough. Knead lightly, wrap in clear film (plastic wrap) and chill in the refrigerator for 20 minutes.

2 Roll out the dough and line a 23cm/9in loose-based flan tin (quiche pan). Prick the pastry base a few times. Line the flan case (pie shell) with foil and baking beans and chill again for about 15 minutes.

3 Preheat the oven to 200°C/400°F/Gas 6. Place a baking sheet in the oven. Stand the flan tin on the baking sheet and bake blind for 15 minutes. Remove the beans and foil and return the pastry case to the oven for 5 minutes more. Reduce the oven temperature to 180°C/350°F/Gas 4.

4 To make the filling, melt the butter in a heavy frying pan. Add the onion and cook over a low heat, stirring occasionally, for 5 minutes, until softened. In a jug (pitcher), beat together the eggs and cream. Add the nutmeg and season to taste with salt and pepper.

5 Spoon the onion mixture into the cooked pastry case and sprinkle over the grated cheese. Pour in the egg and cream mixture. Bake the quiche for 35–40 minutes, or until the filling has just set. Cool, then gently ease the quiche out of the tin and place it on a plate for serving.

VEGETABLE CRUMBLE

This dish is perennially popular with children, and even those who claim to dislike Brussels sprouts will tuck into it eagerly.

SERVES 8

INGREDIENTS
450g/1lb potatoes, peeled and halved
25g/1oz/2 tbsp butter
225g/8oz leeks, sliced
450g/1lb carrots, chopped
2 garlic cloves, crushed
225g/8oz/3¼ cups mushrooms, thinly sliced
450g/1lb Brussels sprouts, sliced
salt and ground black pepper

FOR THE CHEESE CRUMBLE
50g/2oz/½ cup plain (all-purpose) flour
50g/2oz/¼ cup butter
50g/2oz/1 cup fresh white breadcrumbs
50g/2oz/½ cup grated Cheddar cheese
30ml/2 tbsp chopped fresh parsley
5ml/1 tsp English (hot) mustard powder

VARIATIONS
• *Substitute cauliflower or broccoli, broken into small florets or thinly sliced, for the Brussels sprouts.*
• *You could vary the cheeses used for the crumble topping. Try Parmesan or Red Leicester.*

1 Add the potatoes to a pan of lightly salted water. Bring to the boil and cook for about 15 minutes, or until just tender.

2 Meanwhile, melt the butter in a large pan. Add the sliced leeks and chopped carrots and cook over a low heat, stirring occasionally, for 2–3 minutes. Add the garlic and sliced mushrooms and cook, stirring occasionally for 3 minutes more.

3 Add the Brussels sprouts to the pan. Season to taste with pepper. Transfer the vegetable mixture to a 2.5 litre/4 pint/10 cup ovenproof dish.

4 Preheat the oven to 200°C/400°F/Gas 6. Drain the cooked potatoes and cut them into 1cm/½in-thick slices. Arrange them in an even layer on top of the other vegetables in the dish.

5 To make the crumble, sift the flour into a bowl and rub in the butter with your fingertips. Alternatively, process in a food processor until combined. Add the breadcrumbs and mix in the grated Cheddar, parsley and mustard powder. Spoon the crumble mixture evenly over the vegetables, pressing it down gently with the back of a spoon, and bake for 20–30 minutes. Serve hot.

MIDDLE-EASTERN VEGETABLE STEW

Serve this spicy dish of mixed vegetables and chickpeas as a side dish for six or as a main course for four. Children may prefer less chilli.

SERVES 4–6

INGREDIENTS
45ml/3 tbsp vegetable stock
1 green (bell) pepper, seeded and sliced
2 medium courgettes (zucchini), sliced
2 medium carrots, sliced
2 celery sticks, sliced
2 medium potatoes, diced
400g/14oz can chopped tomatoes
5ml/1 tsp hot chilli powder
30ml/2 tbsp chopped fresh mint
15ml/1 tbsp ground cumin
400g/14oz can chickpeas, drained and rinsed
salt and ground black pepper
fresh mint sprigs, to garnish

1 Pour the vegetable stock into a large, flameproof casserole and bring to the boil, then add the sliced pepper, courgettes, carrots and celery. Stir over a high heat for 2–3 minutes, or until the vegetables are just beginning to soften.

2 Add the diced potatoes, tomatoes, chilli powder, chopped mint and cumin. Stir in the chickpeas and bring the mixture back to the boil.

3 Lower the heat, cover the casserole and simmer for about 30 minutes, or until all the vegetables are tender. Season to taste with salt and pepper and serve immediately, garnished with mint sprigs.

COOK'S TIP
Cooking the vegetables in a small amount of stock rather than oil works extremely well, and makes this dish ideal for anyone on a low-fat diet.

AUBERGINE & CHICKPEA RAGOÛT

The perfect dish for a winter supper party, this substantial dish combines two hearty main ingredients with a blend of warming spices.

SERVES 4

INGREDIENTS

3 large aubergines (eggplant), cubed
200g/7oz/generous 1 cup dried chickpeas, soaked overnight in cold water to cover
45ml/3 tbsp olive oil
3 garlic cloves, chopped
2 large onions, chopped
2.5ml/½ tsp ground cumin
2.5ml/½ tsp ground cinnamon
2.5ml/½ tsp ground coriander
3 × 400g/14oz cans chopped tomatoes
salt and ground black pepper
1 onion, sliced and 1 garlic clove, sliced cooked until golden and crisp in 30ml/
   1tbsp olive oil, and fresh coriander (cilantro) sprigs, to garnish
cooked rice, to serve

1 Put the aubergine cubes in a colander, sprinkling each layer with salt. Stand the colander in the sink for 30 minutes, then rinse very well. Drain thoroughly and pat dry with kitchen paper.

2 Drain the chickpeas and put them in a pan with enough water to cover. Bring to the boil, then lower the heat and simmer for 1–1¼ hours, or until tender. Drain thoroughly.

3 Heat the oil in a large, heavy pan. Add the garlic and onions and cook over a low heat, stirring occasionally, for 5 minutes, until softened. Add the cumin, cinnamon and ground coriander and cook, stirring constantly, for a few seconds. Stir in the aubergine until coated with the spice mixture. Cook for 5 minutes.

4 Add the tomatoes and chickpeas and season to taste with salt and pepper. Cover and simmer for 20 minutes. Serve the ragoût with rice, topped with the onion and garlic and garnished with coriander.

Harvest Vegetable & Lentil Casserole

In autumn, thoughts turn to hearty, satisfying food. This sustaining, yet low-fat dish is the ideal choice. It will taste even better the day after it is made.

Serves 6

Ingredients

15ml/1 tbsp sunflower oil
2 leeks, sliced
1 garlic clove, crushed
4 celery sticks, chopped
2 carrots, sliced
2 parsnips, diced
1 sweet potato, diced
225g/8oz swede (rutabaga), diced
175g/6oz/³⁄₄ cup whole brown or green lentils
450g/1lb tomatoes, peeled, seeded and chopped
15ml/1 tbsp chopped fresh thyme
15ml/1 tbsp chopped fresh marjoram
900ml/1¹⁄₂ pints/3³⁄₄ cups vegetable stock
15ml/1 tbsp cornflour (cornstarch)
45ml/3 tbsp water
salt and ground black pepper
fresh thyme sprigs, to garnish

Variation

You can use other root vegetables in season, if you like. Substitute turnip for the swede and eddo for the sweet potato, for example. If you do use eddo, protect your hands with rubber gloves when peeling it, as it can irritate the skin.

1 Preheat the oven to 180°C/350°F/Gas 4. Heat the oil in a large, flameproof casserole. Add the leeks, garlic and celery and cook over a low heat, stirring occasionally, for 3 minutes, or until the vegetables begin to soften.

2 Add the carrots, parsnips, sweet potato, swede, lentils, tomatoes, thyme, marjoram and stock. Stir well and season with salt and pepper to taste. Bring to the boil, stirring occasionally.

3 Cover the casserole, transfer to the oven and bake for about 50 minutes, until the vegetables and lentils are tender, stirring the vegetable mixture once or twice to prevent it from sticking.

4 Remove the casserole from the oven. Blend the cornflour with the water in a small bowl. Stir the mixture into the casserole and heat it gently on the stove, stirring constantly, until the mixture boils and thickens. Lower the heat and simmer gently for 2 minutes, stirring.

5 Spoon on to warmed serving plates or into deep soup bowls, garnish with the fresh thyme sprigs and serve immediately.

Jamaican Black Bean Pot

Molasses imparts a rich treacly flavour to the spicy sauce, which includes black beans, vibrant red and yellow peppers and melting butternut squash.

Serves 4

Ingredients
225g/8oz/1¼ cups dried black beans, soaked overnight in cold water to cover
1 bay leaf
5ml/1 tsp vegetable bouillon powder
15ml/1 tbsp sunflower oil
1 large onion, chopped
1 garlic clove, chopped
5ml/1 tsp English (hot) mustard powder
15ml/1 tbsp blackstrap molasses
30ml/2 tbsp soft dark brown sugar
5ml/1 tsp dried thyme
2.5ml/½ tsp dried chilli flakes
1 red (bell) pepper, seeded and diced
1 yellow (bell) pepper, seeded and diced
675g/1½lb butternut squash, seeded and cut into 1cm/½in dice
salt and ground black pepper
fresh thyme sprigs, to garnish
cooked rice, to serve

Variation
Peas and beans feature in many Caribbean dishes. You could substitute red kidney beans, black-eyed beans or gunga peas, also known as pigeon and Jamaica peas, for the black beans. The initial cooking time in step 1 may vary, depending on the type of pulse used.

1 Drain the black beans, rinse them well and drain them again. Place them in a large, heavy pan, cover with fresh cold water and add the bay leaf. Bring to the boil, then boil rapidly for 10 minutes. Lower the heat, cover, and simmer for 30 minutes, or until tender.

2 Drain the beans, reserving the cooking liquid in a large measuring jug (cup). Stir in the bouillon powder, then make the liquid up to 400ml/14fl oz/1⅔ cups with water. Preheat the oven to 180°C/350°F/Gas 4.

3 Heat the oil in the pan. Add the onion and garlic and cook over a low heat, stirring occasionally, for about 5 minutes, until softened. Stir in the mustard powder, molasses, sugar, dried thyme and chilli flakes. Cook for 1 minute, stirring.

4 Stir in the black beans and reserved bouillon. Spoon the mixture into a flameproof casserole. Cover and bake for 25 minutes.

5 Add the peppers and squash. Season to taste with salt and pepper and mix well. Replace the lid and bake for 45 minutes more, until the vegetables are tender. Serve immediately, garnished with thyme sprigs and accompanied by the rice.

Vegetarian Cassoulet

Every town in south-west France has its own version of this popular classic. Serve this hearty vegetable version with warm French bread.

SERVES 4–6

INGREDIENTS
400g/14oz/2¼ cups dried haricot (navy) beans, soaked overnight
  in cold water to cover, then drained and rinsed
1 bay leaf
1.75 litres/3 pints/7½ cups cold water
2 onions
3 cloves
5ml/1 tsp olive oil
2 garlic cloves, crushed
2 leeks, thickly sliced
12 baby carrots
115g/4oz/1½ cups button (white) mushrooms
400g/14oz can chopped tomatoes
15ml/1 tbsp tomato purée (paste)
5ml/1 tsp paprika
15ml/1 tbsp chopped fresh thyme
30ml/2 tbsp chopped fresh parsley
115g/4oz/2 cups fresh white breadcrumbs
salt and ground black pepper

> COOK'S TIP
> *Originally, cassoulet was made with fresh broad (fava) beans, but now haricot beans are used to extend the season of availability.*

1 Put the beans in a large pan. Add the bay leaf, then pour in the measured water. Bring to the boil and cook rapidly for 10 minutes.

2 Peel one of the onions and spike it with cloves. Add it to the beans and lower the heat. Cover and simmer gently for 1 hour, until the beans are almost tender. Drain, reserving the stock but discarding the bay leaf and onion.

3 Preheat the oven to 160°C/325°F/Gas 3. Chop the remaining onion. Heat the oil in a large, flameproof casserole. Add the chopped onion and garlic and cook over a low heat, stirring occasionally, for 5 minutes, or until softened.

4 Add the leeks, carrots, mushrooms, chopped tomatoes, tomato purée, paprika and thyme to the casserole. Stir in 400ml/14fl oz/1⅔ cups of the reserved stock.

5 Bring to the boil, cover and simmer gently for 10 minutes. Stir in the cooked beans and parsley. Season to taste with salt and pepper, sprinkle with the fresh breadcrumbs and bake, uncovered, for 35 minutes, or until the topping is golden brown and crisp.

Red Bean
& Mushroom Burgers

Whether you cook these tasty burgers under the grill or on the barbecue, they are certain to prove popular with everyone.

Serves 4

Ingredients
15ml/1 tbsp olive oil, plus extra for brushing
1 small onion, finely chopped
1 garlic clove, crushed
5ml/1 tsp ground cumin
5ml/1 tsp ground coriander
2.5ml/½ tsp ground turmeric
115g/4oz/1½ cups finely chopped mushrooms
400g/14oz can red kidney beans, drained and rinsed
30ml/2 tbsp chopped fresh coriander (cilantro)
wholemeal (whole-wheat) flour, for forming the burgers
salt and ground black pepper

To serve
warm pitta bread
Greek (US strained plain) yogurt
salad leaves and tomatoes

Cook's Tip
These vegeburgers are rather more delicate than the store-bought variety and, therefore, need to be handled quite carefully.

---

1 Heat the olive oil in a deep, heavy frying pan. Add the onion and garlic and cook over a medium heat, stirring occasionally, for about 4 minutes, until softened. Add the cumin, ground coriander and turmeric and cook for 1 minute more, stirring constantly.

2 Add the mushrooms and cook, stirring, until softened and dry. Remove the pan from the heat.

3 Tip the beans into a bowl and then mash them with a fork. Stir them into the mushroom mixture, then add the fresh coriander, mixing thoroughly. Season well with salt and pepper.

4 Using floured hands, form the mixture into four flat burger shapes. If the mixture is too sticky to handle, mix in a little flour. Preheat the grill (broiler).

5 Brush the burgers with oil and grill (broil) them for 8–10 minutes, turning once, until golden brown. Alternatively, cook on the barbecue, using a wire rack to turn them easily.

6 Serve immediately with warm pitta bread, Greek yogurt, crisp green salad leaves and tomatoes.

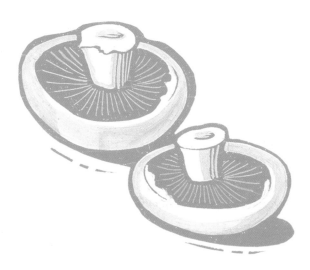

VEGETABLE FAJITAS

A colourful medley of mushrooms and peppers in a spicy sauce, wrapped in tortillas and served with creamy guacamole.

SERVES 2

INGREDIENTS
1 onion, sliced
1 red (bell) pepper, seeded and sliced
1 green (bell) pepper, seeded and sliced
1 yellow (bell) pepper, seeded and sliced
1 garlic clove, crushed
225g/8oz/3¼ cups mushrooms, sliced
90ml/6 tbsp vegetable oil
30ml/2 tbsp medium chilli powder
6 warm wheat flour tortillas
salt and ground black pepper
fresh coriander (cilantro) sprigs and lime wedges, to garnish

FOR THE GUACAMOLE
1 ripe avocado
1 shallot, coarsely chopped
1 fresh green chilli, seeded and coarsely chopped
juice of 1 lime

COOK'S TIP
To heat the tortillas, place them, one at a time, in a heavy, dry frying pan over high heat for a few seconds on each side. Alternatively, stack them interleaved with kitchen paper, and heat through for a minute in the microwave.

1 Combine the onion and red, green and yellow peppers in a large bowl. Add the garlic and mushrooms and mix lightly. Mix the oil and chilli powder in a cup, pour over the vegetable mixture and stir well. Set aside.

2 To make the guacamole, cut the avocado in half lengthways and remove and discard the stone (pit). Scoop the flesh into a food processor or blender, scraping the inside of the skin, and add the chopped shallot, green chilli and lime juice. Process for about 1 minute, until a smooth purée.

3 Empty the guacamole into a small bowl, cover closely with clear film (plastic wrap) and chill in the refrigerator until required.

4 Heat a large, heavy frying pan or wok until very hot. Add the marinated vegetables and stir-fry over a high heat for 5–6 minutes, until the mushrooms and peppers are just tender. Season well with salt and pepper.

5 Spoon a little of the filling on to each warm tortilla and roll up. Place three fajitas on each of two individual serving plates, garnishing them with the fresh coriander and lime wedges. Offer the guacamole separately.

VEGETABLE COUSCOUS WITH SAFFRON & HARISSA

A North African favourite, this spicy dish makes an excellent midweek supper.
Harissa is a fiery chilli paste available from larger supermarkets.

SERVES 4

INGREDIENTS
45ml/3 tbsp olive oil
1 onion, chopped
2 garlic cloves, crushed
5ml/1 tsp ground cumin
5ml/1 tsp paprika
400g/14oz can chopped tomatoes
300ml/½ pint/1¼ cups vegetable stock
1 cinnamon stick
generous pinch of saffron threads
4 baby aubergines (eggplant), quartered
8 baby courgettes (zucchini), trimmed and quartered lengthways
8 baby carrots
225g/8oz/1⅓ cups couscous
400g/14oz can chickpeas, drained and rinsed
175g/6oz/¾ cup prunes
45ml/3 tbsp chopped fresh parsley
45ml/3 tbsp chopped fresh coriander (cilantro)
10–15ml/2–3 tsp harissa
salt

COOK'S TIP
Spices are much more flavoursome and aromatic if you buy them whole and then grind them when needed. An electric coffee grinder will make short work of preparing whole spices. Do not use it for anything else, though.

1 Heat the olive oil in a large pan. Add the onion and garlic and cook gently, stirring occasionally, for 5 minutes, until soft. Add the cumin and paprika and cook, stirring, for 1 minute. Stir in the tomatoes, stock, cinnamon stick, saffron, aubergines, courgettes and carrots. Season with salt to taste. Bring to the boil, lower the heat, cover and cook for 20 minutes.

2 Select a colander or steamer that will fit over the pan of vegetables. Line it with a double thickness of muslin (cheesecloth). Soak the couscous according to the instructions on the packet.

3 Add the chickpeas and prunes to the vegetables and cook for 5 minutes. Fork the couscous to break up any lumps and spread it in the colander or steamer. Place it on top of the vegetables, cover tightly, and cook for 5 minutes until the couscous is hot.

4 Tip the couscous into a warmed shallow dish. Using a draining spoon, add the cooked vegetables. Spoon over a little of the cooking liquid, add the parsley and coriander and toss gently to combine well. Stir the harissa into the remaining sauce and serve separately.

THAI VEGETABLE CURRY

Making your own spice paste gives this curry an authentic flavour. The coconut milk gives it a creamy texture and helps to blend the spices together.

SERVES 4

INGREDIENTS
10ml/2 tsp vegetable oil
400ml/14fl oz/1⅔ cups coconut milk
300ml/½ pint/1¼ cups vegetable stock
225g/8oz new potatoes, halved if large
130g/4½oz baby corn cobs
5ml/1 tsp golden caster (superfine) sugar
175g/6oz/generous 1 cup broccoli florets
1 red (bell) pepper, seeded and sliced lengthways
115g/4oz spinach, tough stalks removed and leaves shredded
30ml/2 tbsp chopped fresh coriander (cilantro)
salt and ground black pepper
cooked jasmine rice, to serve

FOR THE SPICE PASTE
1 fresh red chilli, seeded and chopped
3 fresh green chillies, seeded and chopped
1 lemon grass stalk, outer layers discarded and finely chopped
2 shallots, chopped
finely grated rind of 1 lime
2 garlic cloves, chopped
5ml/1 tsp ground coriander
2.5ml/½ tsp ground cumin
1cm/½in fresh galangal or root ginger, finely chopped
30ml/2 tbsp chopped fresh coriander

COOK'S TIP
The most popular chillies used by Thai cooks are the deceptively innocent-looking bird's eye chillies, which are searingly hot. If you prefer a milder taste, you can use less hot chillies or fewer of them.

1 First, make the spice paste. Place all the ingredients in a food processor or blender and process to a coarse paste.

2 Heat the oil in a large, heavy pan and fry the spice paste for 1–2 minutes, stirring constantly. Add the coconut milk and stock, and bring to the boil.

3 Lower the heat, add the potatoes and simmer gently for 15 minutes. Add the baby corn cobs, season to taste with salt and black pepper and cook for 2 minutes. Stir in the sugar, broccoli and red pepper and cook for 2 minutes more, until the vegetables are tender.

4 Stir in the shredded spinach and half the fresh coriander. Cook for 2 minutes. Serve over jasmine rice, garnished with the remaining chopped coriander.

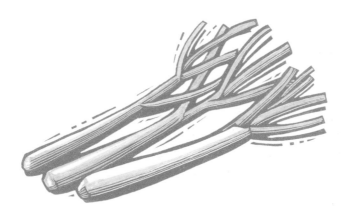

LENTIL DHAL WITH ROASTED GARLIC

This spicy lentil dhal makes a comforting, tasty meal when served with boiled rice or Indian breads and a vegetable dish. Do not be alarmed by the amount of garlic as its flavour softens when roasted.

SERVES 4–6

INGREDIENTS
1 whole bulb of garlic
30ml/2 tbsp extra virgin olive oil, plus extra for brushing
40g/1½oz/3 tbsp ghee or butter
1 onion, chopped
2 fresh green chillies, seeded and chopped
15ml/1 tbsp chopped fresh root ginger
225g/8oz/1 cup red split lentils
900ml/1½ pints/3¾ cups water
5ml/1 tsp ground cumin
5ml/1 tsp ground coriander
2 tomatoes, peeled and diced
a little lemon juice
salt and ground black pepper
30–45ml/2–3 tbsp fresh coriander (cilantro) sprigs, to garnish

FOR THE SPICE MIX
30ml/2 tbsp groundnut (peanut) oil
4–5 shallots, sliced
2 garlic cloves, thinly sliced
15g/½oz/1 tbsp ghee or butter
5ml/1 tsp cumin seeds
5ml/1 tsp mustard seeds
3–4 small dried red chillies
8–10 fresh curry leaves

1 Preheat the oven to 180°C/350°F/Gas 4. Place the garlic in an oiled roasting pan and roast it whole for 30 minutes.

2 Melt the ghee or butter in a pan. Add the onion, fresh chillies and ginger and cook, stirring occasionally, for about 10 minutes, until golden.

3 Stir in the lentils and water. Bring to the boil, then lower the heat and partially cover the pan. Simmer, stirring occasionally, for about 35 minutes, until the mixture looks like a very thick soup.

4 When the garlic is soft and tender, remove it from the oven and leave it to cool slightly. Cut off the top third and, holding the garlic over a bowl, dig out the flesh from each clove so that it drops into the bowl. Mash it to a paste with the oil.

5 Stir the garlic purée, cumin and ground coriander into the lentil mixture and season to taste. Cook for 10 minutes, uncovered, stirring frequently. Stir in the tomatoes, then adjust the seasoning, adding a little lemon juice to taste.

6 For the spice mix, heat the oil in a small, heavy pan and cook the shallots until crisp and browned. Add the garlic and cook until it colours slightly. Remove the mixture from the pan and set it aside.

7 Melt the ghee or butter in the same pan and fry the cumin and mustard seeds until the mustard seeds pop. Stir in the dried chillies, curry leaves and the shallot mixture, then swirl the hot mixture into the cooked dhal. Garnish with the coriander sprigs and serve immediately.

Peppers Filled with Spiced Vegetables

Hot fresh chillies and aromatic Indian spices season the potato and aubergine stuffing in these colourful baked peppers.

SERVES 6 ·

INGREDIENTS

1 aubergine (eggplant)
30ml/2 tbsp groundnut (peanut) oil, plus extra for brushing
6 large even-shaped red or yellow (bell) peppers
500g/1¼lb waxy potatoes
1 small onion, chopped
4–5 garlic cloves, chopped
5cm/2in piece of fresh root ginger, chopped
1–2 fresh green chillies, seeded and chopped
105ml/7 tbsp water
10ml/2 tsp cumin seeds
5ml/1 tsp kalonji seeds
2.5ml/½ tsp ground turmeric
5ml/1 tsp ground coriander
5ml/1 tsp ground toasted cumin seeds
pinch of cayenne pepper
about 30ml/2 tbsp lemon juice
salt and ground black pepper
chopped fresh coriander (cilantro), to garnish

1 Preheat the oven to 230°C/450°F/Gas 8. Cut the aubergine in half lengthways and score the skin. Brush a roasting pan lightly with oil. Put the aubergine halves, cut-side down, in the pan and bake for 20 minutes. Leave to cool.

2 Cut the tops off the peppers and carefully scoop out and discard the seeds. Cut a thin slice off the base of the peppers, if necessary, so they stand upright. Bring a large pan of lightly salted water to the boil. Add the peppers and cook for 5–6 minutes. Lift out with a slotted spoon and drain upside down in a colander.

3 Bring the water used for the peppers back to the boil and cook the potatoes until just tender. Drain, cool and peel, then cut into 1cm/½in dice. Peel the aubergine and cut the flesh into similar dice.

4 Put the chopped onion, garlic, ginger and green chillies in a food processor or blender with 60ml/4 tbsp of the water and process to a purée.

5 Heat half the oil in a large, deep, frying pan and stir-fry the aubergine until browned. Remove from the pan and set aside. Add the remaining oil to the pan and cook the potatoes until lightly browned. Remove from the pan and set aside.

6 Dry-fry the cumin and kalonji seeds in a non-stick pan. When the seeds darken, add the turmeric, coriander and ground cumin. Cook for 15 seconds. Stir in the chopped onion and garlic purée and fry, frequently scraping the pan with a spatula, until it begins to brown.

7 Add the potatoes and aubergines to the pan, and season with salt, pepper and cayenne. Add the remaining water and half the lemon juice and cook, stirring, until the liquid evaporates. Preheat the oven to 190°C/375°F/Gas 5.

8 Place the peppers on a baking sheet and fill with the potato mixture. Brush lightly with oil and bake for 30–35 minutes, until the peppers are cooked. Remove from the oven and leave to cool slightly, then sprinkle with more lemon juice. Garnish with the coriander and serve.

COOK'S TIP
Kalonji seeds are also known as nigella. They are widely used in Indian cooking in dhal and vegetable dishes as well as being scattered over naan bread. Dry-fry them before use to bring out the flavour.

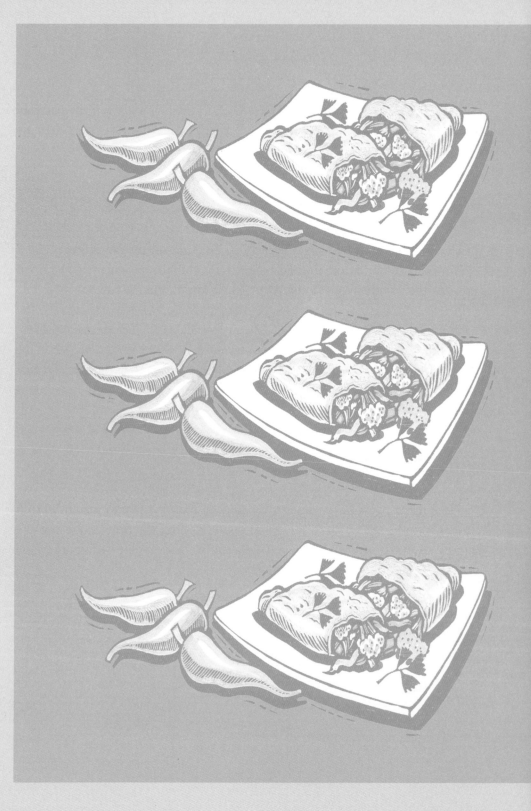

FRESH &
HEALTHY DISHES

A diet which features vegetables and cereals is already a healthy one, but even vegetarians can overdo unhealthy fats or fail to balance their nutrient intake. These are the recipes to turn to when your system needs a boost and you want to increase your sense of wellbeing without having to pore over textbooks on nutrition or even count calories. For low-fat cooking techniques, it is hard to beat stir-frying – try Spring Vegetable Stir-fry to shake off the winter blues. Plenty of fresh vegetables, whether Spaghetti with Fresh Tomato Sauce or Low-fat Vegetable Paella, guarantee a healthy balance of nutrients, including vitamins and fibre.

Spring Vegetable Stir-fry

A dazzling and colourful medley of fresh and sweet young vegetables that can be varied according to availability.

Serves 4

Ingredients
15ml/1 tbsp groundnut (peanut) oil
1 garlic clove, sliced
2.5cm/1in piece of fresh root ginger, finely chopped
115g/4oz baby carrots
115g/4oz small patty pan squash
115g/4oz baby corn cobs
115g/4oz/scant 1 cup green beans, trimmed
115g/4oz sugar snap peas, trimmed
115g/4oz young asparagus, cut into 7.5cm/3in pieces
8 spring onions (scallions), trimmed and cut into 5cm/2in pieces
115g/4oz cherry tomatoes

For the dressing
juice of 2 limes
15ml/1 tbsp clear honey
15ml/1 tbsp soy sauce
5ml/1 tsp sesame oil

1 Heat the groundnut oil in a wok or large frying pan and stir-fry the garlic and ginger over a high heat for 30 seconds.

2 Reduce the heat slightly and add the baby carrots, patty pan squash, baby corn cobs and green beans, and stir-fry for 3–4 minutes more.

3 Add the sugar snap peas, asparagus, spring onions and cherry tomatoes. Toss over the heat for a further 1–2 minutes.

4 Mix the dressing ingredients in a jug (pitcher) and pour them over the stir-fried vegetables. Stir well, cover and cook for 2–3 minutes more, until the vegetables are crisp-tender. Serve immediately.

SPROUTING BEANS & PAK CHOI

Health food stores are a good source of the more unusual sprouting beans, or you can sprout your own easily at home.

SERVES 4

INGREDIENTS
45ml/3 tbsp groundnut (peanut) oil
3 spring onions (scallions), sliced
2 garlic cloves, thinly sliced
2.5cm/1in piece of fresh root ginger, thinly sliced
1 carrot, cut into thin batons
150g/5oz/1¼ cups sprouting beans
200g/7oz pak choi (bok choy), shredded
50g/2oz/½ cup unsalted cashew nuts or halved almonds
salt and ground black pepper

FOR THE SAUCE
45ml/3 tbsp light soy sauce
30ml/2 tbsp dry sherry
15ml/1 tbsp sesame oil
15ml/1 tbsp chilli sauce
150ml/¼ pint/⅔ cup cold water
5ml/1 tsp cornflour (cornstarch)
5ml/1 tsp clear honey
ground black pepper

1 Heat the oil in a large wok or frying pan and stir-fry the onions, garlic, ginger and carrot for 2 minutes. Add the sprouting beans and stir-fry for 2 minutes more, stirring and tossing them together.

2 Add the pak choi and cashew nuts or almonds. Toss over the heat for 2–3 minutes, or until the cabbage leaves are just wilting.

3 Quickly mix all the sauce ingredients in a jug (pitcher) and pour them into the wok, stirring constantly until the sauce is hot and coats the vegetables. Season to taste with salt and pepper, if necessary, and serve immediately.

Quorn with Ginger, Chilli & Leeks

If you have never eaten Quorn, this would be a good recipe to try. It is available from most supermarkets. Serve it over noodles or rice for a well-balanced meal.

SERVES 4

INGREDIENTS
45ml/3 tbsp soy sauce
30ml/2 tbsp dry sherry or vermouth
225g/8oz/2 cups Quorn cubes
10ml/2 tsp clear honey
150ml/¼ pint/⅔ cup vegetable stock
10ml/2 tsp cornflour (cornstarch)
45ml/3 tbsp sunflower oil
3 leeks, thinly sliced
1 fresh red chilli, seeded and sliced
2.5cm/1in piece of fresh root ginger, grated
salt and ground black pepper
1 sheet of nori, toasted and crumpled into pieces, to garnish

1 Mix the soy sauce and dry sherry or vermouth in a medium bowl. Add the Quorn cubes, toss until well coated and leave to marinate for about 30 minutes to absorb the flavours.

2 Using a slotted spoon, lift out the Quorn cubes from the marinade and set them aside. Stir the clear honey, vegetable stock and cornflour into the remaining marinade to make a smooth paste.

3 Heat the oil in a wok or large frying pan. When it is hot, stir-fry the Quorn cubes until they are crisp on the outside. Remove the Quorn and set aside. Reheat the oil and stir-fry the leeks, chilli and ginger for about 2 minutes, until they are just soft. Season lightly.

4 Add the Quorn cubes to the vegetables in the wok and mix well. Stir the marinade mixture, pour it into the wok and stir until it forms a thick coating for the Quorn and vegetables. Serve, garnished with pieces of nori.

SPINACH WITH MUSHROOMS & RED PEPPER

This is a wonderful way to cook three tasty and nutritious vegetables. Serve the stir-fry very hot, with freshly made warm chapatis.

SERVES 4

INGREDIENTS
450g/1lb fresh or frozen spinach
30ml/2 tbsp corn oil
2 onions, diced
6–8 curry leaves
1.5ml/¼ tsp onion seeds
5ml/1 tsp crushed garlic
5ml/1 tsp grated fresh root ginger
5ml/1 tsp mild chilli powder
5ml/1 tsp salt
7.5ml/1½ tsp ground coriander
1 large red (bell) pepper, seeded and sliced
115g/4oz/1⅔ cups mushrooms, coarsely chopped
225g/8oz/1 cup low-fat fromage frais or 250ml/8fl oz/1 cup natural (plain) yogurt
30ml/2 tbsp fresh coriander (cilantro) leaves

1 Blanch fresh spinach briefly in boiling water and drain thoroughly. Thaw frozen spinach, then drain. Set aside.

2 Heat the oil in a wok or large frying pan. Add the onions, curry leaves and onion seeds and cook, stirring occasionally, for 1–2 minutes. Add the garlic, ginger, chilli powder, salt and ground coriander. Stir-fry for 2–3 minutes more.

3 Add half the red pepper slices and all the mushrooms and continue to stir-fry for 2–3 minutes.

4 Add the spinach and stir-fry for 4–6 minutes. Finally, stir in the fromage frais or yogurt and half the fresh coriander, followed by the remaining red pepper slices. Cook over a medium heat, stirring constantly, for 2–3 minutes more before serving, garnished with the remaining coriander.

Black Bean
& Vegetable Stir-fry

The secret of a quick stir-fry is to have everything ready before you begin to cook.
This colourful vegetable mixture is coated in a classic Chinese sauce.

SERVES 4

INGREDIENTS
8 spring onions (scallions)
225g/8oz/3 cups button (white) mushrooms
1 red (bell) pepper
1 green (bell) pepper
2 large carrots
60ml/4 tbsp sesame oil
2 garlic cloves, crushed
60ml/4 tbsp black bean sauce
90ml/6 tbsp warm water
225g/8oz/2 cups beansprouts
salt and ground black pepper

1 Thinly slice the spring onions on the diagonal and slice the button mushrooms. Cut both the peppers in half, remove the seeds and membrane and slice the flesh into thin strips.

2 Cut the carrots in half widthways, then cut each half into thin strips lengthways. Stack the slices and cut through them to make very fine strips.

3 Heat the oil in a large wok or frying pan until it is very hot. Add the spring onions and garlic and stir-fry for 30 seconds. Add the mushrooms, peppers and carrots and stir-fry over a high heat for 5–6 minutes, until the vegetables are just beginning to soften.

4 Mix the black bean sauce with the water. Add to the wok and cook, stirring occasionally, for 3–4 minutes. Stir in the beansprouts and continue to cook, stirring constantly, for 1 minute more, until all the vegetables are coated in the sauce. Season to taste with salt and pepper. Serve immediately.

Spring Vegetable Omelette

This resembles a Spanish omelette in that it is not flipped, but finished off under the grill. Packed with tender vegetables, it makes a very tasty light lunch.

SERVES 4

INGREDIENTS
50g/2oz/½ cup fresh asparagus tips
50g/2oz spring greens (collards), shredded
15ml/1 tbsp sunflower oil
1 onion, sliced
175g/6oz cooked new potatoes, halved or diced
2 tomatoes, chopped
6 eggs
15–30ml/1–2 tbsp chopped fresh mixed herbs
salt and ground black pepper
salad, to serve

1 Steam the asparagus tips and spring greens over a pan of boiling water for 5–10 minutes, or until tender. Drain the vegetables and keep them warm.

2 Heat the oil in a large frying pan, that can safely be used under the grill (broiler). (Cover a wooden handle with foil to protect it.) Add the onion and cook over a low heat, stirring occasionally, for 5–10 minutes, or until softened.

3 Add the new potatoes and cook, stirring constantly for 3 minutes. Stir in the tomatoes, asparagus and spring greens. Beat the eggs lightly with the herbs and season to taste with salt and pepper.

4 Preheat the grill. Pour the egg mixture over the vegetables, then cook over a gentle heat until the base of the omelette is golden brown. Slide the pan under the grill and cook the omelette for 2–3 minutes, until the top is golden brown. Serve immediately, cut into wedges, with salad.

COOK'S TIP
Remember to use a low-fat dressing for the salad, such as cider vinegar and natural (plain) yogurt.

CORIANDER OMELETTE PARCELS WITH ASIAN VEGETABLES

Stir-fried vegetables in black bean sauce make a remarkably good omelette filling, which is quick and easy to prepare. It would also be a suitable filling for pancakes.

SERVES 4

INGREDIENTS

130g/4½oz broccoli, cut into small florets
30ml/2 tbsp groundnut (peanut) oil
1cm/½in piece of fresh root ginger, finely grated
1 large garlic clove, crushed
2 fresh red chillies, seeded and finely sliced
4 spring onions (scallions), sliced diagonally
175g/6oz/3 cups shredded pak choi (bok choy)
50g/2oz/2 cups fresh coriander (cilantro) leaves, plus extra to garnish
115g/4oz/1 cup sprouting mung beans
45ml/3 tbsp black bean sauce
4 eggs
salt and ground black pepper

COOK'S TIP
Black bean sauce is made from fermented soya beans, which are then crushed and mixed with flour and salt. Yellow bean sauce is similar, but much lighter in colour and far less salty. Both are available from most supermarkets and Chinese food stores.

1 Bring a large pan of lightly salted water to the boil, add the broccoli and blanch for 2 minutes. Drain, refresh under cold running water, then drain again.

2 Heat half the groundnut oil in a wok or frying pan and stir-fry the grated ginger, garlic and half the chillies for 1 minute. Add the spring onions, broccoli and pak choi, and stir-fry for 2 minutes more.

3 Chop three-quarters of the fresh coriander leaves and add to the wok or frying pan with the sprouting beans. Stir-fry for 1 minute, then add the black bean sauce and toss over the heat for 1 minute more. Remove the pan from the heat and keep the vegetables hot.

4 Lightly beat the eggs and season well with salt and pepper. Heat a little of the remaining oil in a small frying pan and add one-quarter of the beaten egg. Swirl the egg to cover the base of the pan, then sprinkle over one-quarter of the remaining whole coriander leaves. Cook the omelette until set, then turn it out on to a plate. Make three more omelettes, adding more oil as required.

5 Divide the stir-fry among the omelettes and roll them up. Cut each one in half crossways and arrange the pieces on a plate. Garnish with coriander leaves and the remaining chillies. Serve immediately.

Braised Aubergine
& Courgettes

*Fresh red chillies add a flicker of fire to a dish that is simple, spicy and quite
sensational. If you do not like your food quite so hot, use larger mild chillies or even
sweet red peppers.*

SERVES 4

INGREDIENTS
1 aubergine (eggplant), about 350g/12oz
2 small courgettes (zucchini)
15ml/1 tbsp vegetable oil
2 garlic cloves, finely chopped
2 fresh red chillies, seeded and finely chopped
1 small onion, diced
15ml/1 tbsp black bean sauce
15ml/1 tbsp dark soy sauce
45ml/3 tbsp water
salt

COOK'S TIP
*When stir-frying, always heat the wok or frying pan
thoroughly before adding the oil. When you add the
oil, swirl it around, so that it coats the sides as well
as the base of the pan. Wait for the oil to heat before
adding the first ingredients.*

1 Trim the aubergine and slice it in half lengthways, then cut it across into
1cm/½in slices. Layer the slices in a colander, sprinkling each layer with salt.
Leave the colander in the sink for about 20 minutes, so the liquid that is drawn
from the aubergine drains away.

2 Meanwhile, roll-cut each courgette by slicing off one end diagonally, then
rolling the courgette through 180° and taking off another diagonal slice to form
a triangular wedge. Make more wedges of courgette in the same way.

3 Rinse the salted aubergine slices well under cold running water, drain and dry thoroughly on kitchen paper.

4 Heat the oil in a preheated wok or frying pan. Add the finely chopped garlic, chopped chillies and diced onion and stir-fry over a medium heat for 2–3 minutes. Stir in the black bean sauce, coating the onions well.

5 Lower the heat and add the aubergine slices. Stir-fry for 2 minutes, sprinkling over a little water, if necessary, to prevent them from burning.

6 Stir in the courgette wedges, soy sauce and measured water. Cook, stirring occasionally, for 5 minutes. Serve hot.

Spaghetti with Fresh Tomato Sauce

This famous Neapolitan sauce is very simple, so nothing detracts from the rich, sweet flavour of the sun-ripened tomatoes themselves.

SERVES 4

INGREDIENTS

675g/1½lb ripe Italian plum tomatoes
60ml/4 tbsp olive oil
1 onion, finely chopped
350g/12oz fresh or dried spaghetti
a small handful of fresh basil leaves, shredded
salt and ground black pepper
coarsely shaved Parmesan cheese, to serve

1 Cut a cross in the blossom end of each tomato and put them in a heatproof bowl. Pour over boiling water to cover and leave for about 30 seconds, or until the skins wrinkle and start to peel back from the crosses. Drain, peel off the skins and coarsely chop the flesh.

2 Heat the oil in a large pan and cook the onion over a low heat, for 5 minutes, until softened and lightly coloured. Stir in the tomatoes and season with salt and pepper to taste. Cover the pan and cook over a low heat for 30–40 minutes, stirring occasionally.

3 Bring a large pan of lightly salted water to the boil and cook the spaghetti until it is *al dente*. Dried pasta will take about 8–10 minutes and fresh spaghetti about 3–4 minutes.

4 Remove the sauce from the heat and taste and adjust the seasoning, if necessary. Drain the pasta, tip it into a warmed serving bowl, pour the sauce over and toss well. Sprinkle the fresh basil over the top and serve immediately, with shaved Parmesan handed separately.

Conchiglie with Roasted Vegetables

Nothing could be simpler – or more delicious – than tossing freshly cooked pasta with colourful roasted vegetables.

Serves 4

Ingredients
1 small aubergine (eggplant)
30ml/2 tbsp extra virgin olive oil, plus extra for brushing
1 red (bell) pepper, seeded and cut into 1cm/½in squares
1 yellow or orange (bell) pepper, seeded and cut into 1cm/½in squares
2 courgettes (zucchini), coarsely diced
15ml/1 tbsp chopped fresh flat leaf parsley
5ml/1 tsp dried oregano
250g/9oz baby Italian plum tomatoes, halved lengthways
2 garlic cloves, coarsely chopped
350g/12oz/3 cups dried conchiglie
salt and ground black pepper
4–6 fresh herb flowers, to garnish

1 Preheat the oven to 230°C/450°F/Gas 8. Cut the aubergine in half and score the cut sides deeply. Brush a roasting pan lightly with oil and place the aubergine on it, cut-sides down. Roast for 15 minutes. Remove the aubergine from the oven and lower the temperature to 190°C/375°F/Gas 5.

2 Cut the aubergine halves into chunks and return them to the roasting pan. Add the peppers and courgettes. Pour over the olive oil and sprinkle with the herbs and seasoning. Stir. Roast for 30 minutes, stirring twice. Stir in the tomatoes and garlic, then roast for 20 minutes more, stirring once or twice.

3 Meanwhile, bring a large pan of lightly salted water to the boil. Add the pasta and cook for 12 minutes, or until it is *al dente*. Drain the pasta and tip it into a warmed bowl. Add the roasted vegetables and toss. Garnish with herb flowers.

SPAGHETTI WITH GARLIC & OIL

This classic Italian dish has only a few ingredients, which must be of the very best quality. Chilli is always included to give the dish some bite.

SERVES 4

INGREDIENTS
400g/14oz fresh or dried spaghetti
45ml/3 tbsp extra virgin olive oil
2–4 garlic cloves, chopped
1 dried red chilli
1 small handful of fresh flat leaf parsley, coarsely chopped
salt

1 Bring a large pan of generously salted water to the boil and cook the spaghetti until it is *al dente*. Dried spaghetti will take 8–10 minutes; fresh spaghetti will be ready in 3–4 minutes.

2 While the pasta is cooking, heat the oil in a small frying pan over a very low heat. Add the chopped garlic and whole dried chilli and stir over a low heat until the garlic is just beginning to brown. Remove the chilli and save as a garnish.

3 Drain the pasta and tip it into a warmed serving bowl. Pour on the oil and garlic mixture, add the parsley and toss until the pasta glistens. Serve immediately, garnished with the chilli.

COOK'S TIPS
- *Don't use salt in the oil and garlic mixture, because it will not dissolve sufficiently. This is the reason why plenty of salt is recommended for cooking the pasta.*
- *For an authentic Italian flavour, use peperoncino, fiery, dried, red chillies from Abruzzi. They are so hot that they are known locally as diavoletto – little devils. They are available in packets from some Italian delicatessens.*

WHOLEMEAL PASTA WITH CARAWAY CABBAGE

Quite surprisingly, crunchy cabbage and Brussels sprouts are the perfect partners for a robust pasta in this healthy dish.

SERVES 6

INGREDIENTS
30ml/2 tbsp olive oil
3 onions, coarsely chopped
400ml/14fl oz/1⅔ cups vegetable stock
350g/12oz round white cabbage, coarsely chopped
350g/12oz Brussels sprouts, trimmed and halved
10ml/2 tsp caraway seeds
15ml/1 tbsp chopped fresh dill
200g/7oz/1¾ cups fresh or dried wholewheat pasta spirals
salt and ground black pepper
fresh dill sprigs, to garnish

1 Heat the oil in a large pan. Add the onions and cook over a low heat, stirring occasionally, for 10 minutes, until softened and golden in colour. If they start to stick to the pan, moisten them with a little of the stock.

2 Add the chopped cabbage and Brussels sprouts and cook for 2–3 minutes, then stir in the caraway seeds and chopped dill. Pour in the remaining stock and season with salt and pepper to taste. Cover and simmer for 5–10 minutes, until the cabbage and sprouts are crisp-tender.

3 Meanwhile, bring a pan of lightly salted water to the boil and cook the pasta for 12 minutes, or until *al dente*.

4 Drain the pasta, tip it into a warmed bowl and add the cabbage mixture. Toss lightly, taste and adjust the seasoning, if necessary, and serve immediately while hot, garnished with fresh dill.

TAGLIATELLE WITH PEA SAUCE, ASPARAGUS & BROAD BEANS

A creamy pea sauce provides a wonderful contrast to the crunchy young vegetables.
Later in the season you could use French beans instead of asparagus.

SERVES 4

INGREDIENTS
15ml/1 tbsp olive oil
1 garlic clove, crushed
6 spring onions (scallions), sliced
225g/8oz/2 cups frozen peas, thawed
30ml/2 tbsp chopped fresh sage, plus extra leaves to garnish
finely grated rind of 2 lemons
450ml/³/4 pint/scant 2 cups vegetable stock
350g/12oz fresh young asparagus, trimmed and cut into 5cm/2in lengths
225g/8oz/2 cups frozen broad (fava) beans, thawed
450g/1lb fresh or dried tagliatelle
60ml/4 tbsp low-fat natural (plain) yogurt, whisked

1 Heat the oil in a pan. Add the garlic and spring onions and cook over a low heat, stirring occasionally, for 2–3 minutes, until softened, but not coloured. Add the peas, sage, lemon rind and stock. Stir in one-third of the asparagus stalks. Bring to the boil, lower the heat and simmer for 10 minutes, until tender. Process in a blender until smooth, then scrape into a pan.

2 Pop the broad beans out of their skins and set them aside. Bring a large pan of water to the boil, add the remaining asparagus and blanch for 2 minutes. Transfer the asparagus pieces to a colander with a slotted spoon and set aside.

3 Bring the water in the pan back to the boil, add the tagliatelle and cook for about 10 minutes, or until it is *al dente*.

4 Meanwhile, add the cooked asparagus and shelled beans to the sauce and reheat. Remove from the heat and stir the yogurt into the sauce. Drain the pasta and divide among four warmed plates. Top the pasta with the sauce. Garnish with a few extra sage leaves and serve immediately.

BAKED CHEESE POLENTA WITH TOMATO SAUCE

Polenta, or cornmeal, is a staple food in Italy. It is cooked like porridge and can be eaten soft. This version uses squares of set polenta, baked in a rich tomato sauce.

SERVES 4

INGREDIENTS
1 litre/1¾ pints/4 cups water
5ml/1 tsp salt
250g/9oz/2 cups quick-cook polenta
5ml/1 tsp paprika
2.5ml/½ tsp ground nutmeg
30ml/2 tbsp olive oil, plus extra for greasing
1 large onion, finely chopped
2 garlic cloves, crushed
2 × 400g/14oz cans chopped tomatoes
15ml/1 tbsp tomato purée (paste)
5ml/1 tsp sugar
50g/2oz/½ cup grated Gruyère cheese
salt and ground black pepper

1 Preheat the oven to 200°C/400°F/Gas 6. Line a 28 × 18cm/11 × 7in baking tin (pan) with clear film (plastic wrap). Put the water in a large, heavy pan and add the salt. Bring the water to the boil. Pour in the polenta in a steady stream and cook, stirring constantly, for 5 minutes. Beat in the paprika and nutmeg, then pour the mixture into the prepared tin. Level the surface and leave to cool.

2 Heat the oil in a pan. Add the onion and garlic and cook over a low heat, stirring occasionally, for 5 minutes, until soft. Stir in the tomatoes, tomato purée and sugar, and season with salt and pepper to taste. Simmer for 20 minutes.

3 Turn out the polenta on to a chopping board and cut it into 5cm/2in squares. Place half the polenta squares in a greased ovenproof dish. Spoon over half the tomato sauce and sprinkle with half the grated cheese. Repeat the layers of polenta, sauce and cheese. Bake the polenta for about 25 minutes, until the top is golden and bubbling. Serve immediately.

HERBED RICE PILAFF

The difference between a pilau and a pilaff is largely one of origin. Both are rice dishes, usually with spices and often including a mixture of vegetables for colour and extra flavour. This delightful dish uses a simple herb mixture.

SERVES 4

INGREDIENTS
225g/8oz/scant 1 cup mixed brown basmati and wild rice
15ml/1 tbsp olive oil
1 onion, chopped
1 garlic clove, crushed
5ml/1 tsp ground cumin
5ml/1 tsp ground turmeric
50g/2oz/⅓ cup sultanas (golden raisins)
750ml/1¼ pints/3 cups vegetable stock
45ml/3 tbsp chopped fresh mixed herbs
salt and ground black pepper
fresh herb sprigs and 25g/1oz/¼ cup chopped nuts, to garnish

1 Rinse the rice mixture several times in cold water. If there is sufficient time, leave it to soak for 30 minutes in the water used for the final rinse. Drain well.

2 Heat the oil in a large, heavy pan. Add the chopped onion and garlic and cook over a low heat, stirring occasionally, for about 5 minutes, until the onion is softened but not coloured.

3 Stir in the ground cumin, turmeric and rice and cook over a moderate heat, stirring constantly, for about 1 minute, or until the rice grains are well coated.

4 Stir in the sultanas and vegetable stock. Bring to the boil, stirring frequently. Lower the heat, cover and simmer, stirring occasionally to prevent the rice from sticking, for 20–25 minutes, until the rice is cooked and just tender and almost all the liquid has been absorbed.

5 Stir in the chopped mixed herbs and season to taste with salt and pepper. Spoon the pilaff into a warmed serving dish and garnish with fresh herb sprigs and a sprinkling of chopped nuts. Serve immediately.

RISOTTO PRIMAVERA

*Celebrate springtime with this quick and easy rice dish. Use organic vegetables,
if possible, so that you can really savour the flavour. It makes a perfect stuffing for
lightly grilled red peppers if the vegetables are finely chopped.*

SERVES 4

INGREDIENTS
250g/9oz mixed spring vegetables
10ml/2 tsp olive oil
1 medium onion, sliced
250g/9oz/1¼ cups risotto rice
2.5ml/½ tsp ground turmeric
about 600ml/1 pint/2½ cups vegetable stock
45ml/3 tbsp chopped fresh parsley
salt and ground black pepper

1 Prepare the vegetables according to type, cutting them to more or less the same
size and leaving small ones whole so that they cook evenly.

2 Heat the oil in a large, non-stick pan. Add the onion and cook over a low heat,
stirring occasionally, for 10 minutes, or until softened and golden.

3 Stir in the rice and cook, stirring constantly, for 1–2 minutes, until the grains
are all coated with oil and glistening. Add the turmeric and cook, stirring
constantly, for 1 minute, then add the vegetable stock. Season well with salt and
pepper. Bring to the boil, then add the vegetables.

4 Bring back to the boil, then lower the heat, cover and cook gently, stirring
occasionally, for 20 minutes, or until the rice is tender and most of the liquid
has been absorbed. Add more stock if necessary.

5 Stir in the parsley and fluff up the rice. Transfer the risotto to a warmed serving
dish and serve immediately.

Risotto with Summer Vegetables

This is one of the prettiest risottos, especially if you can get yellow courgettes which contrast so well with the peas and green beans.

SERVES 4

INGREDIENTS

150g/5oz/1¼ cups shelled fresh peas
115g/4oz/1 cup green beans, cut into short lengths
30ml/2 tbsp olive oil
25g/1oz/2 tbsp butter
2 small yellow courgettes (zucchini), cut into thin batons
1 onion, finely chopped
275g/10oz/1½ cups arborio rice
120ml/4fl oz/½ cup Italian dry white vermouth
about 1 litre/1¾ pints/4 cups simmering vegetable stock
50g/2oz/¾ cup freshly grated Parmesan cheese
a small handful of fresh basil leaves, finely shredded, plus a few whole leaves,
    to garnish
salt and ground black pepper

COOK'S TIP
When making an authentic risotto, it is essential to be sure that each addition of stock has been completely absorbed before adding any more.

---

1 Bring a large pan of lightly salted water to the boil and blanch the peas and beans for 2–3 minutes, until just tender. Drain, refresh under cold running water, drain again and set aside.

2 Heat the oil and 15g/½oz/1 tbsp of the butter in a medium pan. Add the courgettes and cook over a low heat for 2–3 minutes. Remove with a slotted spoon and set aside. Add the onion to the pan and cook, stirring occasionally, for about 3 minutes, or until softened.

3 Stir in the arborio rice until coated with the butter and oil mixture, then add the vermouth. When most of it has been absorbed, add a few ladles of the hot vegetable stock and season with salt and pepper to taste. Stir over a low heat until the stock has been absorbed.

4 Continue adding the stock, a little at a time, and stirring constantly for about 20 minutes, until all the stock has been added. The risotto should be moist and creamy and the rice tender.

5 Gently stir in the vegetables, the remaining butter and about half the grated Parmesan. Heat through, then stir in the shredded basil. Transfer to a warmed serving dish and serve immediately, garnished with a few whole basil leaves. Offer the remaining grated Parmesan separately.

LOW-FAT VEGETABLE PAELLA

*Paella, which originated in the town of Valencia, is not actually the name of the dish,
but the heavy, two-handled, cast-iron pan in which it is traditionally cooked. This
vegetarian version is a delicious change from the more traditional shellfish- or
chicken-based paella. It is full of flavour and includes plenty of healthy fibre.*

SERVES 6

INGREDIENTS
1 onion, chopped
2 garlic cloves, crushed
225g/8oz leeks, sliced
3 celery sticks, chopped
1 red (bell) pepper, seeded and sliced
2 courgettes (zucchini), sliced
175g/6oz/2¼ cups brown cap mushrooms, sliced
175g/6oz/1½ cups frozen peas
450g/1lb/2¼ cups long grain brown rice
400g/14oz can cannellini beans, drained and rinsed
900ml/1½ pints/3¾ cups vegetable stock
60ml/4 tbsp dry white wine
a few saffron threads
225g/8oz cherry tomatoes, halved
45–60ml/3–4 tbsp chopped fresh mixed herbs
salt and ground black pepper
lemon wedges, whole cherry tomatoes and celery leaves, to garnish

COOK'S TIP
*Long grain rice works very well in this recipe, but
for a more authentic texture, try to obtain a Spanish
rice, such as calasparra, or even use risotto rice.*

1 Mix the onion, garlic, leeks, celery, red pepper, courgettes and mushrooms in
a large, heavy pan or flameproof casserole.

2 Add the peas, rice, cannellini beans, stock, wine and saffron to the vegetables. Bring the mixture to the boil over a moderate heat, stirring constantly, then lower the heat and simmer, stirring occasionally, for about 35 minutes, until almost all the liquid has been absorbed and the rice is tender.

3 Stir in the tomatoes and chopped herbs, season to taste with salt and pepper and heat through for 1–2 minutes. Serve garnished with lemon wedges, tomatoes and celery leaves.

Roasted Vegetables with Salsa Verde

Fresh herbs are at the heart of the Italian salsa verde (green sauce). It tastes wonderful with the vegetable mixture. Serve it with rice or a mixture of rice and vermicelli.

SERVES 4

INGREDIENTS
3 courgettes (zucchini), sliced lengthways
1 large fennel bulb, cut into wedges
450g/1lb butternut squash, cut into 2cm/³⁄₄in chunks
12 shallots
2 red (bell) peppers, seeded and thickly sliced
4 plum tomatoes, halved and seeded
30ml/2 tbsp olive oil
2 garlic cloves, crushed
5ml/1 tsp balsamic vinegar
salt and ground black pepper

FOR THE SALSA VERDE
45ml/3 tbsp chopped fresh mint
90ml/6 tbsp chopped fresh flat leaf parsley
15ml/1 tbsp Dijon mustard
juice of ½ lemon
30ml/2 tbsp olive oil

> COOK'S TIP
> *Dijon, in France is the mustard capital of the world. The mustard from this region is clean, sharp and creamy. It is widely used for cooking.*

1 Preheat the oven to 220°C/425°F/Gas 7. Make the salsa verde. Place all the ingredients, except the olive oil, in a food processor or blender. Blend to a coarse paste, then add the oil, a little at a time, until the mixture forms a smooth purée. Season to taste with salt and pepper.

2   In a large bowl, toss the courgettes, fennel, squash, shallots, peppers and tomatoes in the olive oil, garlic and balsamic vinegar. Leave for 10 minutes to allow the flavours to mingle.

3   Place all the vegetables – apart from the squash and tomatoes – in a roasting pan. Brush with half the oil and vinegar mixture and season with plenty of salt and pepper.

4   Roast for 25 minutes. Remove the roasting pan from the oven, turn the vegetables over and brush with the rest of the oil and vinegar mixture.

5   Add the squash and tomatoes and cook for 20–25 minutes more, until all the vegetables are tender and lightly charred around the edges. Spoon the roasted vegetables on to a serving platter and serve with the salsa verde.

Bean Feast with Mexican Salsa

Canned beans really come into their own when you need to make a nutritious meal in double-quick time. There are now many types available.

Serves 4

Ingredients
400g/14oz can red kidney beans
400g/14oz can flageolet or small cannellini beans
400g/14oz can borlotti beans
15ml/1 tbsp olive oil
1 small onion, finely chopped
3 garlic cloves, finely chopped
1 fresh red chilli, seeded and finely chopped
1 red (bell) pepper, seeded and coarsely chopped
2 bay leaves
10ml/2 tsp chopped fresh oregano
10ml/2 tsp ground cumin
5ml/1 tsp ground coriander
2.5ml/½ tsp ground cloves
15ml/1 tbsp soft dark brown sugar
300ml/½ pint/1¼ cups vegetable stock
salt and ground black pepper
fresh coriander sprigs, to garnish

For the salsa
1 ripe but firm avocado
45ml/3 tbsp freshly squeezed lime juice
1 small red onion, chopped
1 small fresh hot green chilli, finely sliced
3 ripe plum tomatoes, peeled, seeded and chopped
45ml/3 tbsp chopped fresh coriander

1 Drain all the beans in a colander and rinse thoroughly. Heat the oil in a heavy pan. Add the onion and cook over a low heat, stirring occasionally, for 3 minutes, until soft and transparent. Add the garlic, chilli, red pepper, bay leaves, oregano, cumin, coriander and cloves.

2 Stir well and cook for a further 3 minutes, then add the sugar, beans and stock and cook for 8 minutes. Season to taste with salt and pepper and leave over a low heat while you make the salsa.

3 Cut the avocado in half, remove the stone (pit), then peel it and dice the flesh. Toss it with the lime juice, then add all the remaining salsa ingredients and season with plenty of black pepper. Mix well.

4 Spoon the beans into four serving bowls. Garnish with sprigs of fresh coriander and serve with the salsa.

VARIATION
If you prefer a guacamole, coarsely mash the avocado with a fork before adding the other ingredients, but make sure it still has a little texture.

ENTERTAINING
IN STYLE

Vegetarian dishes are so attractive, colourful, appetizing and tasty that
they can turn any occasion into a party, but this collection of stylish
recipes, from roulade to crêpes and from pasta to pastry, is the perfect
opportunity to show off to friends, family and guests. Whether for an *al
fresco* lunch at the weekend or a formal dinner when you want to
impress, you are sure to find just the dish. Try the elegant Wild
Mushroom Brioche with Orange Butter Sauce or Pumpkin Gnocchi for a
really special occasion or delight your friends with Spring Vegetable &
Pine Nut Pizza or Greek Picnic Pie for an informal fun time.

COURGETTE FRITTERS WITH PISTOU

The delicious sauce is the French equivalent of Italian pesto. It provides a lovely contrast to these delicious fritters.

SERVES 4

INGREDIENTS
450g/1lb courgettes (zucchini), trimmed
75g/3oz/⅔ cup plain (all-purpose) flour
1 egg, separated
15ml/1 tbsp olive oil
75ml/5 tbsp water
vegetable oil, for frying
salt and ground black pepper

FOR THE PISTOU
15g/½oz/½ cup fresh basil leaves
4 garlic cloves, coarsely chopped
75g/3oz/1 cup freshly grated Parmesan cheese
finely grated rind of 1 lemon
150ml/¼ pint/⅔ cup olive oil

> COOK'S TIP
> *Use a bland-tasting oil for frying these fritters, such as rapeseed (canola), sunflower or safflower oil.*

1 Start by making the pistou. Put the basil leaves and garlic in a mortar and crush with a pestle to a fairly fine paste. Work in the grated Parmesan and lemon rind. Gradually blend in the olive oil, a little at a time, until fully incorporated, then transfer the pistou to a small serving dish.

2 Grate the courgettes into a large sieve. Sprinkle with plenty of salt. Place the sieve over a bowl, leave for 1 hour, then rinse thoroughly under cold water. Drain, then dry well on kitchen paper.

3 Sift the plain flour into a bowl and make a well in the centre, then add the egg yolk, olive oil and water to the well. Whisk, gradually incorporating the surrounding flour to make a smooth batter. Season to taste with salt and pepper and set aside to rest for 30 minutes.

4 Stir the courgettes into the batter. Whisk the egg white until stiff, then fold it into the batter.

5 Heat the vegetable oil in a large, heavy frying pan. Add tablespoons of batter to the oil and fry for about 2 minutes, until golden. Lift the fritters out and drain well on kitchen paper. Keep warm while you are frying the remainder. Serve immediately with the sauce.

SUMMER HERB RICOTTA FLAN

Made without pastry, this delicate flan, infused with aromatic herbs, is ideal for a light lunch or picnic.

SERVES 4

INGREDIENTS
olive oil, for greasing and glazing
800g/1¾lb/3½ cups ricotta cheese
75g/3oz/1 cup freshly grated Parmesan cheese
3 eggs, separated
60ml/4 tbsp torn fresh basil leaves
60ml/4 tbsp chopped fresh chives
45ml/3 tbsp fresh oregano leaves
2.5ml/½ tsp salt
2.5ml/½ tsp paprika
ground black pepper
fresh herb leaves, to garnish

FOR THE BLACK OLIVE PURÉE
400g/14oz/3½ cups pitted black olives, rinsed and halved
5 garlic cloves, crushed
75ml/5 tbsp olive oil

COOK'S TIP
Although there is a type of ricotta that is aged and salted, the most commonly used kind – and the one required here – is fresh, unripened ricotta, which has a soft, creamy texture. It does not keep well and should be used within one day of purchase.

1 Preheat the oven to 180°C/350°F/Gas 4. Lightly grease a 23cm/9in springform cake tin (pan) with oil. Mix the ricotta, Parmesan and egg yolks in a food processor. Add the fresh herbs, with the salt, and a little pepper. Process until smooth and creamy, then scrape into a bowl.

2 Whisk the egg whites in a large bowl until they form soft peaks. Gently fold them into the ricotta mixture. Spoon the mixture into the prepared tin and smooth the surface with a metal spatula.

3 Bake for 1 hour 20 minutes, or until the flan has risen and the top is golden. Remove from the oven and brush lightly with olive oil, then sprinkle with paprika. Leave the flan to cool before removing it from the tin.

4 Make the olive purée. Set aside a few olives for garnishing, if you like. Place the remainder in a food processor, add the garlic and process until finely chopped. With the motor running, gradually add the olive oil through the feeder tube or lid, until the mixture forms a coarse paste. Transfer it to a serving bowl. Garnish the flan with the herb leaves, and serve with the black olive purée.

LAYERED VEGETABLE TERRINE

With its wrapping of spinach, this courgette, pepper and potato terrine looks very pretty as a centrepiece for a buffet or dinner party.

SERVES 6

INGREDIENTS
3 red (bell) peppers, halved and seeded
450g/1lb waxy potatoes, peeled and halved
1 medium courgette (zucchini), sliced lengthways
115g/4oz spinach leaves, trimmed
25g/1oz/2 tbsp butter
pinch of freshly grated nutmeg
115g/4oz/1 cup grated Cheddar cheese
salt and ground black pepper
torn lettuce leaves and tomato wedges, to serve

VARIATION
For an even more colourful effect, use a mixture of red and yellow peppers and serve with torn oakleaf lettuce or red escaraole and yellow cherry tomatoes, cut in half.

1 Place the pepper halves, skin-side up, on a grill (broiler) rack and grill (broil) until the skins have blistered and charred. Transfer to a bowl, cover with crumpled kitchen paper and leave to cool.

2 Meanwhile, bring a pan of lightly salted water to the boil. Cook the potatoes for 15 minutes. Drain and set aside. Bring a separate pan of water to the boil and add the courgette slices. Blanch them for 1 minute, then lift out with a draining spoon. Add the spinach to the boiling water, blanch for a few seconds, then drain and pat dry on kitchen paper.

3 Preheat the oven to 180°C/350°F/Gas 4. Line the base and sides of a 900g/2lb loaf tin (pan) with the spinach, overlapping the leaves slightly. Slice the potatoes thinly. Lay one-third of them over the base of the tin, dot with a little butter and season with salt, pepper and nutmeg. Sprinkle some cheese over.

4 Peel the peppers, leaving the halves intact. Arrange half of them on top of the potatoes. Sprinkle with a little cheese and add a layer of courgettes. Lay a further third of the potatoes on top with the remaining peppers and more cheese, seasoning as you go. Top with the final layer of potatoes and sprinkle over any remaining cheese. Fold the spinach leaves over. Cover with foil.

5 Place the loaf tin in a roasting pan and pour in boiling water to come halfway up the sides. Bake for about 1 hour. Turn out the terrine and serve sliced, with lettuce and tomatoes.

Wild Mushroom Brioche with Orange Butter Sauce

A butter-rich brioche, ribboned with a mushroom duxelles would make an impressive centrepiece for a sophisticated dinner party.

SERVES 4

INGREDIENTS
5ml/1 tsp easy-blend (rapid-rise) dried yeast
45ml/3 tbsp milk, at room temperature
400g/14oz/3½ cups strong white bread flour
5ml/1 tsp salt
15ml/1 tbsp caster (superfine) sugar
3 eggs
finely grated rind of ½ lemon
200g/7oz/scant 1 cup butter, diced

FOR THE FILLING
50g/2oz/¼ cup butter
2 shallots, chopped
350g/12oz/5 cups assorted wild and cultivated mushrooms, coarsely chopped
½ garlic clove, crushed
75ml/5 tbsp chopped fresh parsley
salt and ground black pepper

FOR THE SAUCE
30ml/2 tbsp frozen concentrated orange juice
175g/6oz/¾ cup butter, diced
cayenne pepper

1 Dissolve the yeast in the milk, add 115g/4oz/1 cup of the flour and mix to form a dough. Fill a large bowl with lukewarm water, then place the bowl of dough in the water. Set aside for 30 minutes.

2 Place the remaining flour in a food processor fitted with the dough blade. Add the salt, caster sugar, eggs, lemon rind and the risen dough and process briefly to mix. Add the butter, in small pieces, and process until the dough is silky smooth and very slack. Wrap it in clear film (plastic wrap) and chill for 2 hours, until firm.

3 Make the filling. Melt the butter in a large, heavy frying pan. Add the shallots and cook over a low heat, stirring occasionally, until softened and translucent, but not browned.

4 Add the mushrooms and garlic and cook, stirring occasionally, until the juices begin to run. Increase the heat to medium and cook until most of the moisture has evaporated. When dry, tip the mixture into a bowl, add the parsley and season to taste with salt and pepper.

5 Grease and line a 900g/2lb loaf tin (pan). Roll out the dough to a 15 × 30cm/ 6 × 12in rectangle. Spoon the cooked mushroom mixture over the dough and roll up to make a fat sausage. Drop this into the loaf tin, cover with a damp dishtowel and set aside in a warm place for 50 minutes, or until the dough has risen above the level of the rim.

6 Preheat the oven to 190°C/375°F/Gas 5. Remove the dishtowel from the loaf tin, place in the oven and bake the brioche for 40 minutes.

7 Meanwhile, make the sauce. Place the orange juice concentrate in a heatproof glass bowl and heat by standing in a pan of simmering water. Remove from the heat and gradually whisk in the butter until creamy. Season to taste with cayenne pepper, cover and keep warm. When the brioche is cooked, turn it out, slice thickly and serve with the sauce.

ROASTED GEM SQUASH

Gem squash has a sweet, subtle flavour that contrasts well with black olives and sun-dried tomatoes. The rice adds substance and texture.

SERVES 2–4

INGREDIENTS

4 whole gem squashes
225g/8oz/2 cups cooked white long grain rice (65g/2½oz/generous ⅓ cup raw rice)
4 pieces sun-dried tomatoes in oil, drained and chopped, plus 30ml/2 tbsp oil
  from the jar
50g/2oz/½ cup pitted black olives, chopped
15ml/1 tbsp chopped fresh basil leaves, plus fresh basil sprigs, to serve
60ml/4 tbsp soft goat's cheese
Tzatziki, to serve

1 Preheat the oven to 180°C/350°F/Gas 4. Trim away the base of each squash, slice off the top, scoop out the seeds with a spoon and discard.

2 Mix together the rice, sun-dried tomatoes, olives, basil and cheese in a bowl. Stir in 15ml/1 tbsp of the oil from the jar.

3 Use a little of the remaining oil to grease a shallow ovenproof dish that is just large enough to hold the squash side by side. Divide the rice mixture among the squash and place them in the dish. Drizzle any remaining oil over.

4 Cover with foil and bake for 45–50 minutes, until tender. Garnish with basil sprigs. Serve with Tzatziki.

VARIATIONS
- *If you are not keen on olives, use raisins instead.*
- *If gem squashes are not available, serve half an acorn squash per person instead.*

KOHLRABI STUFFED WITH PEPPERS

*If you have not sampled kohlrabi or have eaten it only in stews where its flavour is
lost, do try this delectable dish which makes the most of its taste.*

SERVES 4

INGREDIENTS
4 small kohlrabi, about 175g/6oz each
about 400ml/14fl oz/1⅔ cups hot vegetable stock
15ml/1 tbsp sunflower oil
1 onion, chopped
1 small red (bell) pepper, seeded and sliced
1 small green (bell) pepper, seeded and sliced
salt and ground black pepper

1 Preheat the oven to 180°C/350°F/Gas 4. Trim the kohlrabi. Arrange them in a
single layer in the base of an ovenproof dish. Pour over the hot stock to come
about halfway up the kohlrabi. Cover and braise in the oven for about 30 minutes,
until tender. Transfer to a plate, reserving the stock, and leave to cool. Leave the
oven switched on.

2 Heat the sunflower oil in a large, heavy frying pan. Add the onion and cook
over a low heat, stirring occasionally, for 3–4 minutes, until softened. Add the
red and green pepper slices and cook, stirring occasionally, for 2–3 minutes more,
until the onion is lightly browned.

3 Add the reserved vegetable stock and season to taste, then simmer, uncovered,
until most of the stock has evaporated. Scoop out the flesh from the kohlrabi
and chop it coarsely. Stir the flesh into the onion and pepper mixture, taste and
adjust the seasoning, if necessary. Arrange the shells in a shallow ovenproof dish.

4 Spoon the filling into the kohlrabi shells. Place in the oven for about 10 minutes
to heat through, then serve.

Lentil & Nut Loaf

For a special celebration, serve this with all the trimmings. Roasted potatoes and a green vegetable such as Brussels sprouts or steamed broccoli work well.

SERVES 6–8

INGREDIENTS
115g/4oz/½ cup red lentils
115g/4oz/1 cup each of hazelnuts and walnuts
1 large carrot
2 celery sticks
1 large onion
115g/4oz/1⅔ cups mushrooms
50g/2oz/¼ cup butter, plus extra for greasing
10ml/2 tsp mild curry powder
30ml/2 tbsp tomato ketchup
30ml/2 tbsp vegetarian Worcestershire sauce
1 egg, beaten
10ml/2 tsp salt
60ml/4 tbsp chopped fresh parsley
150ml/¼ pint/⅔ cup water

1 Put the lentils in a bowl and add cold water to cover. Set aside for 1 hour to soak. Grind the nuts in a food processor until quite fine but not too smooth. Tip the nuts into a large bowl. Coarsely chop the carrot, celery, onion and mushrooms, add them to the food processor and process until finely chopped.

2 Heat the butter in a pan. Add the vegetables and cook gently over a low heat, stirring occasionally, for 5 minutes. Stir in the curry powder and cook for 1 minute more. Remove from the heat and set aside to cool.

3 Drain the lentils and stir them into the ground nuts. Add the vegetables, ketchup, Worcestershire sauce, egg, salt, parsley and measured water.

4 Preheat the oven to 190°C/375°F/Gas 5. Grease a 1kg/2¼lb loaf tin (pan) and line with baking parchment or a sheet of foil. Press the mixture into the tin. Bake for 1–1¼ hours, until just firm, covering the top with foil if it starts to burn. Leave to stand for 15 minutes before you turn it out and peel off the paper.

CLASSIC CHEESE SOUFFLÉ

A melt-in-the-mouth cheese soufflé makes one of the most delightful light lunches imaginable. All you need to go with it is salad and a glass of good wine.

SERVES 2–3

INGREDIENTS
50g/2oz/¼ cup butter
30–45ml/2–3 tbsp fine, dried breadcrumbs
30g/1¼oz/5 tbsp plain (all-purpose) flour
pinch of cayenne pepper
2.5ml/½ tsp English (hot) mustard powder
250ml/8fl oz/1 cup milk
50g/2oz/½ cup grated mature (sharp) Cheddar cheese
25g/1oz/⅓ cup freshly grated Parmesan cheese
4 eggs, separated, plus 1 egg white
salt and ground black pepper

1 Preheat the oven to 190°C/375°F/Gas 5. Melt 15g/½oz/1 tbsp of the butter and grease a 1.2 litre/2 pint/5 cup soufflé dish. Coat the inside of the dish with the breadcrumbs, shaking out any excess.

2 Melt the remaining butter in a pan, stir in the flour, cayenne and mustard and cook for 1 minute. Add the milk, whisking constantly, until the mixture boils and thickens to a smooth sauce.

3 Simmer the sauce for 1–2 minutes, then remove from the heat and whisk in all the Cheddar, half the Parmesan and season to taste with salt and pepper. Cool a little, then beat in the egg yolks.

4 Whisk the egg whites to soft, glossy peaks. Add a few spoonfuls to the sauce to lighten it. Beat well, then gently fold in the rest of the whites.

5 Pour the mixture into the prepared soufflé dish, level the surface and sprinkle the remaining Parmesan over. Run your finger around the inside rim of the dish to help the soufflé rise evenly. Place the dish on a baking sheet and bake for about 25 minutes, or until the soufflé has risen and is golden brown. Serve immediately while hot and puffed up.

LEEK ROULADE WITH CHEESE, WALNUTS & PEPPERS

This is surprisingly easy to prepare and makes a good main course. It is impressive enough for a dinner party.

SERVES 4–6

INGREDIENTS

50g/2oz/¼ cup butter, plus extra for greasing
30ml/2 tbsp fine dried white breadcrumbs
75g/3oz/1 cup freshly grated Parmesan cheese
2 leeks, thinly sliced
40g/1½oz/⅓ cup plain (all-purpose) flour
250ml/8fl oz/1 cup milk
5ml/1 tsp Dijon mustard
about 2.5ml/½ tsp freshly grated nutmeg
2 large (US extra large) eggs, separated, plus 1 egg white
2.5ml/½ tsp cream of tartar
salt and ground black pepper

FOR THE FILLING

2 large red (bell) peppers, halved and seeded
350g/12oz/1½ cups ricotta cheese
75g/3oz/¾ cup walnuts, chopped
4 spring onions (scallions), finely chopped
15g/½ oz/½ cup fresh basil leaves

1 Preheat the oven to 190°C/375°F/Gas 5. Grease a 30 × 23cm/12 × 9in Swiss (jelly) roll tin (pan) and line it with baking parchment. Sprinkle the breadcrumbs and 30ml/2 tbsp of the Parmesan evenly over the parchment.

2 Melt the butter in a pan and cook the leeks gently for 5 minutes, until softened but not browned. Stir in the flour and cook for 1 minute, stirring constantly. Add the milk, whisking constantly until the mixture boils and thickens.

3 Stir in the mustard and nutmeg and season to taste with salt and pepper. Reserve 30–45ml/2–3 tbsp of the remaining Parmesan, then stir the rest into the sauce. Cool slightly, then beat in the egg yolks.

4 Whisk the egg whites and cream of tartar until stiff. Stir 2–3 spoonfuls of the egg white into the leek mixture to lighten it, then carefully fold in the rest.

5 Pour the mixture into the tin and level the surface. Bake for 15–18 minutes, until risen and just firm.

6 Make the filling. Grill (broil) the peppers, skin-side uppermost, until black and blistered. Place in a bowl, cover with crumpled kitchen paper and leave for about 10 minutes. Peel off the skin and cut the peppers into long strips.

7 Beat the cheese with the walnuts and spring onions. Chop half the basil and beat it into the mixture. Season to taste with salt and pepper.

8 Sprinkle a large sheet of baking parchment with the remaining Parmesan. Turn out the roulade on to it. Strip off the lining parchment and cool slightly. Spread the cheese mixture over and top with the red pepper strips. Tear the remaining basil leaves and sprinkle them over the top.

9 Using the baking parchment as a guide, roll up the roulade and roll it on to a serving platter. Serve warm or cold.

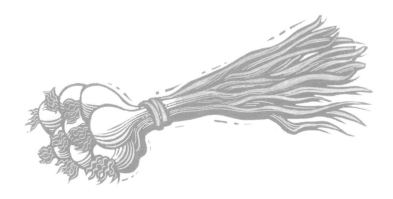

POLENTA CRÊPES WITH BUTTERNUT SQUASH FILLING

These colourful, melt-in-the-mouth crêpes are wonderful served with a fresh-tasting green salad and a rich tomato sauce.

SERVES 4

INGREDIENTS
115g/4oz/1 cup plain (all-purpose) flour
50g/2oz/½ cup polenta or cornmeal
2.5ml/½ tsp mild chilli powder
2 large (US extra large) eggs, beaten
about 450ml/¾ pint/scant 2 cups milk
25g/1oz/2 tbsp butter, melted
vegetable oil, for greasing
salt and ground black pepper

FOR THE FILLING
45ml/3 tbsp olive oil
450g/1lb/3½ cups seeded and diced butternut squash
pinch of dried red chilli flakes
2 large leeks, thickly sliced
2.5ml/½ tsp chopped fresh thyme
3 chicory (Belgian endive) heads, thickly sliced
115g/4oz goat's cheese, cubed
75g/3oz/¾ cup walnuts, coarsely chopped
30ml/2 tbsp chopped fresh parsley, plus extra to garnish
45ml/3 tbsp freshly grated Parmesan cheese

COOK'S TIP
As you cook the crêpes, stack them on a plate, interleaved with baking parchment to prevent them from sticking together. There is no need to keep them warm.

1 Mix the flour, polenta or cornmeal, chilli powder and a pinch of salt in a bowl and make a well in the centre. Add the eggs and a little of the milk. Whisk well, gradually incorporating the flour mixture and adding enough milk to make a creamy batter. Set aside for 1 hour.

2 Whisk the melted butter into the batter. Heat a lightly greased crêpe pan. Pour in about 60ml/4 tbsp of the batter, cook for 2–3 minutes, turn over and cook for 1–2 minutes, then slide out. Make more crêpes in the same way.

3 Make the filling. Heat 30ml/2 tbsp of the oil in a frying pan and cook the squash, stirring frequently, for 10 minutes. Stir in the chilli flakes, leeks and thyme and cook for 5 minutes. Add the chicory and cook, stirring frequently, for 4–5 minutes. Cool, then stir in the goat's cheese, walnuts and parsley. Season well with salt and ground black pepper.

4 Preheat the oven to 200°C/400°F/Gas 6. Lightly grease an ovenproof dish. Stuff each crêpe with 30–45ml/2–3 tbsp of the filling and place in the dish. Sprinkle with the Parmesan and drizzle with the remaining olive oil. Bake for 10–15 minutes, or until the cheese is bubbling and the crêpes are hot. Garnish with parsley and serve immediately.

BAKED HERB CRÊPES

A spinach, cheese and pine nut filling turns crêpes into party food. Use delicate herbs in the summer and stronger ones, such as sage and thyme, in the winter.

SERVES 4

INGREDIENTS

25g/1oz/1 cup chopped fresh herbs
15ml/1 tbsp sunflower oil, plus extra for frying and greasing
120ml/4fl oz/½ cup milk
3 eggs
25g/1oz/¼ cup plain (all-purpose) flour
30ml/2 tbsp olive oil
1 small onion, chopped
2 garlic cloves, crushed
400g/14oz can chopped tomatoes
pinch of soft light brown sugar
450g/1lb fresh spinach, cooked and drained
175g/6oz/¾ cup ricotta cheese
25g/1oz/¼ cup pint nuts, toasted
5 pieces of sun-dried tomato in oil, drained and chopped
30ml/2 tbsp shredded fresh basil
4 egg whites
salt and ground black pepper

1 Process the herbs and oil in a food processor. Add the milk, eggs, flour and a pinch of salt. Process until smooth. Set aside for 30 minutes. Heat a greased crêpe pan and make eight crêpes, cooking them for about 2 minutes on each side.

2 Heat the olive oil in a small pan, and cook the onion and garlic for 5 minutes. Add the tomatoes and sugar and cook for 10 minutes, until thickened. Purée in a blender or food processor, then sieve into a pan and set aside. Mix the spinach, cheese, nuts, sun-dried tomatoes and basil with seasoning. Whisk the egg whites until stiff. Stir one-third into the spinach mixture, then fold in the rest.

3 Preheat the oven to 190°C/375°F/Gas 5. Place one crêpe at a time on a lightly oiled baking sheet, add a spoonful of filling and fold into quarters. Bake for 12 minutes, until set. Reheat the sauce and serve with the crêpes.

GARGANELLI WITH ASPARAGUS & CREAM

*This is a lovely recipe for late spring, when bunches of fresh young asparagus
are on sale everywhere.*

SERVES 4

INGREDIENTS
1 bunch fresh young asparagus, about 275g/10oz
350g/12oz/3 cups dried garganelli
25g/1oz/2 tbsp butter
250ml/8fl oz/1 cup double (heavy) cream
30ml/2 tbsp dry white wine
115g/4oz/1⅓ cups freshly grated Parmesan cheese
30ml/2 tbsp chopped fresh mixed herbs
salt and ground black pepper

1 With your fingers, snap off and discard the woody ends of the asparagus. They
can be used to make a stock for another recipe. Cut off the asparagus tips and
set them aside. Cut the stalks diagonally into pieces that are about the same length
and shape as the garganelli.

2 Bring a large pan of lightly salted water to the boil and blanch the asparagus
stalks for 1 minute. Add the tips and blanch for 1 minute more. Transfer to a
colander with a slotted spoon. Rinse under cold water to prevent them cooking any
further, drain again thoroughly and set aside.

3 Bring the water in the pan back to the boil, add the pasta and cook until it is
al dente. Meanwhile, melt the butter and cream in a pan, season to taste with
salt and pepper and bring to the boil. Simmer for a few minutes, until the cream
thickens, then add the asparagus, wine and about half the grated Parmesan. Taste
for seasoning and leave over a low heat.

4 Drain the cooked pasta and tip it into a warmed bowl. Pour the sauce over,
sprinkle with the fresh herbs and toss well. Serve immediately, topped with the
remaining grated Parmesan.

Sardinian Ravioli

With their unusual potato, cheese and mint filling, these ravioli are certainly special.
The two types of Pecorino give the ravioli a full flavour.

Serves 4–6

Ingredients
plain (all-purpose) flour, for dusting
50g/2oz/¼ cup butter
50g/2oz/⅔ cup freshly grated Pecorino cheese

For the pasta dough
200g/7oz/1¾ cups strong white bread flour
5ml/½ tsp salt
15ml/1 tbsp olive oil
2 eggs, beaten

For the filling
400g/14oz potatoes, diced
65g/2½oz/generous ⅔ cup grated mature (sharp) Pecorino cheese
75g/3oz soft fresh Pecorino cheese
1 egg yolk
leaves from 1 large bunch fresh mint, chopped
good pinch of saffron threads
salt and ground black pepper

Cook's Tip
If you do not have a pasta machine, you can roll out
the dough by hand. Divide it in half and roll out on
a lightly floured surface to a thickness of about
5mm/¼in. Fold the pasta into three and re-roll.
Repeat this up to six times until the dough is smooth
and no longer sticky, rolling the pasta slightly more
thinly each time.

1 Make the filling. Bring a pan of lightly salted water to the boil and cook the potatoes for 15–20 minutes, or until soft. Drain, tip into a bowl, then mash until smooth. Cool, then stir in the cheeses, egg yolk, mint, saffron and salt and pepper.

2 Meanwhile, make the pasta dough. Sift the flour and salt into a blender or food processor. With the motor running, gradually add the oil and eggs through the lid or feeder tube and process to a firm, but smooth dough. Turn out on to a lightly floured surface and knead for 5 minutes. Divide the dough into quarters. Using a pasta machine, roll out one-quarter of the pasta into a 90cm/36in strip. Cut the strip into two 45cm/18in lengths.

3 With a fluted 10cm/4in biscuit (cookie) cutter, cut out 4–5 rounds from one of the strips. Using a heaped teaspoon, put a mound of filling on one side of each round. Brush a little water around the edge of each round, then fold the plain side over the filling to make a half-moon shape. Pleat the curved edge to seal.

4 Put the ravioli on floured dishtowels, sprinkle with flour and leave to dry. Repeat the process with the remaining dough to make 32–40 ravioli altogether.

5 Preheat the oven to 190°C/375°F/Gas 5. Bring a large pan of lightly salted water to the boil and cook the ravioli for 4–5 minutes. Meanwhile, melt the butter in a small pan.

6 Drain the ravioli, transfer to a large ovenproof dish and pour the melted butter over. Sprinkle with the grated Pecorino and bake in the oven for 10–15 minutes, until golden and bubbly. Leave to stand for 5 minutes before serving.

Layered Polenta Bake

When you are entertaining, it is good to serve something a little out of the ordinary. This combination of polenta, tomatoes, spinach and beans fits the bill very well.

SERVES 6

INGREDIENTS

2 litres/3½ pints/9 cups water

5ml/1 tsp salt

375g/13oz/generous 3 cups fine polenta or cornmeal

olive oil, for greasing and brushing

25g/1oz/⅓ cup freshly grated Parmesan cheese

salt and ground black pepper

FOR THE TOMATO SAUCE

15ml/1 tbsp olive oil

2 garlic cloves, chopped

400g/14oz can chopped tomatoes

15ml/1 tbsp chopped fresh sage

2.5ml/½ tsp soft light brown sugar

200g/7oz can cannellini beans, drained and rinsed

FOR THE SPINACH SAUCE

250g/9oz spinach, tough stalks removed

150ml/¼ pint/⅔ cup single (light) cream

115g/4oz Gorgonzola cheese, diced

large pinch of freshly grated nutmeg

1 Pour the water into a large, heavy pan and add the salt. Bring to the boil. Remove the pan from the heat and gradually whisk in the polenta or cornmeal.

2 Return the pan to the heat and simmer over a low heat, stirring constantly, for 15–20 minutes, until the polenta is thick and comes away from the side of the pan. Remove the pan from the heat.

3 Season the polenta to taste with pepper, then spoon it on to a wet work surface and spread it out evenly with a wet spatula until it is about 1cm/½in thick. Leave to cool for about 1 hour, or until set.

4 Preheat the oven to 190°C/375°F/Gas 5. To make the tomato sauce, heat the oil in a pan, then cook the garlic for 1 minute. Add the tomatoes, sage and sugar and season to taste with salt and pepper. Simmer, stirring occasionally, for 10 minutes, until slightly reduced. Stir in the beans and cook for 2 minutes more.

5 Meanwhile, wash the spinach thoroughly and place in a large pan with only the water that clings to the leaves. Cover the pan tightly and cook over a medium heat, stirring occasionally, for about 3 minutes, or until tender. Drain in a colander, squeezing out as much water as possible.

6 Put the cream, cheese and nutmeg in a small pan. Bring to the boil over a medium heat, stir in the spinach and season to taste with salt and pepper. Lower the heat and simmer gently, stirring frequently, until slightly thickened.

7 Cut the polenta into triangles, then place a layer of polenta in an oiled deep ovenproof dish. Spoon over the tomato sauce, then top with another layer of polenta. Cover with the spinach sauce and then the remaining polenta triangles. Brush with olive oil, sprinkle with Parmesan and bake for 35–40 minutes. Brown the top under a hot grill (broiler) before serving, if you like.

Pumpkin Gnocchi

Very much a gourmet dish, this is perfect for when you really want to impress. The chanterelles complement the pumpkin with their colour and flavour.

SERVES 4

INGREDIENTS

450g/1lb peeled pumpkin, chopped
450g/1lb potatoes, unpeeled
2 egg yolks
200g/7oz/1¾ cups plain (all-purpose) flour, plus extra for dredging
pinch of ground allspice
1.5ml/¼ tsp ground cinnamon
pinch of freshly grated nutmeg
finely grated rind of ½ orange
50g/2oz freshly shaved Parmesan cheese
30ml/2 tbsp olive oil
1 shallot, chopped
175g/6oz/2 cups fresh chanterelle mushrooms, sliced
150ml/¼ pint/⅔ cup crème fraîche
a little milk (optional)
75ml/5 tbsp chopped fresh parsley
salt and ground black pepper

1 Preheat the oven to 180°C/350°F/Gas 4. Wrap the pumpkin in foil and bake for 30 minutes until very soft. Cook the potatoes in salted boiling water for 20 minutes, until tender. Drain and peel. Add the pumpkin to the peeled potato and push through a sieve. Mix in the egg yolks, flour, spices, orange rind and seasoning.

2 Bring a pan of lightly salted water to the boil. Dredge a work surface with flour. Spoon the mixture into a piping (pastry) bag with a 1cm/½in plain nozzle. Pipe a 15cm/6in sausage on the surface. Roll in flour and cut into 2.5cm/1in pieces. Mark each lightly with a fork and cook for 3–4 minutes in the boiling water.

3 Heat the oil in a pan and cook the shallot until soft. Add the chanterelles and cook briefly, then stir in the crème fraîche. Simmer and add milk, if required. Add the parsley and season. Transfer the gnocchi to bowls. Spoon the sauce over the top, sprinkle with Parmesan and serve.

ROASTED VEGETABLE PIZZA

This pizza makes the most of the sweet smoky flavours of roasted vegetables while the goat's cheese adds a creamy texture and tangy edge.

SERVES 3

INGREDIENTS
1 aubergine (eggplant), cut into thick chunks
2 courgettes (zucchini), sliced lengthways
1 red (bell) pepper, quartered and seeded
1 yellow (bell) pepper, quartered and seeded
1 small red onion, cut into wedges
90ml/6 tbsp olive oil
1 pizza base, 25–30cm/10–12in in diameter
400g/14oz can chopped tomatoes, drained
115g/4oz goat's cheese, cubed
15ml/1 tbsp chopped fresh thyme
ground black pepper
green olive tapenade (see Cook's Tip), to serve

1 Preheat the oven to 220°C/425°F/Gas 7. Place the vegetables in a roasting pan. Brush with 60ml/4 tbsp of the oil. Roast for 30 minutes, until charred, turning the peppers once. Remove the vegetables but leave the oven switched on.

2 Put the roasted peppers in a bowl and cover with crumpled kitchen paper or clear film (plastic wrap). When cool, peel off and discard the skins and cut the flesh into strips. Brush the pizza base with half the remaining oil and spread over the tomatoes. Arrange the roasted vegetables on top. Dot with the cheese and sprinkle over the thyme. Drizzle over the remaining oil and season. Bake for 15–20 minutes, until crisp. Spoon the tapenade over to serve.

COOK'S TIP
For vegetarian tapenade, process 40 pitted green olives, 5ml/1 tsp capers, four pieces of drained sun-dried tomatoes in oil, 5ml/1 tsp ground almonds, one chopped garlic clove, a pinch of ground cumin and 60ml/4 tbsp olive oil in a food processor.

Spring Vegetable & Pine Nut Pizza

Here is a chance to practise your artistic skills. With its colourful topping of tender young vegetables, nuts and cheese, the pizza looks like an artist's palette and it tastes wonderful. Try to use a buffalo mozzarella as it has the best flavour. You can save time by using a ready-made pizza base.

SERVES 2–3

INGREDIENTS
1 pizza base, 25–30cm/10–12in in diameter
45ml/3 tbsp olive oil
1 garlic clove, crushed
4 spring onions (scallions), sliced
2 courgettes (zucchini), thinly sliced
1 leek, thinly sliced
115g/4oz/1 cup fresh asparagus tips, sliced
15ml/1 tbsp chopped fresh oregano
30ml/2 tbsp pine nuts
50g/2oz/½ cup grated mozzarella, cheese
30ml/2 tbsp freshly grated Parmesan cheese
salt and ground black pepper

FOR THE TOMATO SAUCE
15ml/1 tbsp olive oil
1 onion, finely chopped
1 garlic clove, crushed
400g/14oz can chopped tomatoes
15ml/1 tbsp tomato purée (paste)
15ml/1 tbsp chopped fresh herbs
pinch of sugar

1 Make the tomato sauce. Heat the oil in a pan and cook the onion and garlic over a low heat, stirring occasionally, for about 5 minutes, until softened, but not browned. Add the tomatoes, tomato purée, fresh herbs and sugar, stir well and simmer for 15–20 minutes, or until the mixture is thick and flavoursome.

2 Preheat the oven to 220°C/425°F/Gas 7. Brush the pizza base with 15ml/1 tbsp of the olive oil, then spread the tomato sauce evenly over the top to within 1cm/½in of the edge.

3 Heat half the remaining olive oil in a frying pan and stir-fry the garlic, spring onions, courgettes, leek and asparagus over a medium heat for 3–5 minutes.

4 Arrange the vegetables over the tomato sauce, then sprinkle the oregano and pine nuts over the top.

5 Mix the cheeses and sprinkle over. Drizzle with the remaining olive oil and season well. Bake for 15–20 minutes until crisp and golden. Serve immediately.

Parsnip & Pecan Gougères with Watercress & Rocket Sauce

These nutty puffs always look impressive with their crisp outer shell which conceals a sweet parsnip centre.

MAKES 18

INGREDIENTS
115g/4oz/½ cup butter, plus extra for greasing
300ml/½ pint/1¼ cups water
75g/3oz/⅔ cup plain (all-purpose) flour
50g/2oz/½ cup wholemeal (whole-wheat) flour
3 eggs, beaten
30ml/2 tbsp finely grated Cheddar cheese
pinch of cayenne pepper
75g/3oz/¾ cup pecan nuts, chopped
1 parsnip, cut into 18 × 2cm/¾in pieces
15ml/1 tbsp milk
10ml/2 tsp sesame seeds
fresh watercress or American cress sprigs, to garnish

FOR THE SAUCE
150g/5oz watercress or American cress, trimmed
150g/5oz rocket (arugula), trimmed
175ml/6fl oz/¾ cup low-fat natural (plain) yogurt
freshly grated nutmeg
salt and ground black pepper

> COOK'S TIP
> *The secret of making successful choux pastry is to let the flour-and-butter mixture cool before beating in the eggs, to prevent them from setting.*

1 To make the sauce, bring a pan of water to the boil and blanch the watercress or American cress and rocket for 2–3 minutes to remove any bitter taste. Drain, refresh under cold water, drain again and chop coarsely.

2 Place the watercress or American cress and rocket in a blender or food processor with the yogurt and process until smooth. Add a pinch of nutmeg and season to taste.

3 Preheat the oven to 200°C/400°F/Gas 6. Place the butter and water in a pan. Bring to the boil, then add both the flours. Beat vigorously until the mixture leaves the sides of the pan. Remove from the heat and cool for 10 minutes. Beat in the eggs, a little at a time, until the mixture is shiny with a soft dropping (pourable) consistency. Beat in the Cheddar, cayenne and pecan nuts.

4 Lightly grease a large baking sheet and drop 18 heaped tablespoons of the mixture on to it. Place a piece of parsnip on each and top with another heaped tablespoon of the mixture. Brush with a little milk and sprinkle with sesame seeds. Bake for 25–30 minutes, or until firm and golden.

5 Just before serving, place the sauce in the top of a double boiler or in a heatproof bowl set over a pan of barely simmering water. Heat gently, taking care not to let the sauce curdle.

6 Garnish the gougères with the watercress or American cress sprigs. Serve immediately with the sauce.

Ratatouille & Fontina Strudel

Mix a colourful jumble of ratatouille vegetables with chunks of creamy cheese, wrap in filo and bake for a summery party pastry. Serve with a mixed salad.

SERVES 6

INGREDIENTS
1 small aubergine (eggplant), diced
45ml/3 tbsp extra virgin olive oil
1 onion, sliced
2 garlic cloves, crushed
1 red (bell) pepper, seeded and sliced
1 yellow (bell) pepper, seeded and sliced
2 courgettes (zucchini), cut into small chunks
generous pinch of dried mixed herbs
30ml/2 tbsp pine nuts
30ml/2 tbsp raisins
8 filo pastry sheets, each about 30 × 18cm/12 × 7in, thawed if frozen
50g/2oz/¼ cup butter, melted
130g/4½oz Fontina or Bel Paese cheese, cut into small cubes
salt and ground black pepper

1 Layer the aubergine in a colander, sprinkling each layer with salt. Drain for 20 minutes, then rinse, drain and pat dry.

2 Heat the oil in a large frying pan and gently cook the onion, garlic, peppers and aubergine for about 10 minutes. Add the courgettes and herbs and season with salt and pepper to taste. Cook for 5 minutes, or until softened. Cool to room temperature, then stir in the pine nuts and raisins.

3 Preheat the oven to 180°C/350°F/Gas 4. Brush two sheets of filo pastry lightly with melted butter. Lay the filo sheets side by side, overlapping them by about 5cm/2in, to make a large rectangle. Cover with the remaining filo, in the same way. Spoon the vegetable mixture down one long side of the filo. Sprinkle the cheese over, then roll up to a long sausage. Transfer to a non-stick baking sheet and curl around to form a ring. Brush with the remaining melted butter and bake for 30 minutes, until golden. Cool for 10 minutes, then slice and serve.

ASPARAGUS & RICOTTA TART

The melt-in-the-mouth filling in this summery tart has a much more delicate texture than a quiche – and tastes absolutely wonderful.

SERVES 4

INGREDIENTS
175g/6oz/1½ cups plain (all-purpose) flour, plus extra for dusting
75g/3oz/6 tbsp butter

FOR THE FILLING
225g/8oz asparagus
2 eggs, beaten
225g/8oz/1 cup ricotta cheese
30ml/2 tbsp Greek (US strained plain) yogurt
40g/1½oz/½ cup freshly grated Parmesan cheese
salt and ground black pepper

1 Preheat the oven to 200°C/400°F/Gas 6. Mix the flour and a pinch of salt in a bowl and rub in the butter with your fingertips or a pastry blender, until the mixture resembles fine breadcrumbs. Stir in enough cold water to form a smooth dough and knead lightly on a floured surface.

2 Roll out the pastry on a lightly floured surface and then use to line a 23cm/9in flan ring (quiche pan). Prick the base all over with a fork. Bake the tart case for 10 minutes, until the pastry is firm, but pale. Remove from the oven and reduce the temperature to 180°C/350°F/Gas 4.

3 Make the filling. Snap the asparagus and discard the woody ends. Cut off the tips and chop the remaining stalks into 2.5cm/1in pieces. Bring a pan of water to the boil. Blanch the stalks for 1 minute, then add the asparagus tips. Simmer for 4 –5 minutes, until almost tender, then drain and refresh under cold water. Drain again. Separate the chopped stalks from the asparagus tips.

4 Beat the eggs, ricotta, yogurt and Parmesan in a bowl. Stir in the asparagus stalks, season to taste with salt and pepper and pour the mixture into the pastry case. Arrange the asparagus tips on top, pressing them down slightly into the ricotta mixture. Bake for 35– 40 minutes, or until golden. Serve warm or cold.

SHALLOT & GARLIC TARTE TATIN

Savoury versions of the famous apple tarte tatin have been popular for some years.
Here, caramelized shallots are baked beneath a layer of Parmesan pastry.

SERVES 4–6

INGREDIENTS
300g/11oz puff pastry, thawed if frozen
plain (all-purpose) flour, for dusting
50g/2oz/¼ cup butter
75g/3oz/1 cup freshly grated Parmesan cheese

FOR THE TOPPING
40g/1½oz/3 tbsp butter
500g/1¼lb shallots, peeled but left whole
12–16 large garlic cloves, peeled but left whole
15ml/1 tbsp golden caster (superfine) sugar
15ml/1 tbsp balsamic vinegar
45ml/3 tbsp water
5ml/1 tsp chopped fresh thyme
salt and ground black pepper

1 Roll out the pastry into a rectangle on a lightly floured surface. Spread the butter over it, leaving a 2.5cm/1in border. Sprinkle the grated Parmesan on top. Fold the bottom third of the pastry up to cover the middle and the top third down. Seal the edges firmly, give the pastry a quarter turn and roll out to a rectangle, then fold as before. Chill for 30 minutes.

2 Make the topping. Melt the butter in a 23–25cm/9–10in heavy frying pan that can safely be used in the oven. Add the shallots, garlic and a pinch of salt and cook gently until lightly browned all over. Sprinkle the golden caster sugar over the top and increase the heat slightly. Cook until the sugar begins to caramelize, then turn the shallots and garlic in the buttery juices to coat all over.

3 Add the vinegar, water and thyme and season to taste with salt and pepper. Partially cover the pan and cook for 5–8 minutes, until the garlic cloves are just tender. Remove from the heat and set aside to cool.

4 Preheat the oven to 190°C/375°F/Gas 5. On a lightly floured surface, roll out the pastry to a round slightly larger than the pan and lay it over the shallots and garlic. Tuck the pastry overlap down inside the pan, then prick the pastry all over with a sharp knife.

5 Bake the tart for 25–35 minutes, or until it is risen and golden. Remove from the oven and cool for 5–10 minutes, then turn the tart out on to a serving platter. Serve immediately, cut in wedges.

COOK'S TIP

The secret of a really successful melt-in-the mouth topping is to cook the shallots and garlic as slowly as possible over a very low heat. Adding a pinch of salt when they are first browning in step 2 draws out the juices and slows the process, resulting in an even golden colour. Do not add the sugar until the shallots have softened because it will prevent them from acquiring the right texture. Above all, do not be tempted to speed up the process.

Red Onion Tart with a Polenta Crust

Mild red onions go well with Fontina cheese and thyme in this tasty tart. Polenta gives the pastry a distinctive colour and crispness.

Serves 5–6

Ingredients
60ml/4 tbsp olive oil
1kg/2¼lb red onions, thinly sliced
2–3 garlic cloves, thinly sliced
5ml/1 tsp chopped fresh thyme, plus a few whole sprigs
5ml/1 tsp soft dark brown sugar
10ml/2 tsp sherry vinegar
225g/8oz Fontina cheese, thinly sliced
salt and ground black pepper

For the pastry
115g/4oz/1 cup plain (all-purpose) flour
75g/3oz/¾ cup fine polenta
5ml/1 tsp soft dark brown sugar
5ml/1 tsp chopped fresh thyme
90g/3½oz/7 tbsp butter
1 egg yolk
about 30ml/2 tbsp iced water

Cook's Tip
Fontina is one of Italy's most delicious cheeses. It is made from the milk of cows that graze in the high alpine meadows of the Valle d'Aosta. It has a delicate, slightly nutty flavour with a hint of honey and melts well.

1 Make the pastry. Mix the flour and polenta in a bowl and add salt, pepper, the sugar and thyme. Rub in the butter until the mixture resembles breadcrumbs. Beat the egg yolk with the water and use to bind the pastry, adding more water, if needed. Gather the dough into a ball, wrap and chill for 30–40 minutes.

2 Heat 45ml/3 tbsp of the oil in a frying pan. Add the onions, cover and cook gently, stirring occasionally, for 20–30 minutes.

3 Add the garlic and chopped thyme. Cook, stirring occasionally, for 10 minutes. Increase the heat slightly, then add the sugar and sherry vinegar. Cook, uncovered, for 5–6 minutes more, until the onions start to caramelize slightly. Season to taste with salt and pepper. Remove from the heat and leave to cool.

4 Preheat the oven to 190°C/375°F/Gas 5. Roll out the pastry thinly and use to line a 25cm/10in loose-based flan tin (quiche pan). Prick the pastry with a fork and support the sides with foil. Bake for 12–15 minutes, until lightly coloured.

5 Spread the onions over the base of the pastry. Add the cheese and most of the thyme sprigs and season to taste with salt and pepper. Drizzle over the remaining oil, then bake for 15–20 minutes, until the cheese is bubbling. Serve immediately, garnished with thyme sprigs.

GREEK PICNIC PIE

Aubergines layered with spinach, salty feta cheese and rice make a marvellous filling for a pie – whether eaten on a picnic or served at home.

SERVES 6

INGREDIENTS

375g/13oz shortcrust (unsweetened) pastry, thawed if frozen
45–60ml/3–4 tbsp olive oil
1 large aubergine (eggplant), sliced into rounds
1 onion, chopped
1 garlic clove, crushed
175g/6oz spinach
4 eggs
75g/3oz feta cheese
40g/1½oz/½ cup freshly grated Parmesan cheese
60ml/4 tbsp natural (plain) yogurt
90ml/6 tbsp milk
225g/8oz/2 cups cooked long grain rice
salt and ground black pepper

COOK'S TIP
If you like, you can layer the aubergine slices in a colander, sprinkling each layer with salt. Stand the colander in the sink for 30 minutes, then rinse the slices well and pat dry on kitchen paper. This helps to prevent them from absorbing too much oil during cooking in step 2.

1 Preheat the oven to 180°C/350°F/Gas 4. Roll out the pastry thinly and line a 25cm/10in flan ring (quiche pan). Prick the pastry all over and bake the unfilled case in the oven for 10–12 minutes, or until the pastry is pale golden.

2 Heat 30–45ml/2–3 tbsp of the oil in a frying pan and cook the aubergine slices for 6–8 minutes on each side, until golden. Lift out and drain on kitchen paper.

3 Add the onion and garlic to the oil remaining in the pan and cook gently until soft, adding a little extra oil if necessary.

4 Chop the spinach finely, by hand or in a food processor. Beat the eggs in a large mixing bowl, then add the spinach, feta, Parmesan, yogurt, milk and the onion mixture. Season well with salt and pepper and stir thoroughly.

5 Spread the rice in an even layer over the base of the partially cooked pastry case. Reserve a few aubergine slices for the top of the pie, and arrange the rest in an even layer over the rice.

6 Spoon the spinach and feta mixture over the aubergines and place the remaining aubergine slices on top. Bake for 30–40 minutes, until lightly browned. Serve the pie warm, or cool completely before transferring to a serving plate or wrapping and packing for a picnic.

CHAMPAGNE RISOTTO

This may seem rather extravagant, but it makes a beautifully flavoured risotto, perfect for that special celebratory dinner.

SERVES 3–4

INGREDIENTS
25g/1oz/2 tbsp butter
2 shallots, finely chopped
275g/10oz/1½ cups risotto rice
½ bottle or 300ml/½ pint/1¼ cups Champagne
750ml/1¼ pints/3 cups simmering light vegetable stock
150ml/¼ pint/⅔ cup double (heavy) cream
40g/1½oz/½ cup freshly grated Parmesan cheese
10ml/2 tsp very finely chopped fresh chervil
salt and ground black pepper
white truffle shavings, to garnish (optional)

1 Melt the butter in a large, heavy pan. Add the shallots and cook over a low heat, stirring occasionally, for 2–3 minutes, until softened. Add the rice and cook, stirring constantly, until the grains are coated in butter. Carefully pour in about two-thirds of the Champagne so that it does not bubble over. Cook over a high heat, stirring constantly, until all the liquid has been absorbed.

2 Add the stock, a ladleful at a time, stirring constantly and making sure that each addition has been completely absorbed before adding more. The risotto should gradually become creamy and velvety and all the stock should be absorbed.

3 When the rice is tender but retains a bit of "bite", stir in the remaining champagne with the double cream and Parmesan. Adjust the seasoning. Remove from the heat, cover and leave to stand for a few minutes. Stir in the chervil. If you want to enhance the flavour, garnish with a few truffle shavings.

COOK'S TIP
When cooking a risotto of this calibre, it is especially important to use the correct type of rice. Carnaroli or Vialone Nano would be perfect.

PILAFF WITH SAFFRON & PICKLED WALNUTS

Pickled walnuts have a warm, tangy flavour that is lovely in rice dishes. This Eastern Mediterranean pilaff is interesting enough to serve on its own.

SERVES 4

INGREDIENTS
5ml/1 tsp saffron threads
15ml/1 tbsp boiling water
40g/1½oz/⅓ cup pine nuts
45ml/3 tbsp olive oil
1 large onion, chopped
3 garlic cloves, crushed
1.5ml/¼ tsp ground allspice
5cm/2in piece of fresh root ginger, grated
225g/8oz/generous 1 cup long grain rice
300ml/½ pint/1¼ cups vegetable stock
50g/2oz/½ cup pickled walnuts, drained and coarsely chopped
40g/1½oz/generous ¼ cup raisins
45ml/3 tbsp coarsely chopped fresh parsley or coriander (cilantro), plus whole leaves, to garnish
salt and ground black pepper
natural (plain) yogurt, to serve

1 Put the saffron in a bowl with the boiling water and leave to stand. Heat a large frying pan and dry-fry the pine nuts until they turn golden. Set them aside.

2 Heat the oil in the pan and cook the onion, garlic and allspice for 3 minutes. Stir in the ginger and rice and cook for 1 minute.

3 Add the stock and bring to the boil. Lower the heat, cover and simmer gently for 15 minutes, or until the rice is just tender.

4 Stir in the saffron and liquid, the pine nuts, pickled walnuts, raisins and parsley or coriander. Season to taste with salt and pepper. Heat through gently for 2 minutes. Garnish with the parsley or coriander leaves and serve with yogurt.

COURGETTE ROULADE

This makes an impressive buffet supper or dinner party dish. The addition of rice in the filling makes it more substantial.

SERVES 6

INGREDIENTS
40g/1½oz/3 tbsp butter
50g/2oz/½ cup plain (all-purpose) flour
300ml/½ pint/1¼ cups milk
4 eggs, separated
3 courgettes (zucchini), grated
25g/1oz/⅓ cup freshly grated Parmesan cheese, plus 30ml/2 tbsp for sprinkling
salt and ground black pepper
herb and green leaf salad, to serve

FOR THE FILLING
75g/3oz/scant ½ cup soft goat's cheese
60ml/4 tbsp fromage frais or natural (plain) yogurt
225g/8oz/2 cups cooked long grain rice
15ml/1 tbsp chopped mixed fresh herbs
15ml/1 tbsp olive oil
15g/½oz/1 tbsp butter
75g/3oz/generous 1 cup button (white) mushrooms, very finely chopped

> VARIATION
> *Substitute a selection of wild mushrooms, such as oyster or chanterelles, for the button mushrooms.*

1 Preheat the oven to 200°C/400°F/Gas 6. Line a 33 × 23cm/13 × 9in Swiss (jelly) roll tin (pan) with baking parchment.

2 Melt the butter in a pan, stir in the flour and cook for 1–2 minutes, stirring constantly. Gradually stir in the milk until the mixture forms a smooth sauce. Remove from the heat and cool. Stir in the egg yolks, add the courgettes and the Parmesan and season to taste with salt and pepper.

3 Whisk the egg whites until stiff, fold them into the courgette mixture and scrape into the prepared tin. Spread evenly. Bake for 10–15 minutes, until firm and lightly golden. Carefully turn out on to a sheet of baking parchment sprinkled with 30ml/2 tbsp grated Parmesan. Peel away the lining parchment. Roll the roulade up, using the parchment as a guide, and leave to cool.

4 To make the filling, mix the goat's cheese, fromage frais or yogurt, rice and herbs in a bowl. Season with salt and pepper. Heat the oil and butter in a small pan and cook the mushrooms until soft.

5 Unwrap the roulade, spread with the rice filling and lay the mushrooms along the centre. Roll up again. Serve warm or cold with a herb and green leaf salad.

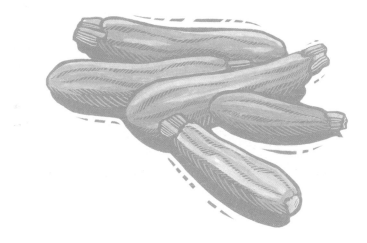

SIDE DISHES

From Lyonnaise Potatoes to Wild Rice Pilaff and from Courgettes in Citrus Sauce to Broccoli & Cauliflower with Apple Mint Sauce, the right choice of a side dish turns any meal into a special occasion. Whether the main course is based around eggs, cheese or vegetables, there will be an accompaniment that complements it perfectly. Sometimes, of course, a simple salad may be all that is required, but at others, a cooked side dish is the only choice – whether you are preparing a hearty midweek supper to satisfy a cold and hungry family on a winter's evening or pulling out the stops for an impressive formal dinner party.

ARTICHOKE RÖSTI

A traditional Swiss dish, rösti is usually made from potatoes alone. The addition of sweet Jerusalem artichokes provides a subtle variation of the flavour.

SERVES 4–6

INGREDIENTS
450g/1lb potatoes
juice of 1 lemon
5ml/1tsp vinegar (optional)
450g/1lb Jerusalem artichokes
about 50g/2oz/¼ cup butter
salt

1 Peel the potatoes and place them in a pan of lightly salted water. Bring to the boil and cook until barely tender – they will take 15–20 minutes.

2 Meanwhile, fill a pan with cold water and add half the lemon juice. Peel the Jerusalem artichokes, dropping them in a bowl of cold water acidulated with a little lemon juice or vinegar to prevent discoloration. Drain and add them to the pan, with a pinch of salt. Bring to the boil and cook for about 5 minutes, until barely tender.

3 Drain and cool both the potatoes and the artichokes, then grate them into a bowl. Mix them with your fingers, without breaking them up too much.

4 Melt the butter in a large, heavy frying pan. Add the artichoke mixture, spreading it out with the back of a spoon. Cook over a low heat for about 10 minutes. Invert the "cake" on to a plate and then slide it back into the pan. Cook the underside for about 10 minutes, or until golden. Serve immediately.

COOK'S TIP
If possible, chill the cooled par-boiled potatoes and artichokes in the refrigerator for 15–30 minutes before peeling. This makes them easier to grate and they will be less likely to break up.

BROAD BEANS WITH CREAM

Tiny new broad beans can be eaten raw with a little salt, just like radishes. More mature beans taste wonderful when cooked and skinned.

SERVES 4–6

INGREDIENTS
450g/1lb/2⅔ cups shelled broad (fava) beans (from about 2kg/4½lb beans in the pod)
90ml/6 tbsp crème fraîche or whipping cream
salt and ground black pepper
finely chopped chives, to garnish

1 Bring a large pan of lightly salted water to the boil over a medium heat. Add the beans. Bring the water back to the boil, then lower the heat slightly and cook the beans gently for about 8 minutes, until just tender. Drain and rinse under cold water, then drain again.

2 To remove the skins, make a slit along one side of each bean with the tip of a sharp knife and then gently squeeze out the kernel with your fingers.

3 Put the skinned beans in a pan with the crème fraîche or whipping cream, season with salt and pepper to taste, cover and heat through gently. Transfer to a warmed serving dish, sprinkle with the chopped chives and serve immediately.

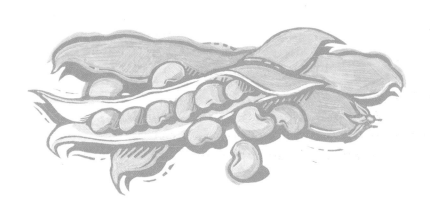

RUNNER BEANS WITH GARLIC

Flageolet beans and garlic add a distinctly French flavour to this simple side dish that is the perfect complement to a rich main course.

SERVES 4

INGREDIENTS
225g/8oz/1¼ cups dried flageolet or cannellini beans, soaked overnight and drained
15ml/1 tbsp olive oil
25g/1oz/2 tbsp butter
1 onion, finely chopped
1–2 garlic cloves, crushed
3–4 tomatoes, peeled and chopped
350g/12oz runner (green) beans, sliced
150ml/¼ pint/⅔ cup white wine
150ml/¼ pint/⅔ cup vegetable stock
30ml/2 tbsp chopped fresh parsley
salt and ground black pepper

1 Place the flageolet or cannellini beans in a large pan of water, bring to the boil over a medium heat, then lower the heat and simmer for 45 minutes–1 hour, until tender. Drain thoroughly and set aside.

2 Heat the oil and butter in a large, heavy frying pan. Add the onion and garlic and cook over a low heat, stirring occasionally, for 3–4 minutes, or until soft.

3 Add the chopped tomatoes to the pan with the onion and garlic and cook over a gentle heat until they are softened.

4 Stir the flageolet beans into the onion and tomato mixture, then add the runner beans, wine and stock and season with a little salt. Stir well. Cover and simmer for 5–10 minutes, or until the runner beans are tender.

5 Increase the heat to medium to reduce the liquid, then stir in the chopped parsley. Check the seasoning, adding a little more salt, if necessary, and pepper. Transfer to a warmed serving dish and serve immediately.

BROCCOLI & CAULIFLOWER WITH APPLE MINT SAUCE

The cider and mint sauce is also ideal for other vegetables, such as celery or beans.

SERVES 4

INGREDIENTS
15ml/1 tbsp olive oil
1 large onion, chopped
2 large carrots, chopped
1 large garlic clove
15ml/1 tbsp dill seeds
4 large fresh apple mint sprigs
30ml/2 tbsp plain (all-purpose) flour
300ml/½ pint/1¼ cups dry cider
500g/1¼lb/4 cups broccoli florets
500g/1¼lb/4 cups cauliflower florets
30ml/2 tbsp tamari (Japanese soy sauce)
10ml/2 tsp mint jelly
salt

1 Heat the olive oil in a large, heavy frying pan. Add the onion, carrots, garlic, dill seeds and apple mint leaves and cook over a low heat, stirring occasionally, for about 5 minutes, or until the vegetables are soft.

2 Stir in the flour and cook, stirring constantly, for 1 minute, then stir in the cider. Bring to the boil, then simmer until the sauce looks glossy. Remove the pan from the heat and set aside to cool slightly.

3 Bring two small pans of lightly salted water to the boil and cook the broccoli and cauliflower separately until just tender. Meanwhile, pour the sauce into a food processor and add the tamari and mint jelly. Process to a fine purée.

4 Drain the broccoli and cauliflower well and mix them in a warmed serving dish. Pour over the sauce, mix lightly to coat and serve immediately.

BAKED CABBAGE

This healthy and economical dish uses the whole cabbage, including the core, which is usually discarded but is very flavoursome.

SERVES 4

INGREDIENTS
1 green or white cabbage, about 675g/1½lb
15ml/1 tbsp light olive oil
30ml/2 tbsp water
45–60ml/3–4 tbsp vegetable stock
4 firm, ripe tomatoes, peeled and chopped
5ml/1 tsp mild chilli powder
15ml/1 tbsp chopped fresh parsley or fennel, to garnish (optional)

FOR THE TOPPING
3 firm ripe tomatoes, thinly sliced
15ml/1 tbsp olive oil
salt and ground black pepper

1 Preheat the oven to 180°C/350°F/Gas 4. Shred the leaves and the core of the cabbage finely. Heat the oil in a frying pan with the water and add the cabbage. Cover and cook over a very low heat, to allow the cabbage to sweat, for 5–10 minutes. Stir occasionally.

2 Pour in the vegetable stock, then stir in the tomatoes. Cook over a low heat for a further 10 minutes. Season with the chilli powder and a little salt.

3 Tip the cabbage mixture into a large, square ovenproof dish. Level the surface and arrange the sliced tomatoes on top. Brush with the oil then sprinkle with salt and pepper to taste.

4 Bake for 30–40 minutes, or until the tomatoes are just starting to brown. Serve hot, with a little parsley or fennel sprinkled over the top, if you like.

CELERIAC GRATIN

It may not look very handsome, but celeriac has a delicious sweet and nutty flavour, which is accentuated in this dish by the addition of Emmenthal cheese.

SERVES 4

INGREDIENTS
juice of ½ lemon
450g/1lb celeriac
25g/1oz/2 tbsp butter
1 small onion, finely chopped
30ml/2 tbsp plain (all-purpose) flour
300ml/½ pint/1¼ cups milk
25g/1oz/¼ cup grated Emmenthal cheese
15ml/1 tbsp capers, rinsed and drained
salt and cayenne pepper

1 Preheat the oven to 190°C/375°F/Gas 5. Fill a pan with water and add the lemon juice. Peel the celeriac and cut it into 5mm/¼in slices, immediately adding them to the pan of acidulated water. This prevents them from discolouring.

2 Bring the water to the boil, then lower the heat and simmer the celeriac for 10–12 minutes, until just tender. Drain the celeriac and arrange the slices, overlapping them slightly, in a shallow ovenproof dish.

3 Melt the butter in a small pan. Add the onion and cook over a low heat, stirring occasionally, for 5 minutes, until soft but not browned. Stir in the flour, cook, stirring constantly, for 1 minute and then gradually add the milk, stirring constantly until the mixture thickens, to make a smooth sauce.

4 Stir in the grated cheese and capers, and season with salt and cayenne to taste. Pour the mixture over the celeriac. Bake for 15–20 minutes, until the top is golden brown. Serve immediately.

COURGETTES IN CITRUS SAUCE

Brightly coloured courgettes are so attractive that their mild taste can sometimes be disappointing. This spicy and piquant sauce makes a satisfying and delicious accompaniment to the baby vegetables.

SERVES 4

INGREDIENTS
350g/12oz baby courgettes (zucchini)
4 spring onions (scallions), thinly sliced
2.5cm/1in piece of fresh root ginger, grated
30ml/2 tbsp cider vinegar
15ml/1 tbsp light soy sauce
5ml/1 tsp soft light brown sugar
45ml/3 tbsp vegetable stock
finely grated rind and juice of ½ lemon and ½ orange
5ml/1 tsp cornflour (cornstarch)
10ml/2 tsp water

1 Bring a pan of lightly salted water to the boil. Add the courgettes, bring back to the boil and simmer for 3–4 minutes, or until just tender.

2 Meanwhile, combine the onions, ginger, vinegar, soy sauce, sugar and stock in a small pan. Add the orange and lemon juice and rind. Bring to the boil, lower the heat and simmer for 2 minutes.

3 Mix the cornflour to a paste with the measured water, then stir the paste into the sauce. Bring to the boil, stirring constantly until the sauce has thickened. Drain the courgettes well and tip them into a warmed serving dish. Spoon over the hot sauce. Shake the dish gently to coat the courgettes, and serve.

BAKED FENNEL

The delicate aniseed flavour and crisp-tender texture of baked fennel makes it a very good accompaniment to pasta dishes and risottos. The crumb crust gives it extra texture and flavour.

SERVES 4

INGREDIENTS
3 fennel bulbs, cut lengthways into quarters
30ml/2 tbsp olive oil
50g/2oz/1 cup day-old wholemeal (whole-wheat) breadcrumbs
1 garlic clove, chopped
30ml/2 tbsp chopped fresh flat leaf parsley
salt and ground black pepper
fennel leaves, to garnish

1 Bring a pan of lightly salted water to the boil over a medium heat. Add the fennel quarters, bring back to the boil, then lower the heat and simmer for about 10 minutes, or until just tender.

2 Preheat the oven to 190°C/375°F/Gas 5. Drain the fennel and place the pieces in an ovenproof dish or roasting pan. Brush with half of the olive oil.

3 Put the breadcrumbs, garlic and parsley in a separate bowl and drizzle over the remaining olive oil. Season to taste with salt and pepper. Mix lightly, then sprinkle the mixture evenly over the fennel.

4 Bake for 30 minutes, or until the fennel is tender and the breadcrumbs are crisp and golden. Serve hot, garnished with feathery fennel leaves.

BRAISED LEEKS WITH CARROTS

Sweet carrots and leeks go well together, especially when married with a little chopped mint, chervil or flat leaf parsley.

SERVES 6

INGREDIENTS
65g/2½oz/5 tbsp butter
675g/1½lb carrots, thickly sliced
2 bay leaves
2.5ml/½ tsp caster (superfine) sugar
75ml/5 tbsp water
675g/1½lb leeks, cut into 5cm/2in lengths
120ml/4fl oz/½ cup white wine
30ml/2 tbsp chopped fresh mint, chervil or flat leaf parsley
salt and ground black pepper

> COOK'S TIP
> *Even commercially grown leeks require thorough washing, and home-grown specimens may have a surprising amount of soil trapped between the leaves. If you are short of time, you could use ready prepared leeks from the supermarket.*

1 Melt 25g/1oz/2 tbsp of the butter in a pan and cook the carrots gently for 4–5 minutes. Do not let them brown.

2 Add the bay leaves, caster sugar and water. Season with salt and pepper to taste. Bring to the boil, cover tightly and cook for 10–15 minutes, or until the carrots are tender, shaking the pan frequently to stop the carrots from sticking to the base. Remove the lid, then boil until the juices have evaporated, leaving the carrots moist and glazed.

3 Meanwhile, melt 25g/1oz/2 tbsp of the remaining butter in a pan that is wide enough to hold the leeks in a single layer. Add the leeks, stir to coat them in butter, then cook over a low heat for 4–5 minutes, without letting them brown.

4 Stir in the wine and half the mint, chervil or parsley, then season to taste with salt and pepper. Heat until simmering, then cover and cook gently for 5–8 minutes, or until the leeks are tender, but have not collapsed.

5 Uncover the leeks and turn them in the buttery juices. Increase the heat, then boil the liquid rapidly until reduced to a few tablespoons.

6 Add the carrots to the leeks and reheat them gently, then swirl in the remaining butter. Adjust the seasoning, if necessary. Transfer to a warmed serving dish and serve sprinkled with the remaining fresh herbs.

Spiced Pumpkin with Salsa

Roasted pumpkin has a rich flavour, especially when served with a tasty salsa.

SERVES 6

INGREDIENTS
1kg/2¼lb pumpkin, cut into large pieces, fibre and seeds removed
50g/2oz/¼ cup butter, melted
10ml/2 tsp hot chilli sauce
2.5ml/½ tsp salt
2.5ml/½ tsp ground allspice
5ml/1 tsp ground cinnamon
chopped fresh herbs, to garnish
crème fraîche, to serve

FOR THE TOMATO SALSA
3 fresh serrano chillies, peeled, seeded and finely chopped
1 large onion, finely chopped
grated rind and juice of 2 limes, plus strips of lime rind, to garnish
8 ripe, firm tomatoes, peeled and diced
large bunch of fresh coriander (cilantro), finely chopped
pinch of caster (superfine) sugar

1 Make the salsa 3 hours in advance. Grill (broil) the chillies until the skins are blistered. Place in a bowl, cover with crumpled kitchen paper and set aside for 20 minutes. Marinate the onion in the lime rind and juice. Add the tomatoes to the onion. Add the chillies with the coriander and the sugar to the bowl. Mix well, garnish with extra lime rind, cover and chill.

2 Preheat the oven to 220°F/425°F/Gas 7. Put the pumpkin pieces in a roasting pan. Mix together the melted butter and hot chilli sauce and drizzle it evenly over the pumpkin. Mix the salt and spices in a bowl and sprinkle over the pumpkin. Roast for 30–40 minutes, or until the pumpkin flesh yields when pressed gently. Transfer to a serving platter, garnish with the chopped herbs and serve with the tomato salsa and crème fraîche.

LEMONY VEGETABLE PARCELS

These handy packages of winter vegetables are pretty and convenient. They are guaranteed to brighten up even the dreariest day.

SERVES 4

INGREDIENTS
2 medium carrots, cubed
1 small swede (rutabaga), cubed
1 large parsnip, cubed
1 leek, sliced
finely grated rind of ½ lemon
15ml/1 tbsp lemon juice
15ml/1 tbsp wholegrain mustard
5ml/1 tsp walnut or sunflower oil
salt and ground black pepper

1 Preheat the oven to 190°C/375°F/Gas 5. Place the carrot, swede and parsnip cubes in a large bowl, then add the sliced leek. Stir in the lemon rind and juice and the mustard. Season to taste with salt and pepper.

2 Cut four 30cm/12in squares of baking parchment and brush them lightly with the oil. Divide the vegetable mixture among them. Roll up the paper from one side, then twist the ends firmly to seal.

3 Transfer the parcels to a baking sheet and bake them for 50–55 minutes, or until the vegetables are just tender. Serve on heated plates, opening each parcel slightly to reveal the contents.

VARIATION
Substitute the same quantity of curry or tikka paste for the mustard and omit the lemon rind and juice.

Mixed Vegetables with Aromatic Seeds

A tantalizing aroma is the first indication of how tasty this vegetable medley will be. Fresh ginger and three different types of seeds create a wonderful flavour.

SERVES 4–6

INGREDIENTS

675g/1½lb small new potatoes
1 small cauliflower
175g/6oz green beans
115g/4oz/1 cup frozen peas
30ml/2 tbsp sunflower oil
a small piece of fresh root ginger, finely chopped
10ml/2 tsp cumin seeds
10ml/2 tsp black mustard seeds
30ml/2 tbsp sesame seeds
juice of 1 lemon
salt and ground black pepper

1 Scrub the potatoes but do not peel them. Cut the cauliflower into small florets, then trim and halve the green beans.

2 Cook the vegetables in separate pans of lightly salted boiling water until tender, allowing 15–20 minutes for the potatoes, 8–10 minutes for the cauliflower and 4–5 minutes for the beans and peas. Drain thoroughly.

3 Heat the oil in a wide, shallow pan. Add the ginger and cumin, black mustard and sesame seeds. Cover the pan and fry until the seeds start to pop.

4 Add the cooked vegetables and toss over the heat for another 2–3 minutes. Sprinkle over the lemon juice and season with pepper. Serve immediately.

Spinach with Raisins & Pine Nuts

Wilted spinach benefits from the slightest touch of sweetness, as this unusual and delicious Spanish dish amply illustrates.

Serves 4

Ingredients
50g/2oz/scant ⅓ cup raisins
1 thick slice crusty white bread
45ml/3 tbsp olive oil
25g/1oz/¼ cup pine nuts
500g/1¼lb young spinach leaves, stalks removed
2 garlic cloves, crushed
salt and ground black pepper

1 Put the raisins in a small bowl. Add sufficient boiling water to cover and leave to soak for 10 minutes. Meanwhile, cut off the crusts from the white bread and discard, then cut the bread into small cubes.

2 Heat 30ml/2 tbsp of the oil in a large, heavy frying pan. Add the bread cubes and fry over a medium heat, stirring and turning frequently, until golden all over. Lift out with a slotted spoon and drain well on kitchen paper.

3 Add the remaining oil to the pan. When it is hot, fry the pine nuts until beginning to colour. Add the spinach and garlic and cook quickly, turning the spinach until it has just wilted.

4 Drain the raisins, toss them into the pan and season lightly with salt and pepper. Transfer to a warmed serving dish. Sprinkle with the croûtons and serve.

Variation
Swiss chard or spinach beet can be used instead of the spinach, but will need to be cooked a little more.

Lyonnaise Potatoes

Two simple ingredients are prepared separately and then tossed together to create the perfect combination. These potatoes go very well with grilled tomatoes and lightly cooked green beans.

SERVES 6

INGREDIENTS
900g/2lb floury potatoes, scrubbed but not peeled
vegetable oil, for shallow frying
25g/1oz/2 tbsp butter
15ml/1 tbsp olive oil
2 medium onions, sliced into rings
salt
15ml/1 tbsp chopped fresh parsley

1 Bring a large pan of lightly salted water to the boil and cook the potatoes for 10 minutes. Drain them in a colander and leave to cool slightly. When the potatoes are cool enough to handle, peel them and slice them thinly.

2 Heat the vegetable oil in a frying pan. Add half the potato slices and fry over a low heat, turning occasionally, for about 10 minutes, until crisp. Remove from the pan with a slotted spoon and drain on kitchen paper. Set aside and keep hot while you fry the remaining potato slices.

3 Meanwhile, melt the butter with the olive oil in a heavy pan. Add the onions and cook over a low heat, stirring occasionally, for about 10 minutes, until golden. Drain on kitchen paper.

4 Remove the second batch of potato slices with a slotted spoon and drain on kitchen paper. Mix the two batches together in a warmed serving dish, toss with salt and carefully mix with the onions. Sprinkle with the parsley and serve.

VARIATION
For garlic-flavoured Lyonnaise potatoes, add about six large unpeeled garlic cloves when you par-boil the potatoes in step 1.

MARQUIS POTATOES

Swirled potato nests filled with a tangy tomato mixture look wonderfully appetizing and taste superb. As a side dish, this recipe will serve six, but could also make a tasty lunch for two or three people accompanied by a salad.

MAKES 6 NESTS

INGREDIENTS
4 large floury potatoes, total weight about 900g/2lb
15ml/1 tbsp olive oil, plus extra for greasing
2 shallots, finely chopped
450g/1lb ripe tomatoes, peeled, seeded and diced
25g/1oz/2 tbsp butter
60ml/4 tbsp milk
3 egg yolks
salt and ground black pepper
chopped fresh parsley, to garnish

1 Peel the potatoes and cut them into small chunks. Put them in a pan of cold water. Add salt, bring to the boil and cook for 20 minutes, or until very tender.

2 Heat the olive oil in a large frying pan. Add the shallots and cook, stirring constantly, for 2 minutes. Add the diced tomatoes and cook over a low heat, stirring occasionally, for 10 minutes more, until all the moisture has evaporated. Keep warm over a low heat.

3 Drain the potatoes in a colander, then return them to the pan so that they can dry off. Cool slightly, then mash with the butter, milk and two of the egg yolks. Season to taste with salt and pepper.

4 Preheat the grill (broiler) and grease a baking sheet. Spoon the potato mixture into a piping (pastry) bag fitted with a medium star nozzle. Pipe six oval nests on to the baking sheet. Beat the remaining egg yolk with a little water and carefully brush over the potato. Grill (broil) for 5 minutes or until golden.

5 Carefully spoon the tomato mixture inside the nests and top with a little parsley. Serve them immediately.

Oven Chip Roasties

An easy alternative to fried chips that tastes just as good and is much easier to cook. They also make very popular canapés to serve with pre-dinner drinks.

SERVES 4–6

INGREDIENTS
150ml/¼ pint/⅔ cup olive oil
4 medium to large baking potatoes
5ml/1 tsp mixed dried herbs (optional)
sea salt flakes
mayonnaise, to serve

1 Preheat the oven to the highest temperature; this is generally 240°C/475°F/ Gas 9. Lightly oil a large, shallow roasting pan and place it in the oven to get really hot while you are preparing the potatoes.

2 Cut the potatoes in half lengthways, then into long, thin wedges, or thicker ones if you like. Brush each side lightly with olive oil.

3 When the oven is really hot, remove the roasting pan carefully and sprinkle the potato wedges over it, spreading them out in a single layer over the hot oil.

4 Sprinkle the potato wedges with the dried herbs, if using, and sea salt flakes. Roast for about 20 minutes, or longer if they are thicker, turning once so that they brown evenly, until they are golden brown, crisp and lightly puffy. Remove from the oven, drain thoroughly on crumpled kitchen paper and serve immediately with a spoonful of mayonnaise.

VARIATIONS
- *Sweet potatoes also make fine oven chips (French fries). Prepare and roast as for regular potatoes, although you may find they cook more quickly.*
- *You can flavour the roasties with mild paprika instead of mixed herbs.*
- *Serve with lemon juice instead of mayonnaise.*

CARIBBEAN ROASTED SWEET POTATOES, ONIONS & BEETROOT

An aromatic coconut and spice paste makes a medley of colourful root vegetables truly memorable.

SERVES 4

INGREDIENTS

30ml/2 tbsp groundnut (peanut) oil
450g/1lb sweet potatoes, peeled and cut into thick strips or chunks
4 freshly cooked beetroot (beet), peeled and cut into wedges
450g/1lb small red or yellow onions, halved
5ml/1 tsp coriander seeds, lightly crushed
3–4 small whole fresh red chillies
salt and ground black pepper
chopped fresh coriander (cilantro), to garnish

FOR THE PASTE

2 large garlic cloves, chopped
1–2 fresh green chillies, seeded and chopped
15ml/1 tbsp chopped fresh root ginger
45ml/3 tbsp chopped fresh coriander
75ml/5 tbsp coconut milk
30ml/2 tbsp groundnut (peanut) oil
grated rind of ½ lime
2.5ml/½ tsp light muscovado (brown) sugar

1 Preheat the oven to 200°C/400°F/Gas 6. Make the paste. Process the garlic, chillies, ginger, coriander and coconut milk in a food processor or blender. Scrape the paste into a small bowl and beat in the oil, lime rind and muscovado sugar.

2 Heat the oil in a roasting pan in the oven for 5 minutes. Toss the next four ingredients in the oil. Roast for 10 minutes. Stir in the paste and the chillies. Season to taste and toss the vegetables to coat them thoroughly with the paste.

3 Roast, stirring occasionally, for a further 25–35 minutes, or until the vegetables are tender. Transfer to a warmed platter and serve, sprinkled with coriander.

PILAU RICE WITH WHOLE SPICES

This fragrant rice dish makes a perfect accompaniment to any Indian vegetarian dish.
Basmati is known as the prince of rices.

SERVES 4

INGREDIENTS
600ml/1 pint/2½ cups hot vegetable stock
generous pinch of saffron threads
250g/9oz/1⅓ cups basmati rice
50g/2oz/¼ cup butter
1 onion, chopped
1 garlic clove, crushed
½ cinnamon stick
6 green cardamom pods
1 bay leaf
50g/2oz/⅓ cup sultanas (golden raisins)
15ml/1 tbsp sunflower oil
50g/2oz/½ cup cashew nuts
naan bread and tomato and onion salad, to serve (optional)

1 Pour the stock into a jug (pitcher) and stir in the saffron threads. Set aside to infuse (steep). Rinse the rice several times in cold water. If there is time, leave it to soak for 30 minutes in the water used for the final rinse.

2 Heat the butter in a pan and cook the onion and garlic for 5 minutes. Stir in the cinnamon, cardamom and bay leaf and cook for 2 minutes. Drain the rice thoroughly, add it to the pan and cook, stirring constantly, for 2 minutes.

3 Add the saffron-flavoured stock and sultanas to the pan. Bring to the boil, stir, then lower the heat, cover and cook gently for about 10 minutes, or until the rice is tender and all the liquid has been absorbed.

4 Meanwhile, heat the oil in a frying pan and fry the cashew nuts until browned. Drain well on kitchen paper. Sprinkle the cashew nuts over the rice. Serve with naan bread and a tomato and onion salad, if you like.

WILD RICE PILAFF

With its wonderful nutty flavour and appealing appearance, wild rice makes a fine addition to this fruity, Middle Eastern mixture.

SERVES 6

INGREDIENTS
200g/7oz/1 cup wild rice
40g/1½oz/3 tbsp butter
½ onion, finely chopped
200g/7oz/1 cup long grain rice
475ml/16fl oz/2 cups vegetable stock
75g/3oz/¾ cup flaked (sliced) almonds
115g/4oz/⅔ cup sultanas (golden raisins)
30ml/2 tbsp chopped fresh parsley
salt and ground black pepper

1 Bring a large pan of water to the boil. Add the wild rice and 5ml/1 tsp salt. Lower the heat, cover and simmer gently for 45–60 minutes, until the rice is tender. Drain well.

2 Meanwhile, melt 15g/½oz/1 tbsp of the butter in another pan and cook the onion over a low heat, stirring occasionally, for 5 minutes, or until it is just softened. Stir in the long grain rice and cook for 1 minute more.

3 Stir in the vegetable stock and bring to the boil. Lower the heat, cover tightly and simmer gently for about 30 minutes, until the rice is tender and the liquid has been absorbed.

4 Melt the remaining butter in a small pan. Add the almonds and cook until they are just golden. Set aside.

5 Tip both types of rice into a warmed serving dish and stir in the almonds, sultanas and half the parsley. Taste and adjust the seasoning if necessary. Sprinkle with the remaining parsley and serve immediately.

MINTED COUSCOUS CASTLES

These pretty little timbales are perfect for serving as part of a summer lunch. They are virtually fat-free, so you can indulge yourself with impunity.

MAKES 4

INGREDIENTS
225g/8oz/1⅓ cups couscous
475ml/16fl oz/2 cups boiling vegetable stock
15ml/1 tbsp lemon juice
2 tomatoes, diced
30ml/2 tbsp chopped fresh mint
vegetable oil, for brushing
salt and ground black pepper
fresh mint sprigs, to garnish

1 Put the couscous in a bowl and pour over the boiling vegetable stock. Cover securely and leave to stand for 30 minutes, until all the stock has been absorbed and the grains are tender and plump.

2 Using a fork stir in the lemon juice with the diced tomatoes and chopped mint. Season to taste with salt and pepper.

3 Brush the insides of four cups or individual moulds lightly with oil. Spoon in the couscous mixture and pack down firmly. Chill for several hours.

4 Invert the moulds on a platter and serve cold, garnished with mint. Alternatively, cover and heat gently in a low oven, then turn out and serve hot.

COOK'S TIP
Only true Moroccan couscous is easily available in an "instant", ready-cooked form, but this is not immediately distinguishable when compared to traditional couscous, so always check the cooking instructions on the back of the packet.

STIR-FRIED NOODLES WITH BEANSPROUTS

A classic Chinese noodle dish that makes a marvellous accompaniment. In China, noodles are served at virtually every meal – even breakfast.

SERVES 4

INGREDIENTS
175g/6oz dried egg noodles
15ml/1 tbsp vegetable oil
1 garlic clove, finely chopped
1 small onion, halved and sliced
225g/8oz/2 cups beansprouts
1 small red (bell) pepper, seeded and cut into strips
1 small green (bell) pepper, seeded and cut into strips
2.5ml/½ tsp salt
1.5ml/¼ tsp ground white pepper
30ml/2 tbsp light soy sauce

1 Bring a large pan of water to the boil. Add the dried egg noodles and remove the pan from the heat. Cover and leave to stand for about 4 minutes, until the noodles are just tender.

2 Heat the oil in a wok or large frying pan. When it is very hot, add the garlic, stir briefly, then add the onion slices. Cook, stirring, for 1 minute, then add the beansprouts and peppers. Stir-fry for 2–3 minutes.

3 Drain the noodles thoroughly, then add them to the wok. Toss over the heat, using two spatulas or wooden spoons, for 2–3 minutes, or until the ingredients are well mixed and have heated through.

4 Add the salt, white pepper and soy sauce and stir thoroughly before serving the noodle mixture in heated bowls.

SALADS

In the long hot days of summer, when it is too much effort to cook, thoughts turn to salads – and the choice is immense, whether for main courses or as accompaniments. However, salads also play an important role at other times of year, when their refreshing flavours can reinvigorate and restore the system. They range from simple dressed leaves, such as Mixed Leaf & Herb Salad, to filling grain-based salads, including Tabbouleh and Spanish Rice Salad. There are also easy family dishes, such as Feta & Mint Potato Salad, or elegant creations for a smart dinner party, such as Springtime Salad with Quail's Eggs.

Springtime Salad with Quail's Eggs

Enjoy some of the best early season garden vegetables in this crunchy green salad. Quail's eggs add a touch of sophistication and elegance.

Serves 4

Ingredients
175g/6oz broad (fava) beans
175g/6oz fresh peas
175g/6oz asparagus
175g/6oz very small new potatoes, scrubbed
45ml/3 tbsp good lemon mayonnaise
45ml/3 tbsp sour cream or crème fraîche
½ bunch fresh mint, chopped, plus whole leaves for garnishing
8 quail's eggs, soft-boiled and peeled
salt and ground black pepper

1 Cook the broad beans, peas, asparagus and new potatoes in separate pans of lightly salted boiling water until just tender. Drain, refresh under cold water and drain again. When the vegetables are cold, mix them lightly in a serving bowl.

2 Mix the mayonnaise with the sour cream or crème fraîche and chopped mint in a jug (pitcher). Stir in salt and pepper, if needed.

3 Pour the dressing over the salad and toss to coat. Add the quail's eggs and whole mint leaves and toss very gently to mix. Serve immediately.

Cook's Tip
For soft-boiled quail's eggs, cook for 1–2 minutes, then refresh under cold running water before peeling off the shells.

Roasted Plum Tomato & Rocket Salad

This is a good side salad to accompany a cheese flan or a fresh herb pizza. It is also substantial enough to serve as a light lunch for two.

Serves 4

Ingredients
450g/1lb ripe baby Italian plum tomatoes, halved lengthways
75ml/5 tbsp extra virgin olive oil
2 garlic cloves, thinly sliced
225g/8oz/2 cups dried pasta shapes
30ml/2 tbsp balsamic vinegar
2 pieces sun-dried tomato in olive oil, drained and chopped
large pinch of sugar
1 handful rocket (arugula) leaves
salt and ground black pepper

1 Preheat the oven to 190°C/375°F/Gas 5. Arrange the halved tomatoes, cut-side up, in a roasting pan. Drizzle 30ml/2 tbsp of the oil over them and sprinkle with the slices of garlic and salt and pepper to taste. Roast for 20 minutes, turning once.

2 Meanwhile, bring a large pan of lightly salted water to the boil and cook the pasta until it is *al dente*.

3 Put the remaining oil in a large bowl with the vinegar, sun-dried tomatoes and sugar with salt and pepper to taste.

4 Drain the pasta, add it to the bowl of dressing and toss to mix. Add the roasted tomatoes and mix gently. Just before serving, add the rocket leaves, toss lightly and taste for seasoning. Serve at room temperature or chilled.

Leek & Grilled Pepper Salad with Goat's Cheese

This is a perfect dish when you are entertaining, as the salad actually benefits from being made in advance. Remember to bring it to room temperature before serving.

SERVES 6

INGREDIENTS
4 × 1cm/½in slices goat's cheese
75g/3oz/generous 1 cup fine dry white breadcrumbs
675g/1½lb young leeks
15ml/1 tbsp olive oil
2 large red (bell) peppers, halved and seeded
few fresh thyme sprigs, chopped
vegetable oil, for shallow frying
45ml/3 tbsp chopped fresh flat leaf parsley
salt and ground black pepper

FOR THE DRESSING
75ml/5 tbsp extra virgin olive oil
1 small garlic clove, finely chopped
5ml/1 tsp Dijon mustard
15ml/1 tbsp red wine vinegar

COOK'S TIP
Goat's cheese may be made purely from goat's milk or a mixture of goat's with up to 75 per cent cow's milk. French cheeses are, by law, respectively labelled chèvre *and* mi-chèvre. *They are best eaten within two days of purchase and are in season from late spring to late autumn (fall).*

1 Roll the cheese slices in the breadcrumbs, pressing them in so that the cheese is well coated. Chill the cheese for 1 hour.

2 Preheat the grill (broiler). Bring a pan of lightly salted water to the boil and cook the leeks for 3–4 minutes. Drain, cut into 10cm/4in lengths and place in a bowl. Add the olive oil, toss to coat, then season to taste with salt and pepper. Place the leeks on a grill rack and grill (broil) for 3–4 minutes on each side.

3 Set the leeks aside. Place the peppers on the grill rack, skin-side up, and grill until blackened and blistered. Place them in a bowl, cover with crumpled kitchen paper and leave for 10 minutes. Peel off the skin and cut the flesh into strips. Place in a bowl and add the leeks, thyme and a little pepper.

4 Make the dressing. Put the oil, garlic, mustard and vinegar in a screw-top jar and season to taste with salt and pepper. Shake vigorously until combined. Pour the dressing over the leek mixture, cover and chill for several hours.

5 Heat a little oil in a heavy frying pan and fry the cheese until golden on both sides. Drain and cool, then cut into bitesize pieces. Toss the cheese and parsley into the salad and serve at room temperature.

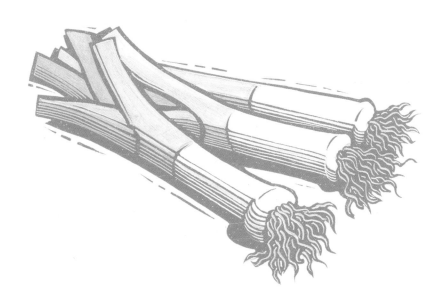

GRILLED ONION & AUBERGINE SALAD WITH TAHINI

Deliciously smoky, this dish balances sweet and sharp flavours. It tastes good with crisp lettuce and sweet, sun-ripened tomatoes.

SERVES 6

INGREDIENTS
3 aubergines (eggplant), cut into 1cm/½in thick slices
675g/1½lb onions, thickly sliced
75–90ml/5–6 tbsp olive oil
45ml/3 tbsp coarsely chopped flat leaf parsley
45ml/3 tbsp pine nuts, toasted
salt and ground black pepper

FOR THE DRESSING
2 garlic cloves, crushed
150ml/¼ pint/⅔ cup light tahini
juice of 1–2 lemons
45–60ml/3–4 tbsp water

COOK'S TIPS
• If you do not have a cast-iron griddle, cook the vegetables under the grill (broiler).
• There are two types of tahini, light and dark. Choose the lighter version for dressings and dips and the darker one for more robust dishes.

1 Place the aubergines in a colander, sprinkling each layer generously with salt. Leave to stand in the sink for about 45 minutes, then rinse thoroughly under cold running water and pat dry with kitchen paper.

2 Thread the onion slices on to skewers (soaked in cold water if wooden or bamboo), to keep them together.

3 Heat a ridged cast-iron griddle. Brush the aubergine slices and onions with about 45ml/3 tbsp of the oil and cook for 6–8 minutes on each side, brushing with more oil, as necessary. The vegetables should be browned and soft when cooked. The onions may need a little longer than the aubergines.

4 Arrange the vegetables on a serving dish and season to taste with salt and pepper. Sprinkle with the remaining olive oil if they look a bit dry.

5 To make the dressing, put the garlic and a pinch of salt in a mortar and crush with a pestle. Gradually work in the tahini. When it has been fully incorporated, gradually work in the juice of 1 lemon, then the water. Taste and add more lemon juice if you think the dressing needs it. Thin with more water, if necessary, so that the dressing is fairly runny.

6 Drizzle the dressing over the salad and set aside for 30–60 minutes for the flavours to mingle. Sprinkle with the chopped parsley and pine nuts. Serve the salad at room temperature, not chilled.

Sweet-&-sour Artichoke Salad

This Italian salad combines spring vegetables with a deliciously piquant sauce called agrodolce.

Serves 4

Ingredients
juice of 1 lemon
6 small globe artichokes
30ml/2 tbsp olive oil
2 medium onions, coarsely chopped
175g/6oz/1 cup fresh or frozen broad (fava) beans (shelled weight)
300ml/½ pint/1¼ cups water
175g/6oz/1½ cups fresh or frozen peas (shelled weight)
salt and ground black pepper
fresh mint leaves, to garnish

For the sauce
120ml/4fl oz/½ cup white wine vinegar
15ml/1 tbsp caster (superfine) sugar
a handful of fresh mint leaves, torn

1 Fill a bowl with cold water and add the lemon juice. Peel the outer leaves from the artichokes and discard them. Cut the artichokes into quarters and place them in the bowl of acidulated water to prevent them from discolouring.

2 Heat the oil in a large, heavy pan. Add the onions and cook over a low heat, stirring occasionally, until they are golden.

3 Stir in the beans, then drain the artichokes and add them to the pan. Pour in the measured water. Bring the water to the boil then lower the heat. Cover and cook for 10–15 minutes.

4 Add the peas, season to taste with salt and pepper and cook for 5 minutes more, stirring occasionally, until the vegetables are tender. Drain them thoroughly. Place them in a bowl, leave to cool, then cover and chill.

5 Make the sauce. Mix all the ingredients in a small pan. Heat gently for 2–3 minutes, or until the sugar has dissolved. Simmer for about another 5 minutes, stirring occasionally. Remove from the heat and leave to cool.

6 To serve, drizzle the agrodolce sauce over the vegetables and garnish with the fresh mint leaves.

VARIATION
Agrodolce dressing is also traditionally served with onions as a hot side dish. Melt 50g/2oz/¼ cup butter in a large pan. Stir in the sugar and when it has dissolved, add the vinegar and 675g/1½lb baby (pearl) onions. Season to taste with salt and pepper, cover and cook over a low heat for about 25 minutes, until tender and golden. Sprinkle with the mint and serve immediately.

FATTOUSH

This simple salad has been served for centuries in the Middle East, but nowadays you are as likely to encounter it in San Francisco as in Syria.

SERVES 4

INGREDIENTS
1 yellow or red (bell) pepper, seeded and sliced
1 large cucumber, coarsely chopped
4–5 tomatoes, chopped
1 bunch spring onions (scallions), sliced
30ml/2 tbsp finely chopped fresh parsley
30ml/2 tbsp finely chopped fresh mint
30ml/2 tbsp finely chopped fresh coriander (cilantro)
2 garlic cloves, crushed
juice of 1½ lemons
45ml/3 tbsp olive oil
salt and ground black pepper
2 pitta breads

1 Place the yellow or red pepper, cucumber and tomatoes in a large salad bowl. Add the spring onions with the finely chopped parsley, mint and coriander.

2 Make the dressing. Mix the garlic with the lemon juice in a jug (pitcher). Gradually whisk in the olive oil, then season to taste with salt and black pepper. Pour the dressing over the salad and toss lightly to mix.

3 Toast the pitta bread, in a toaster or under a hot grill (broiler) until crisp and lightly browned. Serve with the prepared salad.

VARIATION
If you like, make this salad in the traditional way. After toasting the pitta breads until crisp, crush them coarsely in your hand and sprinkle over the top of the salad before serving.

GADO GADO

The crunchy peanut sauce on this traditional Indonesian salad owes its flavour to galangal, an aromatic rhizome that resembles ginger.

SERVES 4

INGREDIENTS
250g/9oz white cabbage, shredded
4 carrots, cut into thin batons
4 celery sticks, cut into thin batons
225g/8oz/2 cups beansprouts
½ cucumber, cut into thin batons
fried onion, salted peanuts and sliced fresh chilli, to garnish

FOR THE PEANUT SAUCE
15ml/1 tbsp vegetable oil
1 small onion, finely chopped
1 garlic clove, crushed
1 small piece galangal, grated
5ml/1 tsp ground cumin
1.5ml/¼ tsp mild chilli powder
5ml/1 tsp tamarind paste or freshly squeezed lime juice
60ml/4 tbsp crunchy peanut butter
5ml/1 tsp soft light brown sugar

1 Steam the cabbage, carrots and celery for 3–4 minutes, until just tender. Cool. Spread out the beansprouts on a serving dish. Top with the cabbage, carrots, celery and cucumber.

2 For the sauce, heat the vegetable oil in a pan, add the onion and garlic and cook gently for 5 minutes, until soft. Stir in the galangal, cumin and chilli powder and cook for 1 minute. Stir in the next three ingredients.

3 Heat gently, stirring occasionally and adding a little hot water, if necessary, to make a coating sauce. Spoon a little of the sauce over the vegetables and garnish with fried onions, peanuts and sliced chilli. Serve the rest of the sauce separately.

Couscous Salad

This classic salad comes from Morocco and is a popular choice for a substantial accompaniment. Make it several hours ahead, so that the flavours can blend.

SERVES 4

INGREDIENTS
275g/10oz/1⅔ cups couscous
550ml/18fl oz/2½ cups boiling vegetable stock
16–20 pitted black olives, halved
2 small courgettes (zucchini), cut in thin batons
25g/1oz/¼ cup flaked (sliced) almonds, toasted
60ml/4 tbsp olive oil
15ml/1 tbsp lemon juice
15ml/1 tbsp chopped fresh coriander (cilantro)
15ml/1 tbsp chopped fresh parsley
good pinch of ground cumin
good pinch of cayenne pepper
salt

1 Place the couscous in a bowl and pour over the stock. Stir with a fork, then set aside for 10 minutes for the stock to be absorbed. Fluff up with a fork. Add the olives, courgettes and almonds to the couscous and mix in gently.

2 Whisk the olive oil, lemon juice, coriander, parsley, cumin, cayenne and a pinch of salt in a jug (pitcher). Pour the dressing over the salad and toss to mix.

VARIATION
You can substitute ½ cucumber for the courgettes and pistachios for the almonds.

TABBOULEH

This traditional bulgur wheat salad remains a winner. Serve it with roasted or barbecue-cooked vegetables or a part of a meze.

SERVES 4

INGREDIENTS
150g/5oz/scant 1 cup bulgur wheat
600ml/1 pint/2½ cups water
3 spring onions (scallions), finely chopped
2 large garlic cloves, crushed
4 firm tomatoes, peeled and chopped
90ml/6 tbsp chopped fresh parsley
60ml/4 tbsp chopped fresh mint
90ml/6 tbsp fresh lemon juice
75ml/5 tbsp extra virgin olive oil
salt and ground black pepper

1 Place the bulgur wheat in a bowl and pour over the water. Leave to soak for 20 minutes.

2 Line a colander with a clean dishtowel. Tip the soaked bulgur wheat into the centre, let it drain, then gather up the sides of the dishtowel and squeeze out any remaining liquid. Tip the bulgur wheat into a large bowl.

3 Add the spring onions, garlic, tomatoes, parsley and mint. Mix well, then pour over the lemon juice and olive oil. Season generously with salt and pepper, then toss so that all the ingredients are combined. Cover and chill in the refrigerator for several hours before serving.

SPANISH RICE SALAD

Ribbons of green and yellow pepper add colour and flavour to this simple salad. The rice makes it almost a meal in itself.

SERVES 6

INGREDIENTS
275g/10oz/1½ cups white long grain rice
1 bunch spring onions (scallions), thinly sliced
1 green (bell) pepper, seeded and sliced
1 yellow (bell) pepper, seeded and sliced
3 tomatoes, peeled, seeded and chopped
30ml/2 tbsp chopped fresh coriander (cilantro)

FOR THE DRESSING
45ml/3 tbsp mixed sunflower and olive oil
15ml/1 tbsp rice vinegar
5ml/1 tsp Dijon mustard
salt and ground black pepper

1 Bring a large pan of lightly salted water to the boil and cook the rice for 10–12 minutes, until tender but still slightly firm at the centre of the grain. Do not overcook. Drain, rinse under cold water and drain again. Leave until cold.

2 Place the rice in a large serving bowl. Add the spring onions, peppers, tomatoes and chopped coriander.

3 Make the dressing. Mix the oils, vinegar and mustard in a jar with a tight-fitting lid and season to taste with salt and pepper. Shake vigorously. Stir 60–75ml/ 4–5 tbsp of the dressing into the rice and adjust the seasoning, if necessary.

4 Cover with clear film (plastic wrap) and chill for about 1 hour before serving. Offer the remaining dressing separately.

VARIATION
Diced carrot, garden peas and drained, canned corn can be added to this salad.

SESAME NOODLE SALAD

Toasted sesame oil adds a nutty flavour to this Japanese influenced salad, which is at its best when served warm.

SERVES 2–4

INGREDIENTS
250g/9oz medium egg noodles
200g/7oz sugar snap peas or mangetouts (snow peas), sliced diagonally
2 carrots, cut into thin batons
2 tomatoes, seeded and diced
30ml/2 tbsp chopped fresh coriander (cilantro), plus coriander sprigs, to garnish
15ml/1 tbsp sesame seeds
3 spring onions (scallions), shredded

FOR THE DRESSING
10ml/2 tsp light soy sauce
30ml/2 tbsp toasted sesame seed oil
15ml/1 tbsp sunflower oil
4cm/1½in piece of fresh root ginger, finely grated
1 garlic clove, crushed

1 Bring a large pan of water to the boil, add the noodles and remove the pan from the heat. Cover and leave to stand for about 4 minutes, until the noodles are just tender.

2 Meanwhile, bring a second, smaller pan of water to the boil. Add the sugar snap peas or mangetouts, bring back to the boil and cook for 2 minutes. Drain and refresh under cold water, then drain again.

3 Make the dressing. Put the soy sauce, sesame seed and sunflower oils, ginger and garlic in a screw-top jar. Close tightly and shake vigorously to mix.

4 Drain the noodles thoroughly and tip them into a large bowl. Add the sugar snaps or mangetouts, carrots, tomatoes and coriander. Pour the dressing over the top, and toss thoroughly with your hands to combine. Sprinkle the salad with the sesame seeds, top with the shredded spring onions and coriander sprigs and serve while the noodles are still warm.

FRAGRANT PUY LENTIL & SPINACH SALAD

This earthy salad has a strong flavour and is great for a picnic or barbecue. If you cannot find Puy lentils use brown ones instead.

SERVES 6

INGREDIENTS
225g/8oz/1 cup Puy lentils
1 fresh bay leaf
1 celery stick
1 fresh thyme sprig
30ml/2 tbsp olive oil
1 onion, thinly sliced
10ml/2 tsp crushed toasted cumin seeds
400g/14oz young spinach leaves
30–45ml/2–3 tbsp chopped fresh parsley, plus a few extra sprigs to garnish
salt and ground black pepper
toasted French bread, to serve

FOR THE DRESSING
45ml/3 tbsp extra virgin olive oil
5ml/1 tsp Dijon mustard
15–25ml/1–1½ tbsp red wine vinegar
1 small garlic clove, finely chopped
2.5ml/½ tsp finely grated lemon rind

> VARIATION
> *Substitute 5 ml/1 tsp balsamic vinegar for the same quantity of red wine vinegar in the dressing.*

1 Rinse the lentils and place them in a large pan. Add sufficient cold water to cover. Tie the bay leaf, celery and thyme into a bundle and add to the pan, then bring to the boil. Lower the heat to a steady boil. Cook the lentils for 30–45 minutes, until just tender.

2 Meanwhile, make the dressing. Mix the olive oil and Dijon mustard with 15ml/1 tbsp of the red wine vinegar. Add the chopped garlic and lemon rind and whisk to mix. Season well with salt and pepper.

3 Drain the lentils and discard the herbs. Tip them into a bowl, add most of the dressing and toss. Set aside and stir occasionally.

4 Heat the oil in a pan and cook the onion for 4–5 minutes, until it starts to soften. Add the cumin and cook for 1 minute.

5 Add the spinach and season to taste, then cover and cook for 2 minutes. Stir, then cook again briefly until wilted.

6 Stir the spinach into the lentils and leave the salad to cool to room temperature. Stir in the remaining dressing and chopped parsley. Adjust the seasoning, adding more vinegar if necessary. Spoon on to a serving platter, sprinkle some parsley sprigs over and serve at room temperature with toasted French bread.

Feta & Mint Potato Salad

The oddly named Pink Fir Apple potatoes are perfect for this salad as they keep their shape when cooked. They taste great with feta cheese, yogurt and fresh mint.

Serves 4

Ingredients
500g/1¼lb salad potatoes, such as Pink Fir Apple
90g/3½oz feta cheese, crumbled

For the dressing
225g/8oz/1 cup natural (plain) yogurt
15g/½oz/½ cup fresh mint leaves
30ml/2 tbsp mayonnaise
salt and ground black pepper

1 Steam the potatoes, without peeling them, over a pan of boiling water for about 20 minutes, or until tender.

2 Meanwhile, make the dressing. Mix the yogurt and mint in a food processor and pulse until the mint leaves are finely chopped. Scrape the mixture into a small bowl, stir in the mayonnaise and season to taste with salt and pepper.

3 Drain the potatoes well and tip them into a large bowl. Spoon the dressing over and sprinkle the feta cheese on top. Serve immediately.

Cook's Tip
Pink Fir Apple potatoes have a smooth, waxy texture and retain their shape when cooked, making them ideal for salads. Charlotte, Belle de Fontenay and other salad potatoes could be used instead.

Avocado, Red Onion & Spinach Salad with Polenta Croûtons

The simple lemon dressing gives a sharp tang to this sophisticated salad, while the croûtons, with their crunchy golden exterior and soft centre, add a contrast.

SERVES 4

INGREDIENTS
1 large red onion, cut into wedges
300g/11oz ready-made polenta, cut into 1cm/½in cubes
olive oil, for brushing
225g/8oz baby spinach leaves
1 avocado
5ml/1 tsp lemon juice

FOR THE DRESSING
60ml/4 tbsp extra virgin olive oil
juice of ½ lemon
salt and ground black pepper

1 Preheat the oven to 200°C/400°F/Gas 6. Place the onion wedges and polenta cubes on a lightly oiled baking sheet and bake for 25 minutes, or until the onion is tender and the polenta is crisp and golden, turning everything frequently to prevent sticking. Leave to cool slightly.

2 Meanwhile, make the dressing. Place the olive oil and lemon juice in a screw-top jar. Add salt and pepper to taste, close the jar tightly and shake vigorously.

3 Place the spinach in a serving bowl. Peel, stone (pit) and slice the avocado, then toss the slices in the lemon juice to prevent them from discolouring. Add them to the spinach with the onions. Pour the dressing over the salad and toss gently. Sprinkle the polenta croûtons on top or hand them round separately.

WATERCRESS, PEAR, WALNUT & ROQUEFORT SALAD

Sharp-tasting blue Roquefort and peppery leaves are complemented in this salad by sweet fruit and crunchy nuts.

SERVES 4

INGREDIENTS
75g/3oz/³⁄4 cup shelled walnuts, halved
2 red Williams pears
15ml/1 tbsp lemon juice
1 large bunch watercress or American cress, about 150g/5oz, tough stalks removed
200g/7oz Roquefort cheese, cut into chunks

FOR THE DRESSING
45ml/3 tbsp extra virgin olive oil
30ml/2 tbsp lemon juice
2.5ml/¹⁄2 tsp clear honey
5ml/1 tsp Dijon mustard
salt and ground black pepper

1 Toast the walnuts in a dry frying pan over a low heat for about 2 minutes, until golden, tossing frequently to prevent them from burning.

2 Meanwhile, make the dressing. Put the olive oil, lemon juice, honey and mustard into a screw-top jar and season to taste with salt and pepper. Close the lid tightly and shake vigorously until thoroughly combined.

3 Core and slice the pears then toss them in the lemon juice to prevent them from discolouring. Place the pear slices in a bowl and add the watercress or American cress, toasted walnuts and Roquefort. Pour the dressing over the salad, toss well and serve immediately.

VARIATION
Roquefort has a unique flavour, but if you like a milder cheese, try using Dolcelatte instead.

FENNEL, ORANGE & ROCKET SALAD

This light and refreshing salad is ideal for serving with spicy or rich foods. Fennel and orange is a classic combination in Italian cooking.

SERVES 4

INGREDIENTS
2 oranges
1 fennel bulb
115g/4oz rocket (arugula) leaves
50g/2oz/½ cup pitted black olives

FOR THE DRESSING
15ml/1 tbsp balsamic vinegar
1 small garlic clove, crushed
30ml/2 tbsp extra virgin olive oil
salt and ground black pepper

1 With a vegetable peeler, cut thin strips of rind from the oranges, leaving the pith behind. Cut the pieces into fine strips. Set them aside.

2 Peel the oranges, removing all the white pith. Slice them into thin rounds and discard any seeds. Bring a small pan of water to the boil, add the strips of rind and cook for 2–3 minutes. Drain and dry on kitchen paper.

3 Cut the fennel bulb in half lengthways and slice horizontally across the bulb as thinly as possible, preferably in a food processor fitted with a slicing disc, or using a mandoline. Combine the orange rounds and fennel slices in a serving bowl and toss with the rocket leaves.

4 Make the dressing. Mix the vinegar and garlic in a bowl. Whisk in the oil, then season with salt and pepper to taste. Pour the dressing over the salad, toss well and leave to stand for a few minutes. Sprinkle with the black olives and garnish with the blanched strips of orange rind before serving.

PANZANELLA

Open-textured, Italian-style bread is essential for this colourful Tuscan salad which makes the most of late-summer tomatoes.

SERVES 6

INGREDIENTS
10 thick slices day-old Italian style bread, about 275g/10oz
1 cucumber, peeled and cut into chunks
5 tomatoes, seeded and diced
1 large red onion, chopped
175g/6oz/1½ cups pitted black or green olives
20 fresh basil leaves, torn

FOR THE DRESSING
60ml/4 tbsp extra virgin olive oil
15ml/1 tbsp red or white wine vinegar
salt and ground black pepper

1 Soak the bread in cold water to cover for about 2 minutes, then lift it out and squeeze gently, first with your hands and then in a dishtowel to remove any excess water.

2 Make the dressing. Place the oil and vinegar in a screw-top jar and season to taste with salt and pepper. Close the lid tightly and shake vigorously. Mix the cucumber, tomatoes, onion and olives in a bowl.

3 Break the bread into chunks and add to the bowl with the basil. Pour the dressing over the salad, and toss before serving.

Mixed Leaf & Herb Salad

This simple salad is the perfect antidote to a rich, heavy meal, as it contains fresh herbs that can aid the digestion as well as tasting wonderful.

Serves 4

Ingredients
115g/4oz/4 cups mixed salad leaves
50g/2oz/2 cups mixed salad herbs, such as coriander (cilantro), parsley, basil and
* rocket (arugula)*
25g/1oz/2 tbsp pumpkin seeds
25g/1oz/2 tbsp sunflower seeds

For the dressing
60ml/4 tbsp extra virgin olive oil
15ml/1 tbsp balsamic vinegar
2.5ml/½ tsp Dijon mustard
salt and ground black pepper

1 Start by making the dressing. Combine the olive oil, balsamic vinegar and mustard in a screw-top jar. Season with salt and pepper to taste. Close the jar tightly, then shake the dressing vigorously until well combined. Mix the salad and herb leaves in a large bowl.

2 Toast the pumpkin and sunflower seeds in a dry frying pan over a medium heat for 2 minutes, until golden, tossing frequently to prevent them from burning. Leave the seeds to cool slightly before sprinkling them over the salad. Pour the dressing over the salad and toss gently with your hands until the leaves are well coated. Serve immediately.

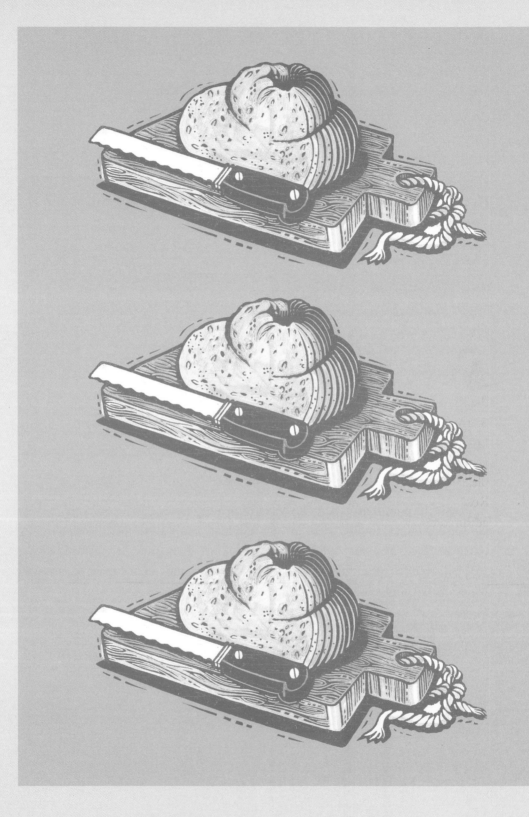

BREADS &
SAVOURY BAKES

Although supermarkets, bakeries and delicatessens stock an unprecedented choice of breads these days, nothing compares with the appetizing aroma and scrumptious flavour of a freshly baked loaf still warm from the oven. Making your own bread, whether a basic Split Tin Loaf or a more exotic Focaccia with Green Peppercorns & Rock Salt, is very easy and extremely satisfying. In fact, baking is always an especially pleasurable kind of cooking. Baked goods, from Shaped Dinner Rolls to Rosemary Crackers and from Irish Soda Bread to Oatcakes, will be admired and appreciated by family, friends and guests.

SPLIT TIN LOAF

As its name suggests, this basic loaf is so called because of the centre split. Some bakers mould the dough in two loaves which join together when the dough rises, but retain the characteristic crack after baking.

MAKES 1 LOAF

INGREDIENTS
vegetable oil, for greasing
500g/1¼lb/5 cups unbleached strong white bread flour,
  plus extra for dusting
10ml/2 tsp salt
15g/½oz fresh yeast
300ml/½ pint/1¼ cups lukewarm water
60ml/4 tbsp lukewarm milk

> ### COOK'S TIP
> *When the dough has risen for the first time, it is knocked back to help disperse the air bubbles evenly throughout. Simply, punch the dough with your fist.*

1 Lightly grease a 900g/2lb loaf tin (pan). Sift the flour and salt into a bowl and make a well in the centre. Mix the yeast with half the lukewarm water in a jug (pitcher), then stir in the remaining water.

2 Pour the yeast mixture into the centre of the flour. Gradually mix in enough of the surrounding flour to make a thick, smooth batter. Sprinkle a little more flour over the batter and leave in a warm place for about 20 minutes, until bubbles appear in the batter. Add the milk and remaining flour and mix to a firm dough.

3 Turn out on to a lightly floured surface and knead for 10 minutes, until smooth and elastic. Place in a lightly oiled bowl, cover with lightly oiled clear film (plastic wrap) and set aside in a warm place for 1–1¼ hours, or until the dough has nearly doubled in bulk.

4 Knock back (punch down) the risen dough, then shape it by hand into a rectangle the length of the tin. Roll up lengthways, tuck the ends under and place, seam-side down, in the tin. Cover and leave in a warm place to rise for 20–30 minutes, or until nearly doubled in size.

5 Using a sharp knife, make one deep central slash along the length of the loaf, then dust the top with plain flour. Leave for 10–15 minutes before baking. Preheat the oven to 230°C/450°F/Gas 8.

6 Bake for 15 minutes, then reduce the oven temperature to 200°C/400°F/ Gas 6. Bake for 20–25 minutes more, or until the bread is golden and sounds hollow when tapped on the base. Turn out on to a wire rack to cool.

GRANT LOAVES

The dough for these quick-and-easy loaves requires no kneading and takes only a minute to mix. The loaves should keep moist for several days.

MAKES 3 LOAVES

INGREDIENTS
vegetable oil, for greasing
1.3kg/3lb/12 cups wholemeal (whole-wheat) bread flour
15ml/1 tbsp salt
15ml/1 tbsp easy-blend (rapid-rise) dried yeast
15ml/1 tbsp muscovado (molasses) sugar
1.2 litres/2 pints/5 cups warm water (35–38°C/95–100°F)

1 Thoroughly grease three loaf tins (pans), each measuring about 21 × 2 × 6cm/ 8½ × 4½ × 2½in and set aside in a warm place. Sift the flour and salt into a large bowl and warm slightly to take off the chill.

2 Stir in the dried yeast and sugar. Make a well in the centre and pour in the water. Mix for about 1 minute, working the sides into the middle. The dough should be slippery. Divide among the prepared tins, cover with oiled clear film (plastic wrap) and leave in a warm place for 30 minutes, or until the dough has risen to within 1cm/½in of the top of the tins.

3 Meanwhile, preheat the oven to 200°C/400°F/Gas 6. Bake for 40 minutes, or until the loaves are crisp and sound hollow when tapped on the base. Turn out on to a wire rack to cool.

COOK'S TIP
Ordinary dried yeast must be mixed with a little warm liquid, and sometimes with sugar as well. When it has dissolved and the mixture is frothy, it can be added to the dry ingredients.

WHOLEMEAL BREAD

This seeded loaf looks rustic and is great for picnics and other al fresco *meals. Try using a stoneground bread flour for the best flavour and texture.*

MAKES 4 ROUNDS

INGREDIENTS
20g/³⁄₄oz fresh yeast
300ml/½ pint/1¼ cups lukewarm milk
5ml/1 tsp caster (superfine) sugar
225g/8oz/2 cups wholemeal (whole-wheat) bread flour
225g/8oz/2 cups unbleached strong white bread flour,
  plus extra for dusting
5ml/1 tsp salt
50g/2oz/¼ cup chilled butter, diced
1 egg, lightly beaten
vegetable oil, for greasing
30ml/2 tbsp mixed seeds

1 Mash the yeast with a little of the milk and the sugar until it dissolves to make a paste. Sift both types of flour and the salt into a large, warmed mixing bowl. Rub in the butter until the mixture resembles breadcrumbs.

2 Add the yeast mixture, remaining milk and egg and mix into a fairly soft dough. Knead on a lightly floured surface for 15 minutes. Place in a lightly oiled bowl, cover with lightly oiled clear film (plastic wrap) and leave to rise in a warm place for at least 1 hour, until doubled in bulk.

3 Knock back (punch down) the dough and knead it for 10 minutes. Divide the dough into four pieces and shape them into flattish rounds. Place them on a floured baking sheet and leave to rise for about 15 minutes more.

4 Preheat the oven to 200°C/400°F/Gas 6. Sprinkle the loaves with the mixed seeds. Bake for about 20 minutes, until golden and firm. Cool on wire racks.

COTTAGE LOAF

Always a good-looking loaf, this makes an attractive centrepiece for a casual lunch or an informal supper party.

MAKES 1 LARGE ROUND LOAF

INGREDIENTS
vegetable oil, for greasing
675g/1½lb/6 cups unbleached strong white bread flour, plus extra for dusting
10ml/2 tsp salt
20g/¾oz fresh yeast
400ml/14fl oz/1⅔ cups lukewarm water

> COOK'S TIP
> *A moist atmosphere in the oven is often conducive to producing a crisp crust on the loaf. If you like, either wipe the floor and inside of the door with a damp cloth or spray them lightly with water, using a mister, before switching the oven on.*

1 Lightly grease two baking sheets. Sift the flour and salt into a large bowl and make a well in the centre. Dissolve the yeast in 150ml/¼ pint/⅔ cup of the water. Add to the flour, with the remaining water and mix to a firm dough.

2 Turn out the dough on to a lightly floured surface and knead for 10 minutes. Place in a lightly oiled bowl, cover with lightly oiled clear film (plastic wrap) and leave in a warm place to rise for about 1 hour, or until doubled in bulk.

3 Knock back (punch down) the risen dough on a lightly floured surface. Knead for 2–3 minutes, then divide the dough into two-thirds and one-third. Shape each piece into a ball shape.

4 Place the balls of dough on the prepared baking sheets. Cover with inverted bowls and leave in a warm place to rise for about 30 minutes.

5 Gently flatten the top of the larger ball of dough and cut a cross in the centre, 5cm/2in across. Brush with a little water and place the smaller ball on top. Make small cuts around each ball.

6 Carefully press a hole through both balls, using the thumb and first two fingers of one hand. Cover with lightly oiled clear film and leave to rest in a warm place for about 10 minutes.

7 Heat the oven to 220°C/425°F/Gas 7 and place the baking sheet on the lower shelf. The loaf will finish expanding as the oven heats up. Bake for 35–40 minutes, or until golden brown and sounding hollow when tapped. Cool completely on a wire rack.

IRISH SODA BREAD

Traditional Irish soda bread can be prepared in minutes and is excellent served warm, with plenty of butter. You can use all white flour, if you like, to create a bread with a finer texture.

MAKES 1 ROUND LOAF

INGREDIENTS
vegetable oil, for greasing
225g/8oz/2 cups unbleached plain (all-purpose) flour
225g/8oz/2 cups wholemeal (whole-wheat) flour, plus extra for dusting
5ml/1 tsp salt
10ml/2 tsp bicarbonate of soda (baking soda)
10ml/2 tsp cream of tartar
40g/1½oz/3 tbsp butter
5ml/1 tsp caster (superfine) sugar
350–375ml/12–13fl oz/1½–1⅔ cups buttermilk

1 Preheat the oven to 190°C/375°F/Gas 5. Lightly grease a baking sheet and set aside. Sift both types of flour and the salt into a large bowl. Add the bicarbonate of soda and cream of tartar, then rub in the butter. Stir in the sugar.

2 Pour in sufficient buttermilk to mix to a soft dough. Do not over-mix or the bread will be heavy and tough. Shape into a round on a lightly floured surface. Place on the prepared baking sheet and mark a cross using a sharp knife, cutting deep into the dough.

3 Dust lightly with wholemeal flour and bake the loaf for 35–45 minutes, or until well risen. The bread should sound hollow when tapped on the base. Cool slightly on a wire rack, but serve warm.

VARIATIONS
- *Shape the dough into two small loaves and bake for 25–30 minutes.*
- *Sour cream may be used instead of buttermilk, as both have a high lactic acid content and so react with the soda.*

SOUR RYE BREAD

You need to plan ahead to make this loaf, as the starter takes a day or two. Caraway seeds are a traditional Eastern European topping but sesame or poppy seeds would work equally well if you are not fond of the pungent taste of caraway.

MAKES 2 LOAVES

INGREDIENTS
450g/1lb/4 cups rye flour
450g/1lb/4 cups strong white bread flour, plus extra for dusting
15ml/1 tbsp salt
7g/¼oz/2½ tsp easy-blend (rapid-rise) dried yeast
25g/1oz/2 tbsp butter, softened
600ml/1 pint/2½ cups lukewarm water
vegetable oil, for greasing
15ml/1 tbsp caraway seeds, for sprinkling

FOR THE SOURDOUGH STARTER
60ml/4 tbsp rye flour
45ml/3 tbsp warm milk

1 For the sourdough starter, mix the rye flour and milk in a small bowl. Cover with clear film (plastic wrap) and leave in a warm place at a constant temperature for 1–2 days, or until the mixture smells pleasantly sour.

2 Sift both types of flour and the salt into a large bowl and stir in the yeast. Make a well in the centre and add the butter, water and sourdough starter. Mix to a soft dough. Turn out the dough on to a floured surface and knead for 10 minutes. Put it in a clean bowl, cover with lightly oiled clear film and leave in a warm place to rise for 1 hour, or until doubled in bulk.

3 Turn out the dough and knead for 1 minute. Divide the dough in half. Shape each piece into a 15cm/6in round. Place on greased baking sheets. Cover with oiled clear film and leave to rise for 30 minutes.

4 Preheat the oven to 200°C/400°F/Gas 6. Brush the loaves with water, sprinkle with caraway seeds and bake them for 35–40 minutes. The loaves should have browned and will sound hollow when tapped on the base. Cool on a wire rack.

WALNUT BREAD

This delicious enriched wholemeal bread is filled with walnuts. It is the perfect companion for cheese and also tastes wonderful with salads.

MAKES 2 LOAVES

INGREDIENTS
vegetable oil, for greasing
50g/2oz/¼ cup butter
350g/12oz/3 cups strong wholemeal (whole-wheat) bread flour, plus extra for dusting
115g/4oz/1 cup unbleached strong white bread flour
15ml/1 tbsp light brown muscovado (molasses) sugar
7.5ml/1½ tsp salt
20g/¾oz fresh yeast
275ml/9fl oz/1 cup lukewarm milk
175g/6oz/1½ cups walnut pieces

1 Lightly grease two baking sheets. Melt the butter in a small pan until it starts to turn brown, then set aside to cool. Mix the flours, sugar and salt in a bowl and make a well in the centre. Cream the yeast with half the milk. Add to the well with the remaining milk. Strain the cooled butter into the well and mix with your hand, gradually incorporating the flour to make a batter, then a moist dough.

2 Turn out on to a lightly floured surface and knead for 6–8 minutes. Place in a lightly oiled bowl, cover with lightly oiled clear film (plastic wrap) and leave in a warm place to rise for 1 hour, or until doubled in bulk.

3 Gently knock back (punch down) the dough on a lightly floured surface. Press or roll it flat, then sprinkle over the nuts, press them in and roll up the dough. Return it to the oiled bowl, re-cover and leave in a warm place for 30 minutes.

4 Turn out on to a lightly floured surface, divide the dough in half and shape each piece into a ball. Place on the baking sheets, cover with lightly oiled clear film and leave in a warm place to rise for 45 minutes, or until doubled in bulk.

5 Preheat the oven to 220°C/425°F/Gas 7. Slash the top of each loaf three times. Bake for 35 minutes, until they sound hollow when tapped. Cool on a wire rack.

FOCACCIA WITH GREEN PEPPERCORNS & ROCK SALT

There is something irresistible about a loaf of freshly baked focaccia with its dimpled surface and fabulous flavour. Serve it with a typical Italian dish.

MAKES 1 LOAF

INGREDIENTS
350g/12oz/3 cups strong white bread flour, plus extra for dusting
2.5ml/½ tsp salt
10ml/2 tsp easy-blend (rapid-rise) dried yeast
10ml/2 tsp drained green peppercorns in brine, lightly crushed
25ml/1½ tbsp fruity extra virgin olive oil
about 250ml/8fl oz/1 cup lukewarm water
oil, for greasing
20ml/4 tsp coarsely crushed rock salt, for the topping
fresh basil leaves, to garnish

1 Sift the flour and salt into a mixing bowl. Stir in the yeast and peppercorns. Make a well in the centre and add 15ml/1 tbsp of the oil, with half the water. Mix, gradually incorporating the surrounding flour and adding more water to make a soft dough.

2 Turn out the dough on to a lightly floured surface and knead for 10 minutes. Press and stretch the dough, using the heel of your hand and turning the dough frequently. Return to the clean, lightly oiled bowl, cover with lightly oiled clear film (plastic wrap) and leave in a warm place until doubled in bulk.

3 Knock back (punch down) the dough and knead lightly for 2–3 minutes. Place on an oiled baking sheet and pat out to an oval. Cover with lightly oiled clear film and leave for 30 minutes.

4 Preheat the oven to 190°C/375°F/Gas 5. Make a few dimples in the surface of the dough with your fingers. Drizzle with the remaining olive oil and sprinkle lightly with the crushed rock salt. Bake for 25–30 minutes, until pale gold all over. Sprinkle with fresh basil leaves and serve warm.

OLIVE BREAD

A mixture of olives combined with olive oil make this wonderful Italian bread.
Choose your olives carefully for the best flavour.

MAKES 1 LOAF

INGREDIENTS
vegetable oil, for greasing
275g/10oz/2½ cups unbleached strong white bread flour, plus extra for dusting
50g/2oz/½ cup strong wholemeal (whole-wheat) bread flour
7g/¼oz/2½ tsp easy-blend (rapid-rise) dried yeast
2.5ml/½ tsp salt
210ml/7½fl oz/1 cup lukewarm water
15ml/1 tbsp extra virgin olive oil, plus extra for brushing
115g/4oz/1 cup pitted black and green olives, coarsely chopped

1 Lightly grease a baking sheet. Mix the flours, yeast and salt in a bowl and make a well in the centre. Add the water and oil and mix to a soft dough. Knead on a lightly floured surface until smooth and elastic, then place in a lightly oiled bowl, cover with oiled clear film (plastic wrap) and leave in a warm place for 1 hour, or until doubled in bulk.

2 Knock back (punch down) the dough on a lightly floured surface. Flatten it and sprinkle over the olives. Fold up and knead to distribute the olives. Leave to rest for 5 minutes, then shape into an oval loaf. Place on the prepared baking sheet.

3 Make six deep cuts in the top of the loaf, and gently spread the sections out. Cover with lightly oiled clear film and leave in a warm place to rise for 30–45 minutes, or until doubled in size.

4 Meanwhile, preheat the oven to 200°C/400°F/Gas 6. Brush the bread with olive oil and bake for 35 minutes. Cool on a wire rack.

VARIATION
Increase the proportion of wholemeal flour to make the loaf more rustic.

THREE-GRAIN TWIST

A mixture of grains gives this close-textured bread a delightfully nutty flavour. You could replace the linseeds with sesame seeds.

MAKES 1 LOAF

INGREDIENTS
30ml/2 tbsp malt extract
475ml/16fl oz/2 cups boiling water
225g/8oz/2 cups strong white bread flour, plus extra for dusting
7.5ml/1½ tsp salt
225g/8oz/2 cups malted brown flour
225g/8oz/2 cups rye flour
15ml/1 tbsp easy-blend (rapid-rise) dried yeast
pinch of sugar
30ml/2 tbsp linseed
75g/3oz/scant 1 cup medium oatmeal
45ml/3 tbsp sunflower seeds
vegetable oil, for greasing

1 Stir the malt extract into the water. Leave the mixture until lukewarm. Sift the white flour and salt into a mixing bowl and add the other flours. Stir in the yeast and sugar. Set aside 5ml/1 tsp of the linseed and add the rest to the flour mixture with the oatmeal and sunflower seeds. Make a well in the centre.

2 Pour the malted water into the well and gradually mix in the flour to make a soft dough, adding extra water if necessary. Knead on a floured surface for 5 minutes, then return to the clean bowl, cover with lightly oiled clear film (plastic wrap) and leave in a warm place to rise for about 2 hours, until doubled in bulk.

3 Flour a baking sheet. Knead the dough again and divide it in half. Roll each half to a 30cm/12in long sausage. Twist them together, dampen the ends and press to seal. Lift the twist on to the prepared baking sheet. Brush it with water, sprinkle with the remaining linseed and cover loosely with a large plastic bag. Leave in a warm place until well risen. Preheat the oven to 220°C/425°F/Gas 7.

4 Bake the loaf for 10 minutes, then reduce the oven temperature to 200°C/400°F/Gas 6 and cook for another 20 minutes. Cool on a wire rack.

CHEESE & COURGETTE CLUSTER BREAD

This unusual bread owes its moistness to grated courgettes, and its depth of flavour to freshly grated Parmesan cheese. You could experiment with different vegetables and cheese. Try a combination of carrot and Cheddar, for example.

MAKES 1 LOAF

INGREDIENTS
4 courgettes (zucchini), coarsely grated
675g/1½lb/6 cups strong white bread flour, plus extra for dusting
2 × 7g/¼oz sachets easy-blend (rapid-rise) dried yeast
50g/2oz/⅔ cup freshly grated Parmesan cheese
30ml/2 tbsp olive oil, plus extra for greasing
milk, to glaze
poppy seeds or sesame seeds, to sprinkle
salt and ground black pepper

1 Put the grated courgettes into a large colander and sprinkle with salt. Stand the colander in a sink for about 20 minutes to drain the juices, then rinse the courgettes thoroughly, drain again and pat dry with kitchen paper.

2 Sift the flour into a large bowl and add the yeast, Parmesan, 2.5ml/½ tsp salt and pepper to taste. Stir in the oil and courgettes, then add enough lukewarm water to make a firm, but still soft dough.

3 Turn out the dough on to a lightly floured surface and knead for about 10 minutes, then return it to the bowl, cover with lightly oiled clear film (plastic wrap) and leave in a warm place for about 1 hour, or until doubled in bulk.

4 Lightly grease a deep 23cm/9in cake tin (pan). Knock back (punch down) the dough and knead it again. Divide it into eight pieces and roll each piece into a smooth ball. Arrange these in the tin, placing one in the centre and the remainder around the outside.

5 Glaze the loaf with a little milk and sprinkle over the seeds. Cover lightly with oiled clear film and leave to rise in a warm place until the balls of dough have doubled in size.

6 Meanwhile, preheat the oven to 200°C/400°F/Gas 6. Bake the loaf for 35–45 minutes, until it is golden brown and sounds hollow when tapped on the base. Cool on a wire rack and eat as soon as possible.

COOK'S TIP

It is possible to speed up the rising process for all yeast breads by using the microwave. Put the dough in an oiled bowl covered with oiled clear film (plastic wrap) and heat in the microwave on HIGH for 10 seconds, then set the bowl aside for 20 minutes, or until the dough has doubled in bulk. If necessary, return it to the microwave and heat on HIGH for a further 10 seconds and then set aside for 10 minutes more. Never put a loaf in a metal tin (pan) in the microwave.

Sun-dried Tomato Bread

This is one bread that absolutely everyone seems to love. Chopped onion and sun-dried tomatoes give it an excellent flavour.

MAKES 4 SMALL LOAVES

INGREDIENTS

675g/1½lb/6 cups strong white bread flour, plus extra for dusting
10ml/2 tsp salt
25g/1oz/2 tbsp caster (superfine) sugar
25g/1oz fresh yeast
400–475ml/14–16fl oz/1⅔–2 cups lukewarm milk
15ml/1 tbsp tomato purée (paste)
75g/3oz/1½ cups sun-dried tomatoes in oil, drained and chopped,
    plus 75ml/5 tbsp oil from the jar
75ml/5 tbsp extra virgin olive oil, plus extra for greasing
1 large onion, chopped

1 Sift the flour, salt and sugar into a bowl and make a well in the centre. Crumble the yeast into a jug (pitcher), mix with 150ml/¼ pint/⅔ cup of the milk and pour into the well in the flour. Stir the tomato purée into the remaining milk, then add to the well in the flour, with the tomato oil and olive oil.

2 Mix the liquid ingredients, and gradually incorporate the surrounding flour to make a dough. Turn out on to a lightly floured surface and knead for about 10 minutes, then return the dough to the clean bowl, cover with lightly oiled clear film (plastic wrap) and leave to rise in a warm place for about 2 hours.

3 Knock back (punch down) the dough, and add the tomatoes and onion. Knead until evenly distributed. Shape into four rounds and place on two greased baking sheets. Cover each pair with a dishtowel and leave to rise again for about 45 minutes.

4 Preheat the oven to 190°C/375°F/Gas 5. Bake the bread for 45 minutes, or until the loaves sound hollow when you tap them on the base. Cool on a wire rack until completely cold before storing.

SHAPED DINNER ROLLS

These rolls are the perfect choice for entertaining as they are elegant and delicate tasting with a crisp top and soft interior.

MAKES 12 ROLLS

INGREDIENTS
vegetable oil, for greasing
450g/1lb/4 cups unbleached strong white bread flour, plus extra for dusting
10ml/2 tsp salt
2.5ml/½ tsp caster (superfine) sugar
7g/¼oz/2½ tsp easy-blend (rapid-rise) dried yeast
50g/2oz/¼ cup butter
250ml/8fl oz/1 cup lukewarm milk
1 egg, beaten
1 egg yolk mixed with15ml/1 tbsp water
poppy seeds and sesame seeds, for sprinkling

1 Grease two baking sheets. Sift the flour and salt into a bowl. Stir in the sugar and yeast. Rub in the butter. Add the milk and egg and mix to a dough. Knead on a floured surface for 10 minutes. Place in a lightly oiled bowl, cover with oiled clear film (plastic wrap) and leave in a warm place for 1 hour, until doubled in bulk. Knock back (punch down) on a floured surface and knead for 3 minutes. Divide into 12 pieces and make shapes.

2 **Plait (braid):** divide a piece of dough into three sausages. Pinch together at one end, plait, then pinch the ends and tuck under.
Baton: shape a piece of dough into an oblong. Slash the surface.
Cottage roll: divide a piece of dough into two-thirds and one-third. Shape into two rounds placing the small one on top of the larger. Make a hole through the centre.
Knot: shape a piece of dough into a rope and tie a single, loose knot.

3 Place the rolls on the baking sheets, cover with oiled clear film and leave in a warm place for 30 minutes, until doubled in bulk. Meanwhile, preheat the oven to 220°C/425°F/Gas 7.

4 Brush the rolls with the egg yolk and water mixture. Sprinkle with poppy seeds or sesame seeds. Bake for 15–18 minutes, or until golden. Cool on a wire rack.

WHOLEMEAL HERB TRIANGLES

Stuffed with salad and cheese, these make a good lunchtime snack. You could vary them by substituting drained sun-dried tomatoes in oil for the herbs.

MAKES 8

INGREDIENTS
225g/8oz/2 cups wholemeal (whole-wheat) flour, plus extra for dusting
115g/4oz/1 cup strong white bread flour
5ml/1 tsp salt
2.5ml/½ tsp bicarbonate of soda (baking soda)
5ml/1 tsp cream of tartar
2.5ml/½ tsp chilli powder
50g/2oz/¼ cup soft margarine
60ml/4 tbsp chopped mixed fresh herbs
250ml/8fl oz/1 cup skimmed milk
15ml/1 tbsp sesame seeds

1 Preheat the oven to 220°C/425°F/Gas 7. Lightly flour a baking sheet. Put the wholemeal flour in a mixing bowl. Sift in the white flour, salt, soda, cream of tartar and chilli powder, then rub in the soft margarine.

2 Add the herbs and milk and mix quickly to a soft dough. Turn out on to a lightly floured surface. Knead only very briefly or the dough will become tough.

3 Roll out to a 23cm/9in round and place on the prepared baking sheet. Brush lightly with water and sprinkle evenly with the sesame seeds.

4 Carefully cut the dough round into eight wedges, separate them slightly and bake for 15–20 minutes. Cool briefly on a wire rack and serve warm.

CHEESE & POTATO SCONES

The addition of creamy mashed potato gives these wholemeal scones an irresistible moist crumb and a crisp crust. Try rosemary or thyme instead of the sage.

MAKES 12

INGREDIENTS

40g/1½oz/3 tbsp butter, plus extra for greasing
115g/4oz/1 cup wholemeal (whole-wheat) flour, plus extra for dusting
2.5ml/½ tsp salt
20ml/4 tsp baking powder
2 eggs, beaten
60ml/4 tbsp semi-skimmed (low-fat) milk
115g/4oz/1⅓ cups cooked, mashed potato
45ml/3 tbsp chopped fresh sage
50g/2oz/½ cup grated mature (sharp) Cheddar cheese
sesame seeds, for sprinkling

1 Preheat the oven to 220°C/425°F/Gas 7. Grease a baking sheet. Sift the flour, salt and baking powder into a bowl. Rub in the butter, then mix in half the beaten eggs and all the milk. Add the mashed potato, sage and half the Cheddar, and mix to a soft dough.

2 Knead the dough lightly on a floured surface until smooth. Roll it out to 2cm/¾in thick, then stamp out nine scones using a sharp 6cm/2½in fluted cutter. Re-roll and cut out more scones until the dough is used up.

3 Place the scones on the prepared baking sheet and brush the tops with the remaining beaten egg. Sprinkle the rest of the cheese and the sesame seeds on top and bake for 15 minutes, or until golden. Cool on a wire rack.

OATCAKES

Old-fashioned they may be, but oatcakes are delicious, especially with cheese. They taste even better when home-made.

MAKES 8

INGREDIENTS
175g/6oz/1½ cups medium oatmeal, plus extra for sprinkling
2.5ml/½ tsp salt
pinch of bicarbonate of soda (baking soda)
15g/½oz/1 tbsp butter, plus extra for greasing
75ml/5 tbsp water

1 Preheat the oven to 150°C/300°F/Gas 2. Mix the oatmeal with the salt and soda in a mixing bowl.

2 Melt the butter with the water in a small pan. Bring to the boil, then add to the oatmeal mixture and mix thoroughly to form a moist dough.

3 Turn out the dough on to a surface sprinkled with oatmeal and knead to a smooth ball. Turn a large baking sheet upside-down, grease it, sprinkle it lightly with oatmeal and place the ball of dough on top. Sprinkle the dough with oatmeal, then roll out to a 25cm/10in round.

4 Cut the round into eight sections, ease them apart slightly and bake for 50–60 minutes until crisp. Leave to cool on the baking sheet, then remove the oatcakes with a metal spatula.

COOK'S TIPS
• To achieve a neat round, place a 25cm/10in cake board or plate on top of the oatcake. Cut away any excess dough with a knife, then lift off the board or plate.
• Medium oatmeal is widely available, but fine is also suitable for oatcakes. Oat flakes, made from steamed rolled oats, are too coarse.

ROSEMARY CRACKERS

The Mediterranean herb rosemary is said to grow best for a strong-willed woman. If you have some (rosemary, not strong-willed women) in your garden, make these excellent crackers, and top them with cream cheese and rosemary flowers.

MAKES ABOUT 25

INGREDIENTS
225g/8oz/2 cups plain (all-purpose) flour, plus extra for dusting
2.5ml/½ tsp baking powder
a good pinch of salt
2.5ml/½ tsp curry powder
75g/3oz/6 tbsp butter, diced
30ml/2 tbsp finely chopped young rosemary leaves
1 egg yolk
30–45ml/2–3 tbsp water
milk, to glaze

TO DECORATE
30ml/2 tbsp cream cheese
rosemary flowers

1 Put the flour, baking powder, salt and curry powder in a food processor. Add the butter and process until the mixture resembles fine breadcrumbs. Add the chopped rosemary, egg yolk and 30ml/2 tbsp of the water. Process again, adding the remaining water, if needed, to make a firm dough. Alternatively, rub the butter into the flour mixture in a bowl, then add the remaining ingredients and combine. Wrap in clear film (plastic wrap) and chill in the refrigerator for 30 minutes.

2 Preheat the oven to 180°C/350°F/Gas 4. Roll out the dough thinly on a lightly floured surface and cut out the crackers using a 5cm/2in fluted cutter.

3 Transfer them to a large baking sheet and prick with a fork. Brush with milk to glaze and bake for about 10 minutes, until pale golden. Cool on a wire rack.

4 Spread a little cream cheese on to each cracker and secure a few rosemary flowers on top, using tweezers to position the flowers, if this makes it easier.

INDEX

broccoli, 16
  and cauliflower with apple
    mint sauce, 247
  pea, leek and broccoli
    soup, 84
Brussels sprouts, 16, 17
buckwheat, 41
  rustic buckwheat pasta bake,
    136–7
burgers, red bean and
    mushroom, 160–1
butterbeans, 43–4
  butterbean, watercress and
    herb dip, 122
buttermilk, 48–9

C
cabbage, 16
  baked, 248
  wholemeal pasta with
    caraway cabbage, 187
caraway, 57
carbohydrates, 9, 11
cardamom, 57
carob, 67
carrots, 14
  with braised leeks, 252–3
  spiced carrot dip, 121
cashew nuts, 54
  Indian stir-fried vegetables
    with cashews, 132
casseroles, harvest vegetable
    and lentil, 154
cassoulet, vegetarian, 158–9
cauliflower, 16
  and broccoli with apple mint
    sauce, 247
  spiced Indian cauliflower
    soup, 85
cayenne, 57

celeriac, 14
  gratin, 249
celery, 22
chanterelles, 24
  cream, 224
chard, Swiss, 17
cheese, 50–1, 235, 270
  asparagus and ricotta
    tart, 231
  baked cheese polenta
    with tomato
    sauce, 189
  brandied Roquefort
    tarts, 119
  butternut squash dip, 120
  celeriac gratin, 249
  and courgette cluster
    bread, 304–5
  and dietary fat, 11
  feta and mint potato
    salad, 284
  leek roulade with cheese,
    walnuts and peppers,
    214–15
  and leek sausages with spicy
    tomato sauce, 146–7
  leeks and grilled pepper
    salad with goat's
    cheese, 270–1
  and onion quiche, 148–9
  pear and Parmesan salad
    with poppy seed
    dressing, 94
  and pesto turnovers, 118
  and potato scones, 309
  ratatouille and Fontina
    strudel, 230
  roasted vegetable
    pizza, 225
  soufflé, 213

summer herb ricotta
    flan, 204–5
  twice baked Gruyère and
    potato soufflés, 110
  watercress, pear, walnut and
    Roquefort salad, 286
cherries, 30
chickpeas, 44
  and aubergine ragoût, 153
  falafel, 112–13
  sprouts, 28
chicory, 22
chillies, 21, 57, 167
  chilli bean dip, 126
  courgette fritters with chilli
    jam, 111
  pasta with sugocasa and,
    135
  peperoncino, 186
  Quorn with ginger, leeks
    and, 176
Chinese gooseberries, 35
Chinese leaves, 16
chives, 26
cholesterol, 10
cilantro see coriander
cinnamon, 57
cloves, 57–8
coconuts, 54, 55
  chilled soup, 71
  milk, 54, 55
  paste, 261
coriander (cilantro), 26, 58
  coriander omelette parcels
    with Asian vegetables,
    180–1
  and garlic soup, 81
corn 19, 40–41
  corn pasta, 61
  corn salad, 25